Blight in the Vineyard

Exposing the Roots, Myths, and Emotional Torment of Spiritual Tyranny

John Immel

Presage Publishing * Ohio

2011 Presage Publishing Print Edition

Copyright © 2011 by Presage Publishing

E-book notice:
All rights reserved. By payment of required fees, you have been granted non-exclusive, non-transferable right to access and read the text of this e-book, on screen. No portion of this book may be reproduced, stored in a retrieval system or transmitted in any form or by any means—electronic, mechanical, photocopy, recording, scanning, or other—except for quotation in critical review or articles, without the prior written permission of the publisher.

Published in the United States by Presage Publishing
PO Box 751492
Dayton, Ohio
45475-1492

www.Presagepublishing.com

Paperback: ISBN: 978-0-9852713-1-2
Electronic: ISBN: 978-0-9852713-3-6
Audio Book: ISBN: 978-0-9852713-5-0

For audio book footnotes and comments visit: Blightinthevineyard.com/audionotes

For articles addressing the ideas and issues around the rise and event of Christian Despotism, visit SpiritualTyranny.com

Cover Design: Lucent Dreams Photography

To the men of virtue who sit quiet in the face of tyranny, who need the moral power to engage the fight: It's time to get in the game.

Contents

1: Noble Goal/Ignoble End   1
2: Lover Of Our Soul   13
3: Meet the Players   21
4: Welcome to the Arena of Ideas   37
5: Let's Practice   49
6: Moral, Authentic Orthodoxy   63
7: Oops, We Got It Right . . . This Time   71
8: That Waskally Critter   85
9: Bonfire-Lighting and a Bucket of Water   101
10: Major Players, Major Thoughts   109
11: Convenient Calvinists   125
12: Three Walls of the Modern Day Romanists   141
13: The Growing Protestant Sainthood   147
14: I Wouldn't Go That Far   161
15: Predestined Eugenics   173
16: Peerless Passion   181
17: Intellectual Beachhead   199
18: Wreckage of Moral Clarity   213
18.5: Why SGM Is Not a Cult   233
19: Morality and the Sociopolitical Thingy   239
20: Covering   249
21: Felt Needs   281
22: Sound Doctrine Subjectivity Beast   297
23: Addicted to Elitism   309
24: Interpersonal Train Wreck   325
25: Getting Healthy   345
26: Group Homoousios and Individual Homoousios   367

Acknowledgments

Thinking and writing are intensely self-appointed, self-driven efforts, but that work is never done in a vacuum. Many people contributed to me as a person or to the actual creation of this work. These few words are only the beginning of my gratitude.

To all the pubs and watering holes near my secret bunker for the Unsound Doctrinal Underground, thanks for letting me camp out with my laptop, library, and practice my barroom theology. The booth rent was never much more than the price of a Diet Coke, a good tip, and the willingness to trade Jägermeister stories for God ideas.

To Dr. William Carpenter, for your perverse pleasure in making me go 9 on 1 in Advanced Systematics for a whole year. It wasn't fair then, but now I understand what you were doing; the best ideas really do prevail, even when they come from a committed C student.

To Dr. James Shelton, for your merciless reading schedule and mandatory class polemics, who could fail to get the tides of Church History? Who could fail to fall in love with this slow motion disaster that is historic Christian thought?

To Dr. Siegfried Schatzmann, you might not want to claim me, but you created a kickass department. Without your vision and curricula, so many young thinkers would be lost to the intellectual vacancy of the Charismatic/Pentecostal movements.

To Dr. Mark McDonald, for your insatiable determination to co-diagnose the philosophical bankruptcy of our culture and the disaster it wrecks on the human psyche and in our relational abilities. Who knows how many hours we've spent haggling over the details of this issue, but I would not trade a minute. Your thoughts, challenges, and additions to my thinking are invaluable tools for understanding the traits of healthy men and women.

To my advanced readers—Mary, Judy, Carl, and Thomas—your comments were essential, encouraging, and challenging. You all gave me some insight into how people read what is on the page and what they hear as a result. You gave me the symptoms, and that made it possible for me to diagnose the problem. I owe a couple of you a drink, a Corona, and a Sam Adams if memory serves. Here is to you. Oops . . . wrong commercial but the sentiment still works.

Leilani, for your tireless editing effort through all my endless dinking and revising and commenting. You are so gracious with my obsession. If there are still errors in the manuscript, it is probably because I had to fiddle just one last time before printing.

Cheri Immel, for being unrelenting in your faith for your favorite son.

Ivan Immel, for being the best employee a manager could ever have, for being the best advanced reader a writer could ever have, and the best father a son could ever imagine.

Introduction

This book has its roots in a condensed version self-published in 1997. Five or six copies of that edition were given to an American ministry organization. Events during my time within that denomination produced grist for the complaint mill. Well, that is an understatement, but it will suffice for the content of this introduction.

I am not a good spectator and don't suffer injustice towards myself or others as a victim, so I did what I have almost always done: I spoke up. Among other things, I fired up my PC and wrote about the problems. The product was a candid, brutally satirical piece. Being a nobody from nowhere and without "authority" or reputation, gave people freedom, at least in their minds, to ignore the point and offer the counter-criticism that my "tone" was disqualifying. Of course, the function of satire is to make a point by defying convention: There is no "qualifying" when addressing tyranny. And tone does not have anything to do with truth. If the house is on fire and a man is angry when he says so, it doesn't make the house any less on fire. Nor are people who hear his angry declaration absolved of the responsibility to judge the reality correctly. I'm still a nobody from nowhere and my tone hasn't improved; only the refinement of my criticisms has gotten better. The house is still on fire, and the flames are spreading.

Sometime after '98 I decided to expand/rewrite *Blight in the Vineyard*, and I finished the foreword of that edition sometime in 2000. I self-published between twenty and forty copies and passed them around Montgomery County, Maryland with the general understanding that I didn't care if it was recopied. The reaction was revealing. On the one hand, people would read *Blight*, cry tears, say thank you for having courage to say hard things, and quietly, by dark of night, pass it along to some other soul they thought had been affected. On the other hand, I'd get calls from people who had read a chapter or two (IF they read anything at all) and thought it their duty to speak the fear of God into my soul for daring to "touch God's anointed." Interestingly enough, these became the conversations of greatest vindication. With wonderful consistency, my tub-thumper of doom would return sometime later, shake my hand, and say, "I owe you an apology. You were exactly right."

And since I love to say I told you so, I did.

Unless the organization is the Catholic Church where the sheer institutional size makes it a distant abstraction, openly criticizing church ministries—naming names and offering judgments—is its own brand of a sticky wicket. The average church fuss often revolves around the color of the carpet, who offended whom at the ice cream social, or a ruckus over Bible verse hairsplitting. But getting into the territory of pastoral conduct and congregation treatment descends into the murky subjective world of perception, and memory, and feelings. It is very easy for offending parties, the people with the power, to dismiss the criticisms with a wave of the "I'm sorry you misunderstood" wand and then quietly exact indirect social retribution. The offended parties are often limited by the terribly embarrassing details of the fight and have narrow ability to impact public perceptions. And if the doctrines taught from the pulpit require people to ignore reports of pastoral misdeeds, no one ever sees enough of the whole picture to really grasp the power and exploitations being executed.

And then someone invented blogs.

The ability to speak candidly has changed because people can use the anonymity of the web browser. They can speak openly about painful, upsetting, demoralizing events and not suffer total humiliation. Over the last few years, many people have told their story, their interaction with the same denomination that was the subject of my early versions of *Blight in the Vineyard*. Some of those stories are the blogging equivalent of the National Enquirer. Some of them are little more than a subjective misunderstanding. But many of the stories are about stunning ill-treatment.

Blogs made it possible for people to compare notes and connect dots. Suddenly, the pixilated events resolve into high definition and the picture shows a breathtaking consistency. The stories contain striking uniformity in pastoral conversations and actions. They contain profound similarities in the emotional, spiritual, and psychological pain of those who have suffered.

That set me to thinking. How was it possible that from state to state, even country to country, people could recount similar life events with stunningly consistent conversations, outcomes, and backlash? What ideas could produce such underlying fear, anxiety, and spiritual frustration? What ironclad logic could cause masses of people to act out similar conduct that produces such invasive outcomes? What thoughts could lurk under the titles of authority that would lead average men to believe they wield unchecked control over people's lives? How could a denomination generate such unswerving reproducibility? By way of comparison, companies spend billions of dollars to produce a brand in the minds of people and they fear the brand name being undone in a blink by the smallest bad press. As far as I know, a church denomination managed to do it without a single TV spot.

I find the scope of these questions and the answers to be fully fascinating. So, I did what I am inclined to do:

Write about it. I combined some specific academic training added to a particular knack at poking tyrants in the eye. Alakazam! Poof! This book follows.

Well, not quite like that.

Ideas have always fascinated me. Why men believe what they believe, how they use that belief structure to fuel the justification of their actions and the subsequent outcomes of those ideas is a captivating study. Since 2007 I've been formalizing my study of the trends of tyranny. I launched a blog called **SpiritualTyranny.com** that has been an almost full-time preoccupation since.

I've come to realize that the authoritarian dynamic is not unique to the Christian organization that I participated in through the early 1990s. Some things do set them apart, but the undergirding ideas are consistent across denominational lines, spiritual movements, and centuries of Christian practice. To be sure, these ideas go deep into Christian ideological history.

The leaders of this group could not have done a better job in making themselves into the poster children for the historic despotism. Indeed, their defiant determination to be "single-minded" in advancing historic doctrine and their zeal to implement the logical next step of the assumptions places them purely on the path. But they are hardly alone. In the pages to come, you will see the concurrent theme of a specific independent church movement evolve into solidarity with a specific body of Christian thought. I am betting that this specific to general relationship will shed the greatest light on the trend towards despotism in American Christianity.

Blight in the Vineyard

1
Noble Goal/Ignoble End

> Of all tyrannies, a tyranny sincerely exercised for the good of its victims may be the most oppressive.
>
> —C. S. Lewis

> Tyrants have always some slight shade of virtue; they support the laws before destroying them.
>
> —Voltaire

> Necessity, the tyrant's plea.
>
> —John Milton

Blight in the Vineyard is about average people, just like you, with hopes and passions and desires. *Blight in the Vineyard* is about single moms who struggle to raise their kids to very exacting ideological values, men pressured to enforce repressive standards on wives in the name of biblical teaching, aspiring ministers eager to find a place in God's vision but never able to measure up, couples who found love and had it crushed under pastoral council, children who suffered horrific treatment and the parents who were talked out of seeking justice in the name of biblical purity, people caught between degenerate spouses and impossible pastoral edicts, and people whose rightful intellectual curiosity is destroyed by a storm of personal criticism.

This is a story about oppression, domination, and coercion.

Real victims exist and their names are many. The

common denominator is a specific body of ideas in the hands of leadership with the will and zeal to press the assumptions to their inevitable ends. Many will recognize the ideas summarized by the doctrines represented by the following words: *Church Polity, Submission, Authority, Leadership Teams, Depravity, Personal Sacrifice, Biblical Headship, Fundamentalism, Orthodoxy* and *Heresy, Sheep Need A Shepherd, Covering,* and *Sound Doctrine*.

I, of course, would love for everyone to read this book, but for those of you who do not immediately hear those concepts echoed from your places of Sunday worship, **this book may not be for you.** All writers must make assumptions about their readership; I will be clear about mine:

- I am writing to an audience with a direct familiarity with the doctrines listed.
- I am writing to people who have been taught to hold an overt expectation that some ideas are more purely Christian, more purely authentic than others.
- I am writing to those who have been taught that church leadership are specifically empowered to enforce doctrines, critique conduct, and organize church resources.
- I am writing to souls that sought to be diligent with everything they were told was authentically Christian, but in the end, the forces of church leadership presumed to dispose of their participation at a whim and pronounce their lives invalid.

If you do not come from this background and the nature of your Christianity is expressed in the broadest acceptance of most any idea and embraces most anyone no matter their ideology, many of the concepts and arguments that follow will be foreign. I suspect that you will find the pains and sufferings discussed are not relatable to your Christian experience. In many ways, you are very, very fortunate, and I wish you the best.

If you ever encounter these ideas and find yourself captured in the mire described above, or you enjoy history and would like to read a unique assessment of Christianity's recorded ideas and how it has affected contemporary American life, you know the resource of choice.

For the rest of you, I was first introduced to what I call the Blight in the Vineyard many years ago. Like most people, I uncritically accepted church doctrine because everyone said it had "biblical" foundation. Church leaders say it would be chaos if someone wasn't in charge of what people believe. Chaos is bad and Man does not know what is good for him, so God appoints some leaders to keep the absolutes of revelation secure against all interlopers.

Historically, the Church's effort to impose intellectual compliance is directly proportional to cultural plurality. That is a wordy way of saying the Church gets nervous over too much free thinking. For the last couple of decades, some men are living in abject terror of Postmodernism. And that is a wordy way of saying some people fear **lots** of free thinking. The Church decides the world's problems are because it doesn't have its mind right, and the remedy for all the bad things is a Christian Enlightened Despotism. The glossy brochure portrays this governance as a cross between a magnanimous father wielding a kitchen spoon and a smothering mother cooing over her precious but unruly children. However, in ages past, in the same ideological free-for-all, her Enlightened Despotism track record reads like Thomas Harris's *Hannibal*, a sociopathic love story told against the backdrop of bloody, "consuming" vindictiveness towards all that offend her. The only thing missing is a doctrinal love for fava beans. Here is the tragedy: She keeps repeating the failure because the roots of this tree are very, very deep in our doctrines and traditions that evolved through Western Europe.

Within the last two hundred fifty years—very briefly in terms of world history—American Christianity progressively abandoned its European roots and offered the world a very different picture. The portrait painted was one of freedom, life, prosperity, and hope. Most of us alive today were brought into the Kingdom of God through this new perspective. Unfortunately, for some, this picture looks like selfishness, chaos, license, and indulgent futility. To "fix" the problem, some in the church returned to the European doctrines claiming they are authentic merely because they are old.

Western culture's philosophical and theological universe has centered on Germany since roughly the 15th century. Most every ideological evolution in the last five hundred years is a byproduct of European intellectuals talking amongst themselves, with American academics offering up an apologetic "me too." Most of our energy is spent repackaging the ideas in modern words and adding a few hedges to make it uniquely American. But at the end of the day, the foundations remain constant.

Few men are intellectual innovators and the ones who are get killed for their heresy before the truth of their observations blazes forth from a bumper sticker.

So, it is no mystery why modern thinkers go looking for answers to our questions, solutions to our problems, and justifications for our actions from those who came before. Why reinvent the wheel if the car already exists? However, driving a car with a steering system that forces you over the same historical cliff is a bad thing. It is scandalous to persist with ideas that have demonstrated bankruptcy. Unfortunately, the ruinous nature is hard to see. The foundations of these ideas have a built-in defense mechanism that undermines critical review.

So, it is no accident that modern American Piety is trending the direction of our intellectual predecessors. After a brief trip into thinking for ourselves—sort of—our intellectual leaders have decided to re-join the "me too" chorus. Only this time it is not so apologetic. This time it is bolstered with zealous moral certainty.

Our ancestors across the Atlantic walked this path repeatedly, galvanized by the arguments that make despotism sound so righteous. American Piety has now been on this path for some decades. I first heard the seeds of this trend thirty years ago in small upstart churches. Now a few of those upstarts are mega churches, with dozens of franchise locations and the authoritarian crop is bountiful. What starts as a noble goal to beat back the chaos and defend the weak eventually reveals that the medicine to cure the ills gives one man, or a group of men, enormous power to dispose of people's lives at a whim. They become unquestionable authorities vested with the moral conviction to demand obedience and brook no challenge. They persist as unquestioning authorities so sure they know all they will ever need to know that they never evaluate the outcomes of their dictates.

It is easy to think that this kind of imbalance only occurs in some fringe super Prophet Jim Jones type who wants lots of money and twenty-three wives. It is hard for us to consider that "real" churches lead by "real" Christians with an effective "biblical" government model would ever, and could ever, act with such despotic indifference. I understand why that makes your brain go tilt, but the dirty little secret of Church history tells a very different story. The core of this tyranny has deep roots in mainstream Christian doctrine. And with profound consistency, those seeking to be the most mainstream, the most authentic, the most purely righteous are the ones who become the greatest perpetrators.

Some years ago, I walked through the doors of a school auditorium in Gaithersburg, Maryland that was pulling double duty as a church; lively music, short songs displayed on the wall, lots of clapping and dancing. They spoke in tongues, laid hands on the sick, and the main preacher cracked jokes during his penetrating social and interpersonal commentary. Even after a decade of Christian life, traveling and being a part of a number of different church flavors and styles, this one stood out.

I was fresh out of a failed attempt at Marine Corps OCS in Quantico and hadn't shed the already habitual parade rest. I stood in the back of the auditorium, in a tweed trench coat, through the entire service. I don't think I moved. This was my first encounter with Covenant Life Church and the ministry team of People of Destiny International (PDI/CLC), located in Gaithersburg, Maryland.

Life was chaos for me then. And like most everyone else, I went looking for someone to order the sloppiness into neat hospital folds. What happened next does not follow any trim and tidy progression where the bad guys have on black hats and the adorably blunt protagonist is sporting a white hat. To be sure, there was a lot of grey in the conflict that occurred. And the glaring moments of white and black hats were subordinated to the proclamations of "authority," and "covering," and "biblical" leadership. Since I had been around similar churches with comparable doctrinal emphasis for the better part of ten years, nothing seemed too terribly out of bounds.

There was no scorching sign that screamed RUN; quite the opposite. One thing led to an assumption that led to another, that led to some friends, which led to a New

Members' class, which led to a host of pastoral interviews. Some months later, I stood—much more relaxed and a smile on my face—with the congregation declaring my commitment to Covenant Life Church and the leaders. They smiled back, shook my hand, looked into my eyes and said, "You belong." They declared their pledge to care for my soul and cover my spiritual welfare.

But in time, the scope and shape of that pastoral pledge became increasingly more disturbing. Eventually, it was clear that belonging had a price, and it was not cheap. To be sure, the real price of inclusion was the very sum of self. It took a while before I realized the commitment's scope was complete abandon to the leadership's "considered" judgments and specific doctrinal mandates. When I challenged the judgments—considered or erroneous—the leaders were not as benign as the glossy brochure insisted. When I asked for specific feedback on the doctrinal mandates, the face of benevolent leadership was revealed for an unmitigated fraud. At the end of the day, the price for my temerity was every church relationship I'd ever invested. The barrage of criticism spanned the spectrum: For questioning the pastors, it was implied that God opposed me. For speaking my mind, the very moral substance of my presence within the church was challenged. Deleterious was the adjective that stands out most.[1]

In the grand scheme, my treatment is little more than a schoolyard scuffle with some boys who were used to intimidating runts on the playground. It only got interesting when they realized that smacking me in the metaphorical spiritual nose did nothing but focus my attention. My specific story is trivial and boring; however, there are other people with stories that will make your heart beat in your

---

1. Look up deleterious in a good dictionary. The one my care group leader used defined it evil, wicked, pernicious, and

chest, your stomach churn, and tears pour out of your eyes.[2]

"Well, all churches have their problems. Why pick on poor PDI/CLC/SGM?"

I will address this comment in much more detail in the pages to come. It is a vague truism that all churches have their problems. But that doesn't mean they should have problems or that all problems are morally equivalent. Just because some churches fuss over the color of the sanctuary carpet does not absolve the Catholic leadership of molesting little boys. And it most certainly doesn't mean the little boys can't complain of the mistreatment.

The elements of Blight in the Vineyard can be seen in many churches in varied measures. My goal is to present the source of this specific problem in the most effective method possible. I don't care for vague academic appraisal of a detached social evolution any more than you. My goal is the highest impact. I am betting that if people see that real names, real faces, real arguments implemented for the broadest church outcomes are behind the tyranny, they will see this is no abstraction.

Mystic Despotism is a coined term I use to describe the manipulation of men's eternal insecurities and spiritual affections to compel earthly action. The blunt version of this is summed up in the following declaration: "Do as I say or you will go to Hell!"

While there are very few preachers with the nerve to make that statement, they don't have any hesitation when dropping this line into a pastoral counseling session: "Well, you know that God opposes the proud." The full implication

---

destructive.

2. This book is not a rehash of mistreatment stories. If you are inclined, browse http://www.sgmrefuge.com and http://www.sgmsurvivors.com for further interpersonal discussions. Then do an internet search for SGM or Sovereign Grace churches' and you will find plenty of smaller blogs

is if you refuse to do what I say, the bad stuff in your life is God's specific retribution.

This manipulation isn't OK.

I am going to talk at length about this very dynamic:
- The motivating power of our love
- The motivating power of our fears
- The assumptions of authority
- The means of manipulation
- The intellectual sleights of hand used to demagogue the sheep
- The power demanded over people's lives
- The specific doctrinal function spread abroad in Christianity

For me to achieve my outcome I am going to:
- Empower you with tools, intellectual tools, so that you gain confidence in your own life with God.
- Equip you so that you can grasp the Arena of Ideas and the tides of Christian thought that are at the root of the practices that drive the error.
- Talk candidly of the PDI/CLC/SGM anecdote, the arguments that support their oppressive practices, so we can see the power of the ideas in action.
- Give a blueprint of what it takes for people to emerge on the other side of such an experience.

But before I do that, I want to preempt three ready objections:
1. I'm divisive.
2. I'm a malcontent with a grudge.
3. I'm harming the Body of Christ.

As for the first objection, I won't pretend otherwise.

---
detailing their own experience.

John Immel

The content of this book is divisive; it says that one thing is right and one thing is wrong. And for that, I am so not sorry.

As for the second objection, the following begins my response:

> I have indeed inveighed sharply against impious doctrines and I have not been slack to censure my adversaries on account, not of their bad morals, but of their impiety. And for this I am so far from being sorry that I have brought my mind to despise the judgments of men and to persevere in this vehement zeal according to the example of Christ who, in his zeal, calls his adversaries a generation of vipers, blind hypocrites, and children of the devil. . . . The ears of our generation have been made so delicate by the senseless multitude of flatterers that go as soon as we perceive that anything of ours is not approved of. We cry out that we are being bitterly assailed. And when we can repel the truth by no other pretense, we escape by attributing bitterness, impatience, intemperance to our adversaries. What would be the use of salt if it were not pungent? Or of the edge of the sword if it did not slay?[3]

This quote is from a key player in our unfolding drama written some centuries ago when responding to the same criticism. A summary of his thoughts is: When we cannot win the argument with our wits, we resort to discrediting our challenger. The *ad hominem* argument was wrong in the 16th century, and it is wrong now.

As to the third criticism that direct conflict harms the Body of Christ, well, if a few words can seriously harm the Body, we are all toast. Humanity is already lost for we Christians then have no fortitude to exist, let alone thrive.

Since I believe that people in general—and the church in particular—is much more robust than is often given

---

3. Letter of Martin Luther to Pope Leo X.

Blight in the Vineyard

credit, I use irreverence to contrast the way most people talk of God stuff, better known as Theology. The tone is outrageous for the sake of my charming orneriness, absurd to illustrate absurdity, and satirical to expose folly. Theology is not a sacred place, though its content is about sacred things. Theology has no Holy Grails but does discuss foundational truths that stand the test of scrutiny. There is no rite of passage and no keepers of the gate: The uninitiated are free to come, and learn, and debate.

And there is the big word: debate.

Since 400 AD, the Church has insisted that men who make their living dispensing God thoughts get to speak without challenge, without scrutiny, without debate. As if once a man becomes a pastor, or a teacher, or an evangelist, the Spirit behind the office is hostile to scrutiny. Christians have fallen mightily with the assumption that intellectual disagreement is equal to divine rebellion. History shows the utter disaster of this perspective.

When leaders obtain power by manipulating our spiritual affections, when leaders sustain power by manipulating our earthly fears, when they hide their failures by exploiting our prejudice, their actions are pure, simple demagoguery. Demagoguery is the exploitation of moral certainty. We are inclined to accept that men are imperfect but government is what God intended. This loose logic lets us evade an overt fight while at the same time accepting a theme circulating pulpits. The theme assumes that our primary Christian responsibility is to avoid all appearances of conflict and unify under the banner of a man in authority. Curiously enough, the men in charge of defining unity are the very people demanding to control without question.

If Jesus and the prophets are our example, then leadership action and government outcome are not the default of God's intent. Their methods for denouncing despotism were hyperbole and satire, and metaphor and satire, and provocation and satire. One divinely inspired insult that comes to mind was uttered by the Prophet Amos. He told the women of Israel that they were fat cows. Make no mistake. There is method to this communication madness: the irreverence, insult, and arrogance. When a culture requires patient, gentle, cautious commentary as the only acceptable means of communication, ears are not circumcised to hear.

Dear Reader, we are at such a place in Christianity concerning leadership method and practice. Far too many people have decided that tone has a moral value. As if everyone must verbalize with patient, benign, tepid, handwringing bromides to qualify to speak at all. I reject the premise that we must talk to each other like a mother to her six-year-old. I choose to have this discussion in the manner of my own adorable bluntness.

Will some of you be offended?

Probably.

I can accept offended. Tyranny, though, I will never accept.

The function of what follows goes to the source of combating despotism: equipping people to use their mind, enter the Arena of Ideas, and roll back the veneer covering the noble goal so we can understand the ignoble outcome.

2
Lover Of Our Soul

I am my beloved's, and his desire is toward me. (KJV)

Song of Solomon 7:10

Thou shalt not be afraid for the terror by night; nor for the arrow that flieth by day. (KJV)

Psalms 91:5

We all met Him one day. Maybe it was as we pointed a gun to our head, despair riddling our mind. Maybe it was at the edge of an altar, after some preacher invited us to come from our seats to bow our heads. Maybe it came while riding in a car, an indescribable joy, an inward assurance that the hostility of our soul was replaced with everlasting love. Maybe it came as the inevitable choice after a long search through every ideology and religion currently known to man. Maybe it came in an endless effort to find relief from guilt and suffering. The list of potential meeting places with the Lover Of Our Soul is as vast as the population of the earth.

It doesn't matter exactly where because the outcomes are strikingly similar. We all heard the essence of the following words ring inside: *"Come to me all you who are weary and heavy laden,"* He said, *"I will give you rest. I will anoint you with my anointing. I will give you my peace and no one shall take it from you."*

The result was a profound affection for the God of Heaven and Earth, and His Son Jesus sprung a well of peace and an endless hunger to know more. As intense as any earthly passion, for us the search for the Lover Of Our Soul is an unquenchable fire. We are finally loved for who we are; known in spite of what that means.

Oh, what a treasure: the life and peace and joy.

But this place of passion, this deep and abiding hunger does not stay stagnant. Eventually, we ask the question: Tell me how to live. Not just how to get up, and go to work, and eat lunch, and feed the kids, and watch some TV.

Tell me how to live! Life with a Capital L! How do we live this life to HIS highest satisfaction?!

We go looking then into a book with a leather cover, the only book that speaks of Truth. But as we consume the writing on the pages, it becomes clear that this testament of God's wisdom is not easy to understand. The mandates in the verses often seem contradictory, if not impossible to perform. How can this be when the love we have is so pure and simple and deep?

They come then with a moral certainty to define "authentic" Christianity. Some speak softly, ever so politely, but still tell us our love affair is lacking without them. Some come and hold our hands, and whisper His sweet nothings in our ears. Others scream from the pulpit their righteous fervor, their unrelenting attack on all things unapproved by their judgments.

The method of delivery does not matter because they all insist qualification to comment on our shortcomings, failures, and inabilities. They might wrap it in a *quid pro quo*, a spiritual tit-for-tat. If you come to me, I will give you "covering." At the root of their appeal is the unmistakable insistence that they are qualified. They are "called." They are "Elders." They are "Authorities." A few even insist that they are Apostles or Prophets. Some

Blight in the Vineyard

make a claim to angelic affirmation, or consecrating visions, or denominational validation. And to prove the point, they grab the book with a leather cover and jab a finger at a verse saying, "This day this saying is fulfilled in your ears." And their right to define how life is supposed to be is settled forever. Amen.

We too read the words on the page: *"I am the vine, you are the branches, and without me you can do nothing. Be a vine, and let the fruit grow."* Where exactly is this vineyard and what is the fruit?

They tell us the vine is their local meeting place, and the fruit is the work around that building, or the conduct demanded from their edicts. **They** might be magnanimous and say, "Go to **any** vineyard, but you must plug in to a vineyard." Or they might be certain: "My Vineyard is best. You will find your highest expression of life here." Once again, they thumb through the pages of the book and find verses that speak of their right to define how life is supposed to be. **They** find the verses that tell us how to look, and act, and eat. **They** tell us our passions and desires are suspect, and our wants and interests are trivial. **They** tell us that their prayers change things. **They** tell us our problems will go away by doing as they do and thinking as they think. And when the problems don't go away, they tell us that we have failed somewhere to do as they ask, to do as God asked. If only our fruit was better, they say, the substance of our lives would change. And when we make the fruit better and the substance of our life does not change, they say, "God is sovereign and He intends this reality. And in light of eternity, the trivial discomfort matters little."

We wonder at this explanation and look around to see if someone can offer a different answer, maybe a solution to the problems. We cannot help but notice that the fruit looks different over there. And what about the branches that don't seem to have any fruit at all, no leaves or anything but nubs? That vineyard over there, it seems, has been told to trim themselves back to almost nothing. To hear them talk they are less than **nothing** and that **nothing** is the fruit of the vine.

We pray to the Lover Of Our Soul and say, "They must really be with you to be sooo . . . sooo . . . empty of self. But I'm not sure. I can't live that way. Is that the point? Should I prune myself to the roots? How do I know that I'm with you? By faith? By your word? By my actions, my conduct, my motives?

It seemed so simple, this life you offered me. How can I know? I don't want to fail you, my love, The Love of My Life. I don't want to disgrace you; I want to be sure.

Why did this get so complicated? I had life but now I have suffering again. What is happening? Show me direction and I will follow. Show me strength and I will not fear my weakness."

Just tell me how to live.
Read the Bible?
Go to church?
What church?
This man says he has miracles.
That man says he has a revelation from God.
This man says angels visit him.
That man says he only preaches sound doctrine.
That man says he preaches by the Spirit.
That man says he is part of a team.
How can I tell who's real and who's not?
Be planted in Good Ground? What is Good Ground?
Submit? To whom?
How come Christians aren't any different than all the other sinners in the world?
Where is the power for this life?
I'm so unsure. I just want you, Lover of My Soul.
But it seems so . . . subjective.

Subjectivity Beast

Lightning scares the sky with wicked preternatural fingers, leaving the lumbering shapes of workers imprinted in his mind's eye. Thunder rumbled in the distance, an ominous omen, hiding the predator as he lurks under cover of darkness. He skulks forward, his footfalls soft, lost in the wind roaring through the vines. He presses between the fruit hanging low nearing his target.

Manacles dangle from his belt by the dozens, enough to go around, enough to capture everyone. The shackle ratchets open like the hiss of a snake, like the slither of a serpent.

The predator waits, knowing his time will come soon.

The dim figure bends and rises, only a step ahead, in an ongoing dance of self-revelation, faster and more dramatic, a whirling blur of human expression.

The predator is patient . . . calm . . . certain. He knows he will succeed. He is experience personified.

There. . . .

The target's hands come into view. Fetters glitter as they descend, encircling the unwary with a cold, hard grip. Captivity!

Laughter bubbles from the predator's belly, deep and wet.

And then he sees another, another human speeding toward self-expression.

The Subjectivity Beast bleeds into the vineyard, his maniacal laughter rising to the stars.

Who Will Brave the Beast?

Who can beat back the evil that lurks under our collective beds?

John Immel

Who can slay the demons of our uncertainties?

Come on, fess up. This is all of us, isn't it? This is our fear that we are somehow seduced, snared by our own narrow perceptions.

So, we flock to local vineyards populated with men that say they are qualified to fill the void, to allay the fears, and affirm our authenticity. The bigger the harvest barn, the brighter the lights, the louder the music, the more inclined we are to think that God must be present. The greater the belonging, the better defined the yardstick, the easier it is to measure authentic Christianity. The neater the answers to life's ambiguities, the more inclined we are to turn ourselves over to their considered judgments.

Nothing grates on the human soul more than chaos. Uncertainty keeps us awake at night and terrorizes us by day. All of our life is spent ordering chaos; some people do it well, and others can barely manage to organize the chaos in their bed sheets. To be sure, the measure of a man's success is directly proportional to his ability to order reality. And man's most debilitating curse is the insurmountable weight of toil as he works with his hands.

This abject terror of chaos is the root of all religions and shows forth man's endless quest to find a way to organize the world he inhabits. In ages past, our forebears looked around and saw a bewildering hostile world with no apparent organization. As man toiled for the smallest relief from the world's beggarly elements, select men raised their hands, insisting that they had the power to beat back the chaos and compel the gods to grant a boon. And the age of the witchdoctor was born. These men interpreted entrails, cast bones, read tea leaves, and sacrificed virgins.

Blight in the Vineyard

It is no accident that at the core of all religions is one uncompromised characteristic: sacrifice. Long before Abram arrived on the scene and instituted a covenant with an obscure god called Yahweh, man was already slaughtering whatever he could see in an effort to appease the powers around him. For the millennia of man's existence, shamans have always said that Death is the coin of the gods' good pleasure. The favors against chaos were always at the price of some loss; the greater the loss, the more profound the death, the better. So potent were the witchdoctor's explanations for man's existence that many of those religions survive in modern minds. Even with the power of reason blazing away as manifest technology, people still consult astrology charts, or read palms, or hang dream catchers, or adorn their houses in fetishes, in an endless effort to find a way to order the chaos.

Some people act like little kids terrified of the monster under the bed: shutting their eyes and plugging their ears, as if ignoring the chaos means it just doesn't exist. And others look at the world and see the inevitability of man's implicit moral depravity. "Don't be shocked at what you see," they say, "but for the Grace of God, there go we all."

To understand the tides of human history and more importantly, the tides of your own history, it is important to grasp these two concepts:
 1. Man abhors chaos.
 2. Man needs a coherent body of ideas to govern his actions.

This principle of human existence is what makes Such and Such for Dummies, Seven Steps to Better Earwax, and preachers pounding pulpits with certainty soooo

John Immel

compelling.

Man needs a place to hang his thinking. He needs the cause and effect, the A, B, C's of his ideas and actions. His greatest psychic pain is the inability to integrate ethical knowledge and moral action. This failure places man at the edge of psychic chaos and over time, disintegrates his existence. So essential is this need that man places the same enormous energy for this pursuit that he uses for getting salt and water.

Man searches for anything or anyone who can help him integrate his ideas and beat back the pending chaos. And since the greatest lever of human existence is our ability to discover wisdom and share our accumulated understanding, he seeks out others who offer answers to these chaos-organizing questions. It doesn't matter if the coherent ideas are right or wrong, wisdom or error; man will embrace any ideas that offer him a cohesive worldview. Then he will act on those ideas until they are fulfilled.

3
Meet the Players

> This and no other is the root from which a tyrant springs; when he first appears he is a protector.
>
> —**Plato**

> Enlighten the people generally, and tyranny and oppressions of body and mind will vanish like evil spirits at the dawn of day.
>
> —**Thomas Jefferson**

> There is only one good, knowledge, and one evil, ignorance.
>
> —**Socrates**

In the self-published, original (1997-ish) version of *Blight in the Vineyard*, my intent was to play on the "I am the vine; you are the branches" metaphor. The combined doctrine and practice to be discussed is blight. People who have suffered under the blight are the vineyard.

Creative, huh?

The title is effective, but the **word** vineyard has been co-opted by that non-denominational denomination called The Vineyard.

Soooo, now the title seems unfortunate because it might lead people to believe this book is specifically about the non-denominational denomination called The Vineyard. Maybe they are inflicted with The Blight, but I am not familiar with the sundry goings-on within that non-denominational denomination. Therefore, they cannot be my object lesson. Sooo . . . what to do?

John Immel

I pondered changing the title because this book is not about the non-denominational denomination called The Vineyard. (There is a test later, so remember this point.)

But then I thought maybe The Vineyard should change the name of their group since I used "The Vineyard" first.

Or maybe I didn't.

It doesn't matter. The more I thought about it, the more sure I was that they should change the name of their non-denominational . . . denomination. So, I considered contacting the headquarters and asking for the change, but then decided that the more spiritual thing was too ardently and often say this book is not about the non-denominational denomination called The Vineyard.

OK, here is the test: Who is this book not about?

Second question on the test: What is this book about?

I've covered this in class a little bit, but I should probably expand. Here is the rub. This book is about a **what**, not a **who**. But we are going to talk about a **who** to dissect the **what**.

The **what** is the stuff that turns very well meaning, very good intentioned, very average people who love God and love his Bible into authoritarian thugs. The **who** is a group called PDI/CLC/SGM.

Hey, I can't help that people like to make acronyms out of their names.

Fine, I'll unravel all of their marketing. Don't ever let it be said that I'm not helpful.

- **PDI** = People of Destiny International = the original international business, publishing, distribution center.
- **CLC** = Covenant Life Church= the mother church in Gaithersburg, Maryland where doctrines, methods, and practices are tested and refined for mass consumption.

22

- **SGM** = Sovereign Grace Ministries = the new name applied to the old ministry after they underwent a "doctrinal refocus" and is now the umbrella name for scads of team-related churches.

In decades past, this group called themselves GOB = Gathering of Believers. And after that they were TAG = Take and Give. Or wait . . . maybe it was the other way around. Who cares? They are the ones addicted to acronyms.

The name on the marquee does not matter because all authoritarian organizations default to one man at the top of the structure. They will try to invent elaborate governmental structures and pretend that everyone gets an equal say in things theological and organizational and governmental, but it isn't true. Look hard enough and long enough and you will find that the compulsion buck stops at one name. Whether by social extortion or direct force or by political intrigue, one man inevitably controls the ideas by a monopoly of government force.

The *El Primo Doctrinal Mover and Shaker* within PDI/CLC/SGM is C. J. Mahaney. It is possible that he is a mere figurehead, a puppet on a theological string, manipulated by shadowy doctrinal masterminds, but it is also possible that pigs fly in a parallel universe. By individual intention (or group objective), he has been fashioned into the point man for all things doctrinal and governmental. And everyone else comes along for the submission and authority ride. [1]

---

1. I heard rumors that they "reorganized" and now grant local churches more autonomy. I wonder if that means those local churches could abandon Reformed Theology, openly disagree with C.J., and still keep the SGM name on the marquee. That will be a fun experiment in co-rulership. Pssst . . . you local pastors, check your charters, and the names on the deeds, and whatever monetary agreements you signed before testing the broad local autonomy.

John Immel

So . . . there is no difference.

PDI/CLC = SGM and SGM = CLC/PDI.
Therefore, CLC = PDI/SGM.

Algebra skills are important. In a few pages you will see why.

When I first started going to (then) PDI/CLC in 1991, I thought I'd found home. The passion and the intellectual energy brought to bear in living the Christian life were infectious. They presented themselves as broadminded thinkers with the zeal to set the standard of Christian living; a model to be emulated and mirrored, an epistle to be read by all men.

Like anyone in love with TRUTH and driven by similar aspirations, I drank deep of the heady tonic. It is a sweet mix: elitism so draped in the language of humility and character that the spice only lingers on the tongue for a moment before the rush of professional, winsome, culturally refined social acceptance slides down the throat and makes a ball of warmth in the soul. And then comes the aperitif of practical life instruction balanced with a lingering spiritual wonder.

The buzz lasts and lasts and lasts.

Not that one has a choice; commitment to the local church is not an option. The definition of what commitment looks like is not negotiable. Submission to the Pastor's authority is not a preference. It is in the Bible after all. And who is going to argue with what is in the Bible?

As long as one keeps drinking and keeps that buzz going, life is good.

Until it is not. . . .

What's Not to Like About Sovereign Grace Ministries?

People of Destiny International was the brainchild of Larry Tomczak and C. J. Mahaney, established 1980-ish in Washington DC and then moved to Gaithersburg, Maryland in 1982. Both men got their preaching start in the Charismatic Renewal thirty plus years ago when people were abandoning the mainline denominational authority in droves. To satisfy their need to preach on Sundays, these men created Covenant Life Church.

Fast forwarding through three decades and a name change to Sovereign Grace Ministries, the organization has grown well beyond the confines of Maryland, spanning in the U.S., Mexico, Canada, the U.K., and Australia. While they boast well into the double digits in local church congregations, their real impact is in publishing books, tapes, and teaching materials; a number of Sovereign Grace Ministries book titles populate Christian bookstore displays. Their broadest reach, however, might be Praise and Worship. They have been very fortunate to have some world-class musicians and songwriters as part of their organization, so the chances are strong that many congregations sing their songs on Sunday.

All of the church-planting and book-writing and tape-teaching and song-singing come from the central authority of SGM. PDI/SGM refers to the publishing, producing, and government wing to their team-related churches. Kind of like the Vatican to the rest of the Holy See. Covenant Life Church is the test bed of all movement practices, doctrines, teaching, and home to the "First Among Equals" leadership/eldership. For the purposes of this book, it doesn't matter the practical or legal distinctions between PDI/CLC/SGM. The point is,

John Immel

the primary shapers of PDI/SGM ideology are (or were) members of Covenant Life Church; hence, my summarizing abbreviation PDI/CLC/SGM.

I will be using the abbreviation PDI/CLC/SGM to remind everyone of the progression from their historic Charismatic Renewal roots to the present day Reformed Theology existence. That evolution is controlled by a central authority: CLC. The reality of this progression, controlled by this central authority, has a direct bearing on the unfolding drama. They are pretty good at rewriting the particulars of their own history so I must remind everyone of their real legacy. So from the outset, I will be using that acronym to reinforce this specific evolution.

OK, they say of themselves:

> Our primary purpose is to establish and nurture local churches to God's glory. Indeed, our greatest desire is that the members of these churches both corporately and as individuals—would bring glory and honor to God in their public and private lives.[2]

That is pretty good, isn't it? That purpose statement is hard to argue with, and I could place a safe bet that most Christian institutions across the world would attribute the same purpose to themselves.

For those of you who have never been to an SGM Church, let me tell you what you would casually experience on a given Sunday. In Gaithersburg you would find a big bright building, full of fathers, and sons, and grandsons. The children are socially obedient and polite saying, "Yes, sir," and "No, sir," while shaking your hand and looking you in the eye. People all seem to be about the same things—a striking corporate single-mindedness,

---

2. From the old, now defunct PDI website, http://www.pdinet.org home page.

Blight in the Vineyard

a conspicuously homogeneous methodology. They talk a little differently using words like, Indwelling Sin, and Conflict Resolution, and Anthropomorphism. The music is loud, and people jump around like they're at a '60s rock concert. Near the podium sits neat rows of men, very pleased, very affirming of everyone who sits in the padded seats. Virtue seems to embody every motive, and those motives deemed bad come under immediate scrutiny.

So what is the objection? Who wouldn't want to be a part of that? And—if one is not inclined to move to Maryland—who wouldn't want to import the same single-mindedness, the same intensity, the same culture-enforced virtue to where they live, and work, and serve God? Where do you get it? What is it called?

> We call it Impassioned Orthodoxy," the back of old PDI magazine reads. "It's a one-two punch this generation doesn't get much of sound doctrine combined with a passion for the presence of God.

Sounds great! Sign me up! There must be something to this passion and sound doctrine. They are growing, so God must be blessing them. What could be better? What is not to like about Sovereign Grace Ministries?

It does sound infectious doesn't it? This is the reaction of thousands of people and dozens of congregations who experience this firsthand and wanted it for themselves. They were so impressed that they did everything in their power to import this mindset to cities and states and countries.

But wait. Hang on a second. What is this thing that **this** generation doesn't get much of? Sound Doctrine? What is that exactly? And do I read that last sentence right? Are they saying that few other churches have passion for the presence of God, and they are somehow

John Immel

unique?

Mmmmm . . . That claim would be a touch on the presumptuous side, so maybe we should give them the benefit of the doubt. It is early in the book, and some of you, dear readers, are not so sure about this gig. Let me try again to decipher that sentence. I think there is only one other possible meaning. SGM is saying that others have **passion**, but it is somehow inferior when absent "sound doctrine"?

Hmm . . . I'm not sure that is any less presumptuous, but it is just one paragraph; a mini blurb on a house rag. It doesn't have any context and there probably isn't anything else like that in their literature. All other written materials are full of humility, good intentions, peace, love, and rainbows.

Or maybe not.

"But what are many Christians and Christian leaders paying close attention to today?" asks Brent Detwiler, a contributor to Sovereign Grace July/August 1998, the magazine of PDI ministries. He goes on to say:

> They're paying close attention to dreams, visions, and prophecy; to conferences, reports of revival, and unusual physical manifestations. They're paying close attention to trends, marketing techniques, and principles of church growth. They're paying close attention to the size of their church, budget, staff, and building. They're paying close attention to sociology, psychology, and psychiatry. They're paying close attention to the latest hot Christian band. **But they are not paying equally close attention either to their lives or their doctrine.** [Emphasis his]

So, all you preachers out there, how could you do such a thing?! How did you get caught up in all those trivialities? When Brent Detwiler showed up to your churches to check your social preoccupations, why didn't you hide it for one day? And you got your doctrine from the local psychiatrist?!

Shame on you!

"**But they are not paying equally close attention either to their lives or their doctrine.**" This sentence should ring some bells with the resident Bible scholars. "Watching your life and doctrine," is the exhortation in the book of Timothy. So by saying that other Christians are watching other things, they are failing to live to a biblical standard. That is pretty bold.

When Brent Detwiler wrote this article, he was part of the "Apostolic Team" within Covenant Life Church, and then he got "promoted" to some "apostolic" church plant.[3] I don't really keep up with the tides of appointments within the group, but now I think he is on the outs with the SGM organization. Or maybe he is back. Who knows? But this we do know: They didn't oust him over this article from ten years ago. So that probably means they liked what he said, which means that his words reflect the broadest assumptions of Sovereign Grace Ministries. Their specific evaluation of ". . . many Christians and Christian leaders" is that they lack true substance and they are not paying attention to the Bible.

This, of course, begs the question: What is this doctrine that everyone else is failing to pay attention to? So we check out some prophecies and some visions. What is the harm? And is anyone going to say that the church budget doesn't really matter?

Really? Is SGM going to say that they fired the

---

3. OK . . . another rumor. They no longer have "apostolic" teams. Or maybe now they are saying they never had them? Or now that they are hobnobbing with the Southern Baptist Convention, they have decided there is a more politically correct name for top leadership. Whatever the truth of the matter, it begs a lot of questions about submission and authority.

John Immel

accountants so they could really, really, really focus on some doctrinal navel-gazing?

What is the big flipping dealeo?

Dave Harvey, another member of their "apostolic leadership" team, wrote of it this way in his article *Workmen or Captives? Avoiding the Snare of Subjectivity* (Sovereign Grace July/August 1998). In classic Dave Harvey style, there is lots of preamble and a handful of side trips that surround his specific point. The temptation is to reproduce the whole article so you can get the full flavor, but that would be tedious. I've still got this magazine, so I guess if I'm accused of somehow misrepresenting, it can be reproduced. But in the interest of brevity, I will summarize Dave's primary and secondary point that brings out his foundational assumption.

Let us begin with the secondary point: Dave Harvey is trying to persuade people who are not inclined to use their mind that thinking is a primary Christian responsibility. Failure to place the mind in the correct spiritual place is a failure of Christian doctrine and ultimately, the source of moral degeneration, spreading heresy, and a deteriorating allegiance to scripture. I suspect that most Christians have this basic assumption. They might not venerate the mind so much but they tend to assume that failing to make scripture primary is the source of the world's woes.

Dave echoes the general consensus in a section called *A Context for Truth*:

> Most Christians are probably comfortable with the idea that the foundation of theology is the Bible. By itself that statement leaves us free to interact with Scripture in a way that can seem fairly autonomous. It places the primary emphasis, appropriately, on an individual relationship with God, through his Word.

Mr. Harvey makes this comment because he is interested in advocating the study of Theology. He knows that most people do not approach their Christianity by using their mind, and most specifically, reading weighty tomes written by historic thinkers. I will address this in much more detail as the book unfolds, but right now I want you to notice the following appeal:

> But do we readily accept the testimony of Scripture itself that the foundation of the Bible is . . . the church? "If I am delayed," Paul wrote to Timothy, "you will know how people ought to conduct themselves in God's household, which is the church of the living God, the pillar and foundation of the truth. (1 Ti 3:15)

Since Dave is asking people to think, pause, and reflect on what he said. This paragraph means that the TRUTH is the specific property of the Church. And if that isn't direct enough for you, his next two sentences say this: "Paradoxically, although truth is indeed the foundation of the church (Eph 2:20), the church is also the foundation for truth. . . . Truth must be anchored and applied within the local church."

This means that TRUTH is specifically confined to a specific body of ideas administrated by some governing organization. This is the preamble to the real point of the article. His closing thoughts sum up the foundational premise well. In the section titled *Subjectivity and Experience*, Dave says:

> It comes down to an issue of authority. For Christians ensnared in subjectivity, spiritual experience can carry an implicit authority that has the effect of overriding Scripture. Such expediencies are commonly used to validate an ungodly decision, justify disassociation from the local church, or claim the right to live a life

John Immel

> unexamined by others. {. . .} Such is the fruit of a church in captivity.

And then under the last section *Workmen or Captives*, he adds this:

> As Christians we must never forget that our remaining sin nature will continually drive us to subordinate the objective truth of Scripture to subjective impressions. We really only have two choices: to become skilled workmen in the rich, timeless, and objective truth of God's Word, or to remain captives—each in our own cramped, subjective little universe of personal impressions.

"It comes down to an issue of authority."

What does?

TRUTH comes down to an issue of authority. The discussion about emotions, experience, and all the subjective rest is merely peripheral to this foundational premise. Authority determines TRUTH because TRUTH is the property of the Church.

Why is TRUTH the property of the Church?

The answer is because the sinful natures of men "drive them to subordinate objective truth." The nature of his corruption drives man to "claim the right to live a life unexamined by others."

This means that even if a man uses his mind, he ultimately cannot be trusted with the conclusions of the mind, because something within him inevitably corrupts the conclusions. Therefore, man cannot claim a right to his own life. Dave Harvey's entire article is in service to this premise: TRUTH is the property of the Church, the lives of men are the property of the church and subordinate to a specific authority.

OK . . . fine. But here is a question: Who within the church determines if we have got the right understanding? Who determines if we have watched the right doctrine? Who determines if we have successfully watched our lives?

Dave Harvey answers that question in a book called *Sovereign Grace Perspectives: Polity*. (Notice page 12). He is evaluating the source of authority for "biblical" government. He is seeking to draw out specific understanding from Romans 12:6-8. His concluding exegesis says this:

Let's track Paul's progression of thought here:
1) We all have different gifts (v.6a).
2) Our gifts are the result of a prior work of grace (v.6b).
3) The grace God has given determines the boundaries of our gifts and service (v.6).35
4) Some have been given a distinct grace to lead (v.8).
5) The grace to lead is exhibited by a "zealous and diligent concern" 36 (v.8).⁴

Whatever Paul's progression of thought may be, notice the implicit presumptions Mr. Harvey is advocating. His effective logic is:

1. Our different gifts are given to us (not earned).
2. Grace determines/necessitates boundaries.
3. Leadership is God's manifest boundary on gifts and talents.
4. "Zeal" and "Concern" is tantamount to Leadership.
5. Leadership is tantamount to Government.

Anyway, Dave's progression above is a direct way of saying, "You don't own you; the **Leadership** does." God's

---

4. Dave Harvey, *Polity: Serving and Leading the Local Church* (Gaithersburg: Sovereign Grace Media, 2004).

gifts are not yours to lay claim. Therefore, you are not justified in doing what you want or exercising initiative with those gifts. Since God limits you by grace, he limits you by leadership because leadership is a manifestation of grace.

Leadership, therefore, means government. By the hallmark of their "zeal" and "concern," they are distinguished to perform the appointed job of administering your life in God's stead. This means that Christian leaders get to organize your life. And since the content of doctrine is the primary force of good action, that means they get to tell everyone what to think.

Hmm . . . interesting.

OK . . . for the sake of generosity, amicability, and Christian love, let us ask these questions. Maybe they are right. Just because PDI/CLC/SGM make a bold proclamation doesn't mean the assertion is wrong. Just because a few men say they have found the TRUTH doesn't make them, by default, presumptuous. If they, in fact, have the best ideas, doesn't it make sense that they should be able to tell people what to think?

In light of the claim that bad ideas are the driving force of snares and bondage and immorality, then shouldn't somebody with the right answers **do something** about it? Maybe man really does need protection from himself. Maybe everyone would do well to believe what SGM is unabashed in advocating.

Grace = leadership = government = truth.
Therefore,
Man = subjective = deceived = immorality.

True or not?

How can we know if this is true?

Well, answering this question poses a challenge,

because on the one hand, we are being told that the use of our mind is a primary Christian expression. But on the other hand, we are told that TRUTH is in fact the property of the Church, which really means the property of leadership.

"Oh John, they can't possibly mean that. PDI/CLC/SGM doesn't want mindless obedience?"

Well, part of Dave's article seems to say men can't be trusted with the truth, but other places he seems to say something else.

Notice the section *A Good Workman*:

> Theology literally means the study of God. And because the foundation of theology is the Bible, a good theologian is simply a Christian who takes Scripture seriously.
>
> The last letter of Paul's life, his second letter to Timothy—**reinforces the centrality**—of good theology. [Emphasis mine] Paul's final words of instruction had one clear goal: Timothy must keep his pattern of sound teaching and guard the good deposit of sound doctrine (2Ti 1:13-14). Above all else, Paul stresses, Timothy must remain a good **theologian**.

According to Dave's comment, Paul is telling us that we must be good theologians to be good Christians. And since I happen to like theology, that sounds pretty good to me. How can they argue with someone who is doing what Paul commands? We just want to be good workman and study theology . . . study ideas . . . study the TRUTH, right?

And Dave adds this gem:

> Under the inspiration of the Holy Spirit, Paul is teaching that correct handling of Scripture springs from correct thinking about Scripture.

John Immel
> True insight is always preceded by mental reflection.

Hmm . . . "True Insight is always preceded by mental reflection." So just in case the TRUTH isn't the property of a select group of men, let's mentally reflect.

4
Welcome to the Arena of Ideas

Don't worry about people stealing your ideas. If your ideas are any good, you'll have to ram them down people's throats.

—Howard Aiken

Human history is, in essence, a history of ideas.

—H.G. Wells

It is not once nor twice but times without number that the same ideas make their appearance in the world.

—Aristotle

Do you feel the expanse of the coliseum, and the crowd looking on, and the tides of opinion ebbing and flowing? Stoicism, Platonism, Neo Platonism, Augustinianism, Taoism, Romanticism, Rationalism, Skepticism, Subjectivism, Nihilism, Modernism, Post Modernism, Determinism, Empiricism, Marxism, Socialism, Liberalism, Logical Positivism, Conservatism, Islam, Judaism, Christianity . . . and the list goes on and on.

Do you feel the wind whipping around your mind?

Do you feel the soft cool sand under your feet? The Latin word *hara* is sand, and *harna* came to mean the part of the Roman amphitheater that was covered with sand. In the ancient Roman coliseums, they put sand on the floor to soak up the blood.

How is that for a vivid image? Do you have the courage

John Immel

to stay here? Or does the thought of shedding blood for Ideas bring a tremble to your soul? This place is not for the faint of heart or mind.

The dictionary says that arena means:
1. a place or scene where forces contend or events unfold.
2. any place of public contest or exertion, any sphere of action as in the arena of debate, or the arena of life.

Arenas are for competition. Arenas are for the public, for humanity, to watch and see. In arenas people cheer for their teams: celebrating victories and mourning defeats. In arenas we see the best of the best excel over the worst of the worst.

The greatest battles are fought here in The Arena of Ideas because this is where freedoms are won, liberties are secured, and lives restored.

Our earliest recorded contenders, the peoples of the Ancient Near East, 3100–2000 BCE, dealt with the heady question of our origin; they developed a story to illustrate human beginnings called *The Epic of Gilgamesh*. The Babylonians, circa 2000–1600 BCE, entered the Arena of Ideas with astrological charting and the measuring of time. The Far Eastern culture contributed with *Shintoism, Daoism, Confucianism,* and *Buddhism*.

Our roots in the West begin in Greece and the contributions of the Hellenistic thinkers and historians Herodotus (c.490–c.425 BCE), Thucydides (c.460/455–c.399 BCE), Xenophon (c.428–c.354 BCE), Plato (c. 428–c.347) Aristotle (384–323 BCE), Plutarch (c.46–c.120 CE), Pausanias (fl.c.160 CE). But while our western roots have thousands of years of historic depth, our United States heritage is a collision of two recent developments in the Arena of Ideas: The Reformation and The Enlightenment.

When the boats landed in the New World, they were filled

with human heads packed with Reformation/Enlightenment thinking. Reformation additions to the Arena of Ideas in American thought were advanced by men like Martin Luther (1483–1546) John Calvin (c 1509–1564), John Owen (1616–1683), Cotton Mather (1663–1728), and Jonathan Edwards (1703–1758). Enlightenment additions to American thought came from men like, Saint Thomas Aquinas (1225–1274), Francis Bacon (1561–1626), Rene Descartes (1596–1650), Isaac Newton (1642–1727), and John Locke (1632–1704).

Do you feel the expanse of the coliseum yet? Do you see the historic crowd looking on? Can you feel the power of the tides of opinion threatening to wash you this way and that? Rather more like a maelstrom tossing about your head than a small wind whipping around your mind, don't you think?

Great men and evil men alike have fought here—fought for the spoils of the human mind and soul and spirit. Some great men with ignoble ideas have fought here. And fortunately for us, in spite of their greatness, they lost. Some ignoble men with great ideas fought here. And to our great fortunes, in spite of their ignobility, they won. Some evil men with ignoble purpose have entered the arena and spread disaster when good men did nothing.

For convenience and clarity, the conflicts in the Arena of Ideas get segmented into economics, or politics, or religion. Sometimes people forget that the names are just designed to give us a starting place and exclude people from commenting out of their disciplines. This is a mistake because all ideas are connected somehow.

The connection of ideas is called Philosophy. Unfortunately, in the mind of many, this word is synonymous with useless ideas batted around like so many beach balls at the intellectual equivalent of a Thelonious Monk concert: really abstract with endless indecipherable phrases. Or they tend to assume that philosophy is an atheistic alternative to theology. And since the Apostle Paul aired out his full distaste of "vain philosophies," most Christians treat the word like a synonym for fornication: something never uttered, never discussed, and roundly condemned.

The tragedy of this scorn is everyone seeks to integrate their ideas into a cohesive whole. The absence of awareness only means people evade a key element of their own consciousness and abandon the means to find governing principles. The abandonment of governing principles means that the results are a hodgepodge of competing, conflicting thoughts in endless competition with emotion, and sensation. The science of organizing human consciousness into a system of effective ideas is called philosophy. And without such a practice, ideas exist in an unconnected, disjointed, causeless vacuum. Man cannot live this way any more than he can give up breathing, so he defaults to whatever ideas fill up the void.

So, irrespective of Paul's problem with his intellectual contemporaries, philosophies don't magically disappear because men forsake the field of ideas. No amount of theological whitewash will prevent men from seeking to answer these fundamental questions.

- How we define the nature of existence.
- How we know what we know.
- How we value what we know.
- How we interact with other people.

These questions represent the four primary branches of philosophical study: Metaphysics, Epistemology, Ethics, and Politics.

Of course, Christians believe that the Bible has answered these questions, and we integrate our thinking accordingly. So, when we say, "Jesus died for our sins . . ." we are actually making a metaphysical summation of what we believe about the nature of human existence. These five words are an abbreviation for Original Sin and Federal Guilt, and the doctrine of Atonement. This is one of many examples of how man integrates his ideas into a cohesive whole.

Men are the sum of their collective ideas. From the time we are born, we are integrating the world from concrete to abstract ideas. The baby who realizes that mommy under a blanket does not disappear is making a philosophic discovery about the nature of existence. Men who put rockets into space are exploiting the metaphysical nature of the universe by manipulating their epistemology. People are forever taking ideas, categorizing them, and placing them in systems for use. Without this ability, we would still be waiting for the gods to manifest fire.

Humans are built to think, to engage the world we live in with our judgment. The way we get better at thinking is by accumulating effective ideas. The way we decide what ideas we have, where we got them, and which ones are good or bad, and how we should use those ideas in context to other people is the progression from Metaphysics to Epistemology, to Ethics, to Politics. Or said another way, this progression starts with the most basic truths of the world in which we live to how we know what we know, to how we should treat other people, to how government is empowered to enforce our ethical assumptions.

So now you know when I talk about philosophy, I am not tossing about intellectual beach balls. I am referring to the integration of ideas: how we know what we know, where ideas came from, their objective value, and how those ideas impact our (human) interaction.

In the pages to come, this might be important.

So, here we are, taking a broad look around the panorama of human thought and its vast rich history.

John Immel

Now I must draw your attention to one of the segments I mentioned: religion. Religion is where warriors are clad for battle in Christian Theology; it is here that we will take up Mr. Harvey's call for mental reflection. Here, we will apply our intellectual passion! Here, we will engage ideas for the spoils of the human mind and soul and spirit.

Theology: That Four-Letter Word

The section title is pretty cool, huh?

People don't much like Theology. The word implies a lot, sounds ominous and deep, but says very little. If I insisted that you needed to know Theology, you would roll your eyes, and sigh, and think, *I've lived twenty years as a Christian and I've done pretty well without.*

You would do it in that order, just like that.

So, the trick here is for me to zig when you think I'm going to zag.

I think this four-letter word stuff is fun, fun, fun, but I'd rather spend my time making money. Was that too transparent? Oh well, my deep, complex, flawed character lends to the charm of being the protagonist.

By the way, for the last twenty years that you **haven't** been studying Theology, that isn't entirely true. You've got a Theology: a Doctrine of God. You have a set of theories that you believe because of the ideas you have accumulated over that time.

No big deal, everybody does.

We all have an intellectual process created to systematize who God is in context to us and who we are in context to God. As I said above, this is the insatiable human drive to integrate ideas in action.

No big deal, everybody does.

So, why does everybody roll their eyes and insist that

that they don't need theology?

Here is the answer: We take our beliefs very personally; our beliefs are our self-image. We believe **what** we believe because . . . we just do. We don't want someone to crush the faith out of us, crush us with our wrong beliefs. We don't want to risk hearing that what we believe is not right because that would mean that we are not right. That makes looking at ideas the same thing as looking at ourselves. And who has the time to do that?

Let me show you the theology secret handshake: the better your ideas, the better your identity. Warriors are confident because they are competent. In the Arena of Ideas, people are trying to unmake you, but you can never escape the Arena. The choice before you is competence or capitulation. Your current fear, and pain, and suffering are embedded in capitulation. I have walked this path. Come with me, aspiring Jedi, and let me give you a brief glimpse of the arena that is Theology.

Here is a lightsaber for your protection.

Jedi, Tai Chi, Kung Fu, and Karate

Trust me this is going somewhere. I like metaphors and we are already talking about the Arena of Ideas where fighting goes on. The following is a small breakdown of the avenues of Theological combat, oops, I mean, studies; see it's a cool metaphor . . . or maybe it's a simile . . . Who can tell?

I am about to give some general definitions. What follows is not designed to be comprehensive. My goal is to give you, dear aspiring Jedi, a sense of scope, the highpoints of sub-disciplines. This will give those new to the arena of Theology a sense of the breadth of formal inquiry into Bible ideas.

Biblical Theology seeks to understand the progression of God's revelation as He introduced himself in context to culture, social political, and theological understanding.

John Immel

Since the term "biblical" tends to be broadly applied to most any academic effort that addresses Bible understanding, Biblical Theology tends to be co-opted to mean many things. But in this instance, the term is applied to the specific perspective. In each book, the audience understood specific "truths" about the world. To understand what God was saying and doing requires understanding this broad conventional wisdom in context, and then limiting interpretive conclusions to those guidelines.

For instance, Gerhard von Rad identified the theme of covenant.[1] Then he read Bible books in light of this theme as the foundation of his interpretive methodology.

Historical Theology is the study of Christian thought through the succeeding centuries of Church history. One can study the entire body of thought of say, 100 CE to 200 CE. Or one can study the Theology of a given thinker or schools of thought, like Augustine and his intellectual children, Luther and Calvin.

Practical Theology or Task Theology is really just a fancy name for "How the heck do we apply all these big words and big ideas to people living their life and paying their bills and raising their kids?" (The scholar types reading this are going to luuuvvvv me.)

Systematic Theology seeks to give an ordered account of major themes in scripture, taking each reference and compiling it with all others to form a systematic picture of Bible ideas. The major themes are designated by some big Greek words that are easy to get once you understand the root words. *Logos* means teaching, or words, or doctrine. The prefixes tell us what the words or teachings are about.

Theo*logy* then would be easily translated: Doctrines of

---

1. Gerhard von Rad, *Old Testament Theology: The Theology of Israel's Historical Traditions*, vol. 1, intro. Walter Brueggemann, trans. D. M. G. Stalker (Louisville: Westminster John Knox Press, 2001).

God. The remaining six themes are:
- **Anthropology:** doctrines of Man
- **Christology:** doctrines of Christ
- **Soteriology:** doctrines of Salvation
- **Pneumatology:** doctrines of the Spirit
- **Ecclesiology:** doctrines of the Church
- **Eschatology:** doctrines of End Things

An example of a Systematic Theology related to our current discussion is John Calvin's *Institutes of the Christian Religion*. But to be sure, there are many, many others with various doctrinal assumptions, presuppositions, and historic filters.

All right, we're studying and studying and studying, compiling our stack of scriptures, reading each passage as if it can be cut and paste together to make our 21st century doctrinal point.

Lo and behold, some bright boy raises his hand and says, "But what did those Israelites think about God? I mean, they were closer to the source. Wouldn't that make their understanding better?"

So people with intellectual integrity say, "Oh, darn. Now we have to figure out what their culture and politics and so forth were to understand what they believed, because that background probably affects what I should think those passages mean. We can't use scriptures like so many Legos to make our doctrinal point. We have to draw out the meaning from their culture."

Yes, they say all of that.

The process of drawing out, of evaluating, what the original audience understood is what people call Exegetics. But the process is far from done. Now the task is to integrate what historic people thought and practiced with how to apply it to our 21st century brains and make our own

John Immel

practice. This is called Hermeneutics.

Exegetics is the science of extracting biblical information.

Hermeneutics is the science of interpretation and application.

Hold your lightsaber high. Protect yourself. Quick now, Jedi, on guard: stick and move, slash and burn. Whewww! You are safe for the moment. You interpret, Jedi. But do you do it well? Are you qualified, young Jedi? Can you use the force?

Exegetics in Brief

Thomas Aquinas introduced Aristotle into Christian Theology in the 13th century. This means that he introduced the primary elements of reason and modern intellectual inquiry into the biblical realm. From him, over a few hundred years and many, many fits and starts, Higher Critical Methodology has evolved with different influences until it took its full shape through the early 20th century.[2]

What does Critical mean? It means that man must use his brain to make effective distinctions; he must apply reason and logic to the content of Bible ideas to successfully grasp the broader intent, meaning, and application. While the Bible does speak of truth, it is no mere talisman to be blindly followed, but rather something to be studied and understood in full. For about one hundred fifty years, theologians have employed an increasingly complex science to draw out the details of Bible texts and the subsequent understanding. A few of the disciplines are Historical Criticism, Redaction Criticism, Textual Criticism, Literary-Source Criticism, and Form Criticism.

Think of a belt full of weapons. Having the right weapon

---

2. Higher Critical Methodology is the umbrella term for a whole bunch of sub-disciplines.

for the fight decides whether you live or die. Or maybe those timid souls amongst the readership would like a more pacifistic metaphor or simile . . . Who can tell?

Think of a belt full of tools. Having the right tools means you can build the right house.

Hermeneutics in Brief

Taking what you have drawn out of scripture and finding a way to apply it to your own life is the essence of Hermeneutics. Interpretation is an iterative process done by everyone. Most people interpret by saying to themselves, "Well, this means to me . . ." The "This means to me. . ." approach to interpretation is of the flip-open-the-Bible-and-point variety. It is self-actualization at its highest expression. Henry David Thoreau would be proud. For most, this is not a terribly disastrous methodology. But trust me, it is very limiting.

How people have interpreted has changed drastically over the centuries.

Allegory was the primary interpretive method for most of Church history. It treated Bible passages as symbolic designed to represent a broader moral or religious principle. A great example would be the two swords the disciples showed Jesus at the Last Supper. The Universal Church allegorized them to represent the sword of the state and the sword of the Spirit, or temporal power and spiritual power.

Most all historic doctrines turn on interpretive methodology. Meaning, the doctrine has less to do with what the Bible **says** and more to do with the **specific method** of reading, extracting, and applying the interpretation.

Reading the Bible requires the action of interpretation. It doesn't matter what level of comprehension—from a child's beginning effort to grasp John 3:16, to a seminary graduate wrestling with Theodicy (the problem of evil)—they are engaged in some form of interpretation. And therefore, by default, they are applying critical thinking to what they read.

The science behind the Exegetics and Hermeneutics are the methods and questions a person learns to ask. The better one gets at asking the right questions, the better one becomes at getting the right answers from the Bible.

"Uh . . . John, are there basic questions that the average Joe Sixpack can ask without having to learn about all that . . . that . . . that four-letter word stuff?"

A compelling question, aspiring Jedi. And by the way, I am assuming that your Joe Sixpack is drinking Coke or something. Certainly, there is a Christian version of Mr. Sixpack. We've got a Christian version of everything else.

Anyway, back to this theology stuff.

What are the most basic questions of Higher Critical Methodology? Take notes, there is a quiz later.

Here they are:
- Who is talking/writing?
- Who is listening?
- What is the occasion?

Say them out loud. Learn these questions. Live these questions. Love these questions.

5
Let's Practice

> Let it be your constant method to look into the design of people's actions, and see what they would be at, as often as it is practicable; and to make this custom the more significant, practice it first upon yourself.
>
> —Marcus Aurelius

You read about candles under bushels in the New Testament. Your Historical Criticism helps pinpoint that a candle is strikingly similar in use to a flashlight. Now, young Jedi, use your questions. Jesus is talking to a bunch of everyday folks, trying to explain a spiritual principle. What did they hear? What would be the application today? They heard candle. But in today's vernacular, it would be synonymous with flashlight.

Jesus would tell us not to put our flashlight under a cover.

Aha, very good, young Jedi. The resulting cosmetic interpretation yields interesting possibilities.

All right, another test. You have just read Matthew and noticed that he repeatedly says "Kingdom of Heaven," and you noticed that other Gospel writers call it "Kingdom of God." Is there something to be drawn out here? Maybe. Ask your questions, young Jedi. Once again, your Historical Criticism reveals that Matthew wrote his book to Jews. But what does it mean? Young Jedi, use the force. What would the original hearers have heard? Matthew is making a theological translation because saying "Kingdom of God" would have put off his

John Immel

audience: Jews. The Hebrew for God was never spoken.

Now, the last test. When reading Romans 10:4, you encounter ". . . Christ is the end of the law." What is contained within these seven words, young Jedi? Is there a sermon here worth preaching? To whom was Paul writing? What would these men have heard? This one is hard. Be patient with yourself. Cultural/religious interpretation is needed, young Jedi.

I submit that the rendering should be ". . . the goal at which the *Torah* aims is the *Messiah*." Study, young Jedi, and find out why.

Our questions really help us draw out some potent meaning. So, do we know we have the truth yet?

Ah, my young Jedi, we are getting the pith of the issues at hand. We are treading dangerously close to the dark side of the force, the conflict of our story. I first must show you the last part of the secret handshake so that we can fight off the perils ahead. The secret handshake is important because it helps identify those things that skew the process.

Assumptions, Presuppositions, Filters

I've never heard anyone else talk about these three things in context to Bible interpretation. So, you may be witnessing a first, an innovation, a wonder of the modern world. Or, maybe I just haven't read that book yet. I'm sure somebody will set me straight.

Anyway, you will remember that I zigged when you thought I was going to zag, right? And you remember that I talked about people's reluctance to study Theology, right? For most people, their beliefs, their ideas, and their identities are the same. Deliberately walking into an Arena where people try to change your ideas is similar

Blight in the Vineyard

to walking into a lion's cage and realizing he's trying to change you into lunch. To have someone change their ideas is tantamount to death.

As a rule, people believe what they believe just because they do. Maybe they can make a case for themselves about why they believe, but **believing** for most people is an inexplicit function that when pressured is not much deeper than the polish on a dresser. Assumptions, presuppositions, and filters go to the root of human conviction, the bedrock of human belief. These words describe the visceral, the human part of the interpretive process and are therefore, the stuff of fear, the stuff of ego, the stuff of self-worth, the stuff of intellectual myopia.

We must then make ourselves use the tools of Higher Critical Methodology to pull back the veneer and scratch what is underneath. The **art** of interpretation is learning to identify your presuppositions and checking them against the intent and purpose of the Bible text and God's revelation as a whole. Can you test your assumptions, young Jedi? Can you separate your presuppositions, your unstated foundational truths? Can you remove your filters from your ears and know that ideas are not identity? Many cannot. They will never be Jedi Masters.

A test on assumptions:

What do you think "Doctrine" is? Can you give a definition? Write it down. It is important to engage this here because we are going to compare notes later. What did you write?

A test on presuppositions:

Every time you read "Doctrine," you have a

nomenclature in your mind as to what the writer means. I am using the word "nomenclature" to describe your interpretive tradition: all the sources that have molded your understanding of the word. For example, when you read "Doctrine," you automatically fill in the blank with what your pastor told you doctrine meant, your given Bible understanding, and what books you've read, and your own personal prejudices. All of these sources get tossed into a pot to simmer, and what comes out is what you think the writer meant. This is the nomenclature of the word "Doctrine." Now, go back and write down what you think the Bible writers meant by "Doctrine." This is your presupposition about what was in the mind of the writer.

A test on filters:

When you read, how do you process what you hear? Filters are like the lenses of a camera: shading and coloring, preventing certain types of light from invading the picture.

Christian filters are the combination of assumptions and presuppositions that limit and bend ideas to conform to root/core beliefs. Certainly, you have encountered people who cannot change their mind, even though the product of their thinking is disaster. This is because the filters on their thinking bend, shade, and color the communicated words/ideas.

So when you read, how does your understanding of the word "Doctrine" bend, shade, and color HOW you hear? If you worked through this little test, you will start to see you're sponsoring thoughts that affect your believing.

Now, young Jedi, you're ready to venture into the world of Theology. You now know the secret handshake. Go forth and do well. But beware, the Subjectivity Beast

lurks ahead.
   'Cause now I'm gonna mess with your mind.
   Boowwaaah ha ha haha hahah!

"I Have You Now . . ."

   You read the Bible.
   You interpret.
   You stand up and tell people you have the truth.
   Do you teach rightly?
   Do you have Sound Doctrine?
   Are you sure?
   Why are you sure? Because Paul told you to have it? Do you have Sound Doctrine because you agree with some 16th century thinker?
   Are doctrine and theology the same?
   Did Paul mean have sound Theology when he spoke to Timothy about sound doctrine: ". . . the sound doctrine that conforms to the glorious gospel of the blessed God . . ."?
   What did Paul say doctrine was?
   Did he say what doctrine was?
   What are your presuppositions, Jedi? Look deep because you've got some.
   Does it mean theology?
   What nomenclature pervades your mind, Jedi, when you filter the word "doctrine" with theology? With that nomenclature in your mind, what does it do to the word "Gospel"? How does it shade the meaning?
   What does "Gospel" mean?
   Can you look past your filters to see the word "Gospel" afresh? Does it mean literally "Good News" or is it nomenclature for Jesus dying on a cross, buried, and resurrected on the third day? Or does the word "Gospel" the totality of thinking contained in the twenty-seven

John Immel

books of the New Testament?

Come on, Jedi, review your notes quickly because the men are coming and they are going to tell you that your beliefs are wrong.

Hurry!!!!

What are the questions to ask and what answers do you get? And when you get the answers, do you have the courage to hear the answers?

Jesus came preaching the Gospel, yes? That Gospel was Good News, yes? That Good News was about a New Covenant, yes? The New Covenant he brought destroyed yokes of bondage and lifted burdens, yes? God preached the Gospel BEFORE to Abraham when he said, "In Him all the nations of the Earth would be blessed." Long before the Cross, the Gospel was preached.

So what is the "Gospel," Jedi? And how do you know you have apprehended rightly? Justify your doctrine, Jedi.

Did I mess with your mind?

I'm not done.

Some Plagiarism

I didn't write what you are about to read. And for my own reasons, I am not going to give credit to who it was; hence, the section title. The following is from a Jedi who tackled the question concerning Sound Doctrine and Theology.

A Word About Doctrine[1] [sic]

---

1. doctrine (d¼k"tr´n) n. − a) a body of principles presented for acceptance or belief, as by a religious, political, or philosophic group; b) a statement of official government policy, especially in foreign affairs. [From Latin doctr°na, teaching.] doctri"nal adj.

The American Heritage® Concise Dictionary," (c) 1994

So, what is doctrine in scripture[2]? Doctrine is the basic tenet of the Gospel. Jesus came. He was anointed (good news: he came to destroy burdens and yokes and to heal the sick). He was crucified. He was resurrected. He ascended into heaven so that he could send the Holy Spirit (good news: the Holy Spirit was far better, he said). Jesus is the source of salvation, and truth, and an abundant life. These things are plain. These things are clear. These things do not require vast amount of interpretation.

So, what is soundness[3]? If doctrine is the basic truth that governs us, then soundness relates not to the nature of that truth but to the effort that we exert in adhering to the TRUTH we see in scripture. How we live and what we believe are inextricably intertwined (watch your life and your doctrine).

That is supported in Paul's writings to Timothy and Titus:

> 9 We also know that law is made not for the righteous but for lawbreakers and rebels, the

---

Houghton Mifflin Company. (c) 1994 INSO Corporation. All rights reserved.
    2. 1319. didaskalia, did-as-kal-ee'-ah; from G1320; instruction (the function or the information):--doctrine, learning, teaching.
    1320. didaskalos, did-as'-kal-os; from G1321; an instructor (gen. or spec.):--doctor, master, teacher.
    1321. didasko, did-as'-ko; a prol. (caus.) form of a prim. verb dao (to learn); to teach (in the same broad application):--teach.
    3. 12 5198. hugiaino, hoog-ee-ah'ee-no; from G5199; to have sound health, i.e. be well (in body); fig. to be uncorrupt (true in doctrine):--be in health, (be safe and) sound, (be) whole (-some).
    5199. hugies, hoog-ee-ace'; from the base of G837; healthy, i.e. well (in body); fig. true (in doctrine):--sound, whole.
    837. auxano, owx-an'-o; a prolonged form of a prim. verb; to grow ("wax"), i.e. enlarge (lit. or fig., act. or pass.):--grow (up), (give the) increase

ungodly and sinful, the unholy and irreligious; for those who kill their fathers or mothers, for murderers, 10 for adulterers and perverts, for slave traders and liars and perjurers--and for whatever else is contrary to the sound doctrine 11 that conforms to the glorious gospel of the blessed God, which he entrusted to me.

1 Timothy 1

16 Watch your life and doctrine closely. Persevere in them, because if you do, you will save both yourself and your hearers.

1 Timothy 4

3 **For the time will come when men will not put up with sound doctrine.** Instead, to suit their own desires, they will gather around them a great number of teachers to say what their itching ears want to hear.

2 Timothy 4

9 He must hold firmly to the trustworthy message as it has been taught, so that he can encourage others by sound doctrine and refute those who oppose it.

13 This testimony is true. Therefore, rebuke them sharply, so that they will be sound in the faith 14 and will pay no attention to Jewish myths or to the commands of those who reject the truth.

Titus 1

So when we read about "sound doctrine" and "watching our doctrine carefully," what should we make of that? Was Paul advocating one superior, infallible

Blight in the Vineyard

belief system? Was he foretelling Calvinism[4] or Arminianism[5]?

No. Calvinism and Arminianism are not doctrines in the sense that Paul was talking about. (They are certainly not the Gospel). They are really theologies[6] and are the result of much more interpretation than the doctrine that Paul was talking. Jesus healing people is doctrine; the Trinity is theology. You can read about Jesus healing people and gain understanding without any interpretation. It takes miles of interpretation to get the Trinity.

A Word about Theology

Theology is essentially a manmade creation. Theology is developed when any person reads and interprets the

---

4. Calvinist doctrine lies within the Augustinian theological tradition. Its central tenets include belief in the absolute sovereignty of God and the doctrine of justification by faith alone (see Faith). As did the German religious reformer Martin Luther, Calvin denied that human beings were capable of free will after the Fall of Adam, but he went farther than Luther in elaborating a doctrine of predestination, that certain persons are elected by God to salvation while others are rejected by him and consigned to eternal damnation.

"Calvinism," Microsoft(R) Encarta(R) 97 Encyclopedia. (c) 1993-1996 Microsoft Corporation. All rights reserved.

5. Arminianism, a doctrine in Christianity formulated in the 17th century, which declares that human free will can exist without limiting God's power or contradicting the Bible. Named for the Dutch Calvinist Jacobus Arminius, the doctrine gradually became a liberal alternative to the more rigid belief in predestination held by High Calvinists in Holland and elsewhere (see Calvinism, predestination).

"Arminianism," Microsoft(R) Encarta(R) 97 Encyclopedia. (c) 1993-1996 Microsoft Corporation. All rights reserved.

6. The•ol•o•gy (th¶-¼l". . .-j¶) n. pl. the•ol•o•gies
    1. The study of the nature of God and religious truth.
    2. A system or school of opinions concerning God and religious questions.
-- the"o•lo"gi•an (-. . .-1½"j. . .n) n. -- the"o•log"i•cal (-. . .-1¼j"¹-k. . .l) adj. -- the"o•log"i•cal•ly adv.

John Immel

Word of God, systematizes it, and forms a belief system out of it. And if we understand anything about the deficiencies of man, how completely sound could any theology really be? Unless we rely on divine revelation, and soundness comes into question there, too.

Therefore, we essentially have an intellectual process implemented by less than perfect creatures to explain who God is in the context of us and who we are in the context of God. That's good. We need a framework to operate in. But when our theological focus becomes explaining what does and does not happen (which is how we sell and use theology), then we have a problem.

Both Calvinism and Arminianism are systematic belief systems that, in this day and age, are primarily used to explain why the good things that we see in the Bible don't happen to us—either God didn't want it to happen (Calvinism) or we caused it not to (Arminianism).

So, why are we so interested in explanations?

I guarantee that anyone walking around in Abraham's day did not need to ask when and why the provision and blessing of God occurred. They took it for granted that it did. Why else would any grown man (Abraham and all of his servants) be circumcised (ouch!) to participate in a covenant? That was no kind of Santa Claus faith. They would have to have seen it to believe it. If the covenant were conditional on God (Calvinism) or on the participants (Arminianism), then who would sacrifice to participate in that?

A covenant is a formal binding agreement; compact or contract. A covenant is not a possibility. It is ridiculous to talk about new conditions or requirements once a contract has been ratified. God gave a promise: He does not then get to say which circumstantial provisions of that promise don't bring him glory or aren't good for the participants. (Calvinism) God gave a promise: Is that covenant so weak that I can prevent the results of it with my own will? (Arminianism)

What did Paul say doctrine was? The Truth. The Gospel. The Good News (. . . *the sound doctrine that conforms to the glorious gospel of the blessed God – 1 Timothy*). Jesus came bringing the Truth, the Gospel, a new covenant, a better covenant, and one that would be ratified by his blood. This was good news. He came to destroy bondage, lift burdens, and heal people. This was the manifestation of the covenant that he brought.

Why do we spend so much time talking about why these things do not happen? How little we expect of God today. People who walked with Jesus and saw Jesus touch others were not asking why—they were asking how. How do I participate in that? How do I get some of that? Jesus did not offer any condition that had to be met other than faith. There were no conditions about my sanctification or his glory—those things are natural outworkings of faith! Yeah, I know. Paul talked about those things. But do we interpret Jesus by Paul or Paul by Jesus? Paul was all about further describing the Covenant, not adding conditions to it.

Here Ends My Plagiarism

Now aspiring Jedis say, "Amen, Sister Jedi." And yes, the person who wrote this was a woman. Can you believe it? She did it all by her female self. She used big words and talked about Theology. GASP!

Did you see what the Jedi did? Did you watch as she asked the right questions?

Who is talking?

Who is he talking to?

John Immel

What is the occasion?

It doesn't matter if you happen to agree with her conclusions; the point of the section is to illustrate someone seeking to use the methodology I have been talking about. Did you watch as she tested assumptions, exposited presuppositions, and addressed the misapplication of filters? It is all here, aspiring Jedi, a brief example of the basic tools of Higher Critical Methodology used to arrive at some solid understanding.

And notice how much the methodology opens ideas and concepts. Notice how much understanding comes from the demonstrated critical thinking. Notice how the conclusions are not a vague product of subjectivism. To the exact opposite, the tools give definition and limitation to the resulting conclusions. And more importantly, never once did Sister Jedi have to appeal to an overt authority to compel an intellectual outcome.

Do you see the possibilities? Do you have the strength to ask the questions? Do you have the courage to hear the answers?

Resulting Mental Reflection

So, have I done it yet? In chapter 1 I defined my goals:
- Empower you with tools, intellectual tools, so that you gain confidence in your own life with God.
- Equip you so that you can grasp the Arena of Ideas and the tides of Christian thought that are at the root of the practices that drive the error.

Everything to this point has been directed toward showing you the content and context of The Arena of

Blight in the Vineyard

Ideas. Here is what I want you to see. The Arena of Theology is huge. Christian thought has undergone massive evolution: from some very simpleminded beginnings to a very complex art/science. I suspect you are seeing by now that The Arena of Theology is a vast complex place and all I have done is give the barest overview. This brief tour is designed to give you a sense of proportion, and context to evaluate the claims being made by the denomination under discussion.

So with that proportion in place, I'm going to start on my last objective listed in chapter 1: Talk candidly of the PDI/CLC/SGM anecdote, the arguments that support their practices, so we can see the power of the ideas in action. Therefore, let's do a brief tour around their leading ideas. Are you ready?

Let us start with good old Dave Harvey. Do you remember what he said?

". . . Paul's final words of instruction had one clear goal: Timothy must keep his pattern of sound teaching and guard the good deposit of sound doctrine.

. . .

Above all else, Paul stresses, Timothy must remain a good **theologian**."

Jedi, Let us do the work. What are his assumption, his presuppositions, his filters?

Do you see Mr. Harvey's explicit assumption that to Paul, Doctrine and Historic Theology are the same? The PDI/CLC progression is **"watch your life and your doctrine" = mentally reflecting + historic theology = sound doctrine.**

Now evaluate. Reflect back on Sister Jedi's thoughts. Use the tools. Ask the questions. Make sure for yourself. If you have to put this book down, grab your Bible, and think through what is being said, do so. Let's not let Mr.

John Immel

Harvey down: mentally reflect! The tools to evaluate what Paul was saying have been provided to you.

Is Mr. Harvey's progression sound? No, it is not. And you know why, don't you?

That is right. How can historic theology be the subject of Paul's affirmation? By definition, those ideas as presented would not have been on Paul's mind. Are you satisfied? Are you with me? Because we can't rest here; we must press on to mentally reflect on the rest of what is being said.

> We call it Impassioned Orthodoxy . . . . It's a one-two punch this generation doesn't get much of—sound doctrine combined with a passion for the presence of God.

Sound Doctrine? Impassioned Orthodoxy? And do I infer correctly that sound doctrine is that Orthodoxy? What does that mean?

This is the next question that must be answered. What are the leaders at PDI/CLC/SGM saying when they make these claims of Impassioned Orthodoxy and Sound Doctrine?

Now we are going to evaluate the next part of the progression: **Sound Doctrine = A Specific Theological System = Orthodoxy = Authentic Christianity.**

6
Moral, Authentic Orthodoxy

When the churches literally ruled society, the human drama encompassed:

a) slavery
b) the cruel subjection of women
c) the most savage forms of legal punishment
d) the absurd belief that kings ruled by divine right
e) the daily imposition of physical abuse
f) cold heartlessness for the sufferings of the poor
g) (g) as well as assorted pogroms ('ethnic cleansing' wars)between rival religions, capital punishment for literally hundreds of offences, and countless other daily imposed moral outrages. . . . [I]t was the free-thinking, challenging work by people of conscience, who almost invariably had to defy the religious and political status quo of their times, that brought us out of such darkness. Of all tyrannies, a tyranny sincerely exercised for the good of its victims may be the most oppressive.
—**Steve Allen**

Fear is the mother of morality.

—**Friedrich Nietzsche**

Biblical orthodoxy without compassion is surely the ugliest thing in the world.

—**Francis Schaeffer**

"Um, yeah. So, how do we know if we've got Sound Doctrine?"

Give the Jedi new batteries for his lightsaber. That is the money question.

Remember the plagiarized section from Sister Jedi?

John Immel

Remember how the equation went? Do you remember Mr. Harvey's explicit assumption that to Paul, Doctrine and Theology are the same? The progression is **"watch your life and your doctrine" = mentally reflecting + Good Theology = Sound Doctrine = Study of specific theology = Reformed Theology.**

We have not discussed Reformed Theology yet. Before we do, we need to wrap our minds around the driving force behind the study of a specific theological belief system first. Remember how PDI/CLC/SGM set out to define their unique place in the world: Impassioned Orthodoxy? How does this Orthodoxy play into the whole picture? Orthodoxy? Why does anyone care about "orthodoxy"?

The following is an article by Joshua Harris of *I Kissed Dating Goodbye* fame as he set out to define "Impassioned Orthodoxy" in an article by that name. This 2,500-word editorial was originally published in 1999 online at the PDI Sovereign Grace website.[1] The link no longer works, but I do have the full article if it is necessary to establish context. Because of length, I selected sections that reflect the article's presumption. This article represents the inevitable evolution of thought captured roughly eight years after the start of their "Doctrinal Refocus." I want you to notice that Joshua's article reveals their hive mind advocacy of the theological algebra detailed above.

> Welcome to PDI. We place a high value on sound teaching and doctrinal integrity. We also believe in the present ministry of the Holy Spirit and love to worship God expressively. At this point in church history, that does make us an odd mix. For many people today, we don't fit into any familiar

---

1. Sovereign Grace magazine online July/August 1999 http://www.pdinet.org/sovgrace/v17no4/

Christian category. We bring together two streams that are typically kept separate—a deep dedication to sound doctrine and a passionate pursuit of the experience of God and the gifts of the Spirit. What words do we use to describe this? The best phrase I've come across is "impassioned orthodoxy."

What is impassioned orthodoxy? This seemingly incongruous pairing refers to something that, from my perspective, lies at the very heart of our calling as Christians. . . .

. . .

The place of orthodoxy in loving God with our whole being is explained in this first simple truth: *You can't truly love what you don't know.* . . .

. . .

The same must be true, in a sense, of our love for God. If we're to truly love God as Jesus describes in Mark 12, our lives must be marked by an ever-increasing desire to know him. Puritan pastor Thomas Watson writes:

"The antecedent of love is knowledge. The Spirit shines upon the understanding and discovers the beauties of wisdom, holiness, and mercy in God. These are the magnet to entice and draw out love for God. . . . If the sun be set in the understanding, there must be night in the affections."

Put another way, if the light's off in your understanding of who God is, then your feelings toward him will be dark and cold.

John Immel

> Knowledge of God comes before love for him, and in this life the only infallible source of the knowledge of God is Scripture. That's what orthodoxy is all about. Orthodoxy is a commitment to the teaching and application of the established, proven, and cherished truths of the Bible. It's about loving the truths of God's Word.
>
> **Enemies of Orthodoxy.** *Postmodernism.* The need for orthodoxy cannot be overstated, for we live in an age that has turned its back on absolute truth. Postmodern thinking says that "truth is whatever's true to you." Sadly, we Christians have allowed ourselves to be influenced by the popular lie that truth is relative. As a result, we've devalued truth in the church. The lack of theological study among many Christians and the widespread abhorrence for any doctrinal debate, no matter how critical the issue, reveal the present apathy towards truth.
>
> . . .
>
> Ultimately, we have no excuse for not pursuing deeper knowledge of God. We can't allow our culture's apathy towards truth, or our own laziness, or wrongheaded ideas to keep us from the study of biblical doctrine and theology. Without it, we cannot love God with all that we are.

This editorial's implicit assumption is that theological study = orthodoxy. I will address the meaning of the "Puritan" writer's cameo role in Joshua's article—how it shapes theological pedigree in chapter 11. For now let us focus on the article's assumption. Joshua Harris's critique goes like this: You don't really love God unless you are willing to study theology. And if you study theology, you must study orthodoxy, which is "a commitment to the teaching and application of the established, proven," Bible truth. This TRUTH = theological study = sound doctrine = orthodoxy. But he doesn't want you to pursue being intellectual too far. Postmodernism allows for too much free thinking. . . .

We will tell you what to think. . . .

Just close your mind. . . .

Bwaaahahahahahaha!

BUAHAHAHAAHahahahahah!

But beyond Joshua Harris's abject terror of Postmodernism, notice the progression of his ham-fisted argument. He starts with your love, or maybe better said, he starts with a challenge to the measure and purity of your love of God. He defines love proportional to the study of God, which really equals the study of theology. I want to pause right here. Remember what I said at the outset (page 11) that I was going to talk about this very dynamic: the motivating power of our love and the motivating power of our fears?

Joshua's article is the manipulation of our affections and our fears in full relief. This juxtaposition calls into question the fundamentals of our moral existence. Unless we concede the ideas within this "orthodoxy," we are not authentic in our love for God. We will talk in detail about the specifics of these ideas momentarily, but I want you to notice the fulcrum of our fears and affections can be used to leverage **any** moral standard. The above article could easily have been written about our love of Allah, tarot cards, or peanut butter. The power of the demand is proportional to our highest value. Any Puritan of Peanut Butter could have said:

> What is impassioned Peanut Butter? The place of orthodoxy in loving Peanut Butter with our whole being is explained in this first simple truth: You can't truly love what you don't know. Knowledge of

John Immel

> Peanut Butter comes before love of the Nut. And in this life, the only infallible source of the knowledge is the Skippy food label.

In as much as we fear judgment, we flock to Skippy to buy our orthodoxy, to purchase the absolution of the Peanut Butter god's wrath. The moral demagoguery works like this:

(Our) love = highest values
(Our) morality = authenticity
(Our) fear = moral judgment

A tyrant exploits this by successfully equating his standards to our highest value. If he succeeds, he is then free to demand any action.

- **Love = Highest Values = Peanut Butter = Skippy.**
- **Morality = Questionable Authenticity = Jiff.**
- **Fear = Moral Judgment = How dare you fail Skippy Orthodoxy?**

Do you think this is a silly illustration?
Really?
Have you ever heard the marketing slogan: "Choosy mothers choose Jiff?" This is a moral manipulation. The marketing plays on a mother's fear of failing to provide the best for her kids. If she chooses any other product, it is because she is not sufficiently particular. She is failing in peanut butter orthodoxy, which is really a failure of motherhood. Jiff successfully positions their peanut butter with the highest motherly value: her kids. By implication, mothers who buy some other peanut butter brand are not very good mothers. They are not good because they are not discriminating; they are not choosy enough and therefore do not really love their kids.

Joshua Harris's argument is the same moral fulcrum.

Equal to man's abhorrence of chaos is his deep-seated drive to integrate his ethical knowledge with his moral action. The leading reason man works so hard to integrate his ideas is in service to this fundamental center of man. The more important his action, the more man seeks a moral justification for that action. Failure to achieve harmony between ethical knowledge and moral action destroys us from the inside out. This is of course why the nature of Grace is specifically designed to blot out our sins and clean our conscience. Fixing this specific human disharmony is at the core of God's plan.

Once you understand the power of this lever, once you grasp how potent a drive this is within human nature, it is simple to grasp why despots use morality to manipulate human action. It is a powerful, powerful, powerful motivator for human action. This is why moral demagoguery works in behalf of Jim Jones, and David Koresh, and the People State of China, and the Workers Paradise of Russia, and Hezbollah. The list is endless because the power of the argument is deeply embedded within human nature: our love and our fear.

The more **moral** men think they are, the more **authentic** they believe their lives to be, the more **action** they will take in service to that **authenticity**. We are not within miles of what defines good morality or effective ethical human action. Only that morality and authenticity and action—their specific relationship—are key elements of man existence.

Some people's morality tells them to take a man's extra money and give it to those who do not have the same amount.

Other people's morality tells them to strap on bombs and kill infidels. And still others just become sanctimonious insufferable little twerps who are just positive they are the most moral amongst men.

Speaking of which . . .

Joshua Harris's article is really an effort to redefine Christian morality because it gives him the power to make a specific body of ideas the highest moral expression.

The logic progresses:

> **True spiritual commitment = morality = a willingness to pursue God intellectually = the explicit commitment to "Absolute Truth" = a synonym for "orthodoxy."**

Since everyone who fails to read my books does not have a commitment to a "high value of doctrinal integrity," let us mentally reflect, because unless we continue to read ". . . we cannot love God with all that we are."

See how easy it was to compel you to read the next chapter?

7
Oops, We Got It Right . . . This Time

> The basic tool for the manipulation of reality is the manipulation of words. If you can control the meaning of words, you can control the people who must use the words.
>
> **—Philip K. Dick**

> Oh well, we almost had a romantic ending!
>
> **—Bugs Bunny**

> History will be kind to me for I intend to write it.
>
> **—Winston Churchill**

Contrary to Mr. Harris's article, spiritual commitment is not directly related to one's willingness to crack open books and read about God, and Orthodoxy is not a product of academic study. As you will soon see, such an equation is devoid of mental reflections.

What follows is not a full progression of doctrinal thought that evolved within PDI/CLC/SGM since 1982. That would be an almost impossible feat in light of their penchant to rewrite their history. Or maybe better said: Rewrite the meaning of their doctrinal foci (and its fallout) and re-arrange the deck chairs on their bus; they manage to focus on many foci depending on the day or the feng shui.

Uhh . . .

Err . . .

Ehem . . .

John Immel

But I need to give this brief overview to acquaint all dear readers with their evolution because it bears on the scope of this unfolding drama.

For all intents and purposes, PDI/CLC/SGM's uniqueness is part of its charm, and there is nothing implicitly scandalous in the charm or the uniqueness.

Way back in the dark ages of the Charismatic Movement, oh, around the mid 1970s, there were impromptu gatherings that started in Washington, D.C. led by none other than Catholic Larry Tomczak. He is no longer with the Catholic Church or SGM. Well, maybe he is back as a "special guest," whatever that is. But for the better part of a decade, if you ask about Larry they said: "Who?"

Just kidding.

Anyway . . .

These get-togethers were named **TAG** and **GOB**, meaning **T**ake **A**nd **G**ive and **G**athering **O**f **B**elievers. The history of **TAG** and **GOB** is readily available in Larry's book, *Clap Your Hands*.[1] Or if you don't like the sanitized version, scratch any four people in Montgomery County, Maryland behind the ear and at least one of them will give the unfiltered version.

Anyway, this informal fellowship, inspired by the exodus from mainline denominational churches, got its life because people found the existing Church structure oppressive. These sectarian rebels thumbed their nose at the current appointed authorities, and flouted their ministerial vetting process. Time passed and lo and behold, the "leaders" of the "informal" TAG and GOB got together and decided they needed structure—much like what they abandoned. (Go figure.) So, Larry Tomczak and

---

1. Larry Tomczak, *Clap Your Hands* (Florida: Strang Communications, 1988).

Blight in the Vineyard

C. J. Mahaney said Eureka! or Holy Spirit! or John Calvin! and decided to create PDI/CLC circa 1980.

For reasons I don't precisely grasp, the leadership of early PDI/CLC was desperate to find and maintain a Christian counterculture identity.[2] The result is inevitable; bouncing around the doctrinal map, defining and redefining words and doctrines, and always seeking to measure themselves against social trends. This means they have flirted with—and certainly not limited to—Faith and Prosperity teaching,[3] Shepherding[4] (though they refuse to call it that) amongst other doctrinal fads. However, whatever ideas they were trying on at the moment, the assumptions that drove the doctrine were essentially charismatic . . . until recently.

I know, I know. Charismatic is a terribly vague word that means a lot and says very little. So, let me draw a picture with crayons, not a fine point pen.

Whatever PDI/CLC aspired to, the spiritual pedigree had all the hallmarks of the independent church movement: independent church government, extemporaneous preaching, dramatic presentation, enthusiasm expected and expressed from the pulpit and the pew, church building was a rented school auditorium, no hymnals (words on the wall), loud

---

2. There are two versions of this book. If you can find a copy of the 1988 version, note the underlying theme in chapter 9, specifically Larry's preoccupation with Mr. Perlis's rebuttal and what that spurred him to conclude about the nature of Christian practice and the specific organization of the "Local Church."

3. The Father of the Faith Movement was a minister from Texas, Kenneth E. Hagin. Prosperity teaching was a faith submovement that teaches people can obtain wealth from tithing, giving, and proclaiming "God's promises."

4. A movement attributed to Bob Mumford, Derek Prince, and Charles Simpson that places primary emphasis on highly involved discipleship and known for subordinating church members' life choices to rigorous approval of church authorities.

music, praise and worship that seems like a rock concert, calls for the laying on of hands (this used to be Gary Ricucci's gifting), prophesying from a mic for the whole church to hear, lots of speaking in tongues a.k.a. Baptism in the Spirit, worship in the spirit, (Vikki Cook used to have some amazing spiritual songs. She probably still does. She is a wonderful talent) and teaching prosperity from the act of giving/tithing. (One PDI pastor reportedly gave himself into wealth, a hallmark of Prosperity teaching. But I don't remember his name.)

I suspect some of you, dear readers, cannot relate to what I just described. So if you are inclined, go to the Yellow Pages and find four Pentecostal/Independent churches in your area and visit different locations for about a month. Nothing will rub off and infect you. It will be a learning experience. Trust me, you will get an object lesson for my generalization.

Anyway . . . a formal definition of a Charismatic Church maybe doesn't exist, but this is one of those deals where if it walks like a duck and quacks like a duck . . . then it probably isn't an elephant.

It is important to understand the origins of this church group. From the outset, they were an independent church movement with all that implies. When John F. MacArthur wrote his book, *Charismatic Chaos*, they would have been guilty by tongue-talking association, assuming he even knew they existed. And the people who attended their churches had every reason to believe that leadership was charismatic-ish in doctrinal pedigree.

Continuing with our recap of PDI/CLC history, sometime around 1990 this bunch of '60s retreads looked at the panorama of Christianity and decided they were going to be doctrinal movers and shakers. So they did what they had always done. They said, "Oops, whatever

Blight in the Vineyard

we said before, never mind. We want to be different than everybody else in the Charismatic world." And they subsequently started to reinvent the substance of their doctrine.

So, now let's talk about what that meant.

We All Live in a Reformed Theology Bus

Heheheheheh . . .

A nostalgia trip for you hippy types. Sing with me now.

We all live in a yellow submarine . . .

The Beatles would be proud.

PDI/CLC/SGM starts its dash towards "authentic" Christianity scouring the pages of weighty tomes from ages past. It took a while before existing members of PDI/CLC started to catch on that something was different down on the farm around 1993-ish. The leaders of PDI/CLC had been bitten by the academic Reformed Theology bug, and names like Edwards and Owens started peppering sermons—oops, I mean theological monologues on Sunday morning.

You're saying to yourself, "So what? Isn't it a good thing for people to reevaluate their doctrine?"

Un momento por favor. This is going somewhere.

While their overt musings were about this "Sound Doctrine," the heart of then PDI/CLC's concern was "How we can define authentic Christianity?" Maybe they've never said those words, but their internal concern was they had been preaching another gospel. For years they had led with "Jesus is Lord," as the core of the Gospel, but on further review, they decided maybe not. The inevitable question then is: How can we know? This, of course, is the question we are currently evaluating now. Remember the Subjectivity Beast? How do we know if we have Christianity right? How do we know if we believe right? As a charismatic, non-denominational, independent church, what is the measure of doctrinal accuracy?

In the late '80s and early '90s, the winds of doctrine were tumultuous, and rumor had it that charismatic chaos washed across American Piety. How to combat the chaos? This question is what prompted Brent Detwiler's comments in the article at the beginning of this book. People are watching all sorts of things that may or may not be God. So, how do we identify an effective measuring stick?

The deeply embedded PDI/CLC/SGM assumption is this: Correct doctrine manifests in specific conduct and doctrine is enforced by Pastoral decree.

Here is the spiritual algebra:
- Sound doctrine = Character.
- Sound doctrine = Leadership Arbitration.
- Character + Leadership Arbitration= Specific Social Action.

Are you scandalized yet?
No, huh?
You think this is reasonable Bible algebra?
So consider the implications in light of these questions:
- What does that character specifically look like?
- What specific social action makes someone authentic?
- What demands can church leaders make?
- What force is leadership empowered to take in pursuit of this character?
- Is leadership the same as governance?
- Is a call to preach the same as a call to govern?

- Is there such a thing as a "call" to govern?
- Are there limits to their governing power?
- What are the limits to their government power?
- Can they enforce ideas?
- Is a man's salvation suspect if he believes wrong things?
- What then must a man think to be saved?
- Can leadership remove people from social participation if they fail to conform to pastoral edicts about precise thinking?
- In light of the Parable of the Wheat and Tares, how can "leadership" be sure they have judged rightly?

It's Our Bus

You already know that I like word pictures, but I can't claim originality on this one. The precise context of the conversation I no longer remember, but the statement I will never forget. Robin Boisvert, my pastor for the years that I was at CLC, said to me during one of his inquisitions, "John, this is a **Reformed Theology** bus, and you can get on or get off."[5] This proclamation came before they got plain about their "doctrinal refocus." They were *not* a Reformed Theology bus from their

---

5. When I attended CLC, each member is assigned a pastor who oversees a section of care groups. Care groups are like home groups, or small groups, or outside Bible studies. The leaders of those care groups report to their pastor, and the pastor reports back to a central planning about the sundry goings-on. So, when one goes to seek pastoral counsel directly, they are referred to the pastor that rules the care groups under his auspice. Robin was (is?) a pastor within the then PDI structure. He was my appointed pastor for my time within the hallowed halls. As you will see, we had lots of conversations. Pssst . . . Robin, the Deleterious Problem Child is back.

inception, and they weren't one when I first set foot in their hallowed halls. Robin's proclamation was a bold, absolute statement at the time.

So, can they drive the bus where they want?

Really?

Ladies and gentlemen, this is where the realm of the theoretical starts rubbing oppressively against the tangible, chaffing the lives of people.

Let us mentally reflect about Robin's declaration.

Is it a bad thing to believe you have the truth?

I hope not, I believe I have it. I am confident that preachers from Toronto to Geneva, from Brownsville to Antioch have spoken, affirmed in their own minds that what they were saying was truth. For that matter, I would imagine that the Maharishi Mahesh Yogi and the Dalai Lama, and every Pope since Gregory the Great believe that they have the truth. So, yes, in as much as free men can choose to define for themselves their walk with God, it is good that thing for them to believe they have truth.

Do you want to go be a Calvinist and cry over the great depravities of man? You can go be about that. Do you want to offer up penance and ask the Pope for absolution? You can go be about that. Do you want to sit cross-legged and chant "ooooohhhhhmmmmm" to the Universe? You can go be about that.

Men are free to pursue truth, which means they are free to fail or succeed in that effort: fine and all right.

But what responsibility does a man bring on himself when he specifically says that TRUTH is defined by submission to **his** authority and **his** proscribed conduct? Said another way, what responsibilities does a man bring on himself when he insists that he has "Sound Doctrine" and that is code for "you **must** believe exactly what I teach?"

Herein is the issue: PDI/CLC/SGM has set themselves up as arbitrator of this dynamic—the doctrine, the socially prescribed actions, the pastoral decree, and the monopoly of force to achieve their dictated outcomes. It is important for one and all to get this point, because it is to this intersection that everything else flows, all roads collide here: **Anyone** who insists that he is in charge of thinking and the monopoly of force to achieve rational subordination is at the crossroad of authoritarian conflict.

Perspective

Some might suggest, "Well, just leave."

This assumption of religious freedom is uniquely American. "Piffle . . . if you don't like what you hear, bolt out the door and find someone who lets you believe what you want. It isn't like they can burn you at the stake or anything."

This specific expectation is why religious wars have been nonexistent in American history. Culturally, we expect the absolute freedom to choose where we worship and it never crosses our minds that there is a compelling force that will prevent such a decision. Long before fights of doctrine turn to bloodshed, congregations pick sides and move to respective buildings with new signs on the front door. And so goes the endless tide of American church splits and denominational evolutions.

Of course, our medieval religious forbearers had never conceived such freedom, and the choice they did exercise was fraught with all manner of civil danger. Being Lollard on Thursday didn't mean you wouldn't be hung for heresy by Sunday. From nation to nation, duchy to duchy, even city to city, the combination of civil authority and religious orthodoxy determined the nature and substance of congregational faith on pain of death. This merging of Church and State and the tides of war waged in the name of God was fresh and vivid in our Founding Fathers' minds. This is why we can even consider such a question as leaving a church if we don't happen to like the pastor's choice of decor.

But the use of violence to shape doctrinal adherence is only part of the compulsion equation. There are many ways to manipulate intellectual compliance. Men can be denied access to the collective resources: money. Unless a member shows mental fealty, they cannot eat at the public trough. Men can be prevented social participation, like care group involvement or church events, unless they recant "deleterious" ideas.[6] Unless they are of the same mind, they cannot participate in the inner social circles. The more accolades and benefits those inner social circles offer, the greater the conformity. And last but certainly not least is extortion by eternal threat. The soul of Mystic Despotism is the declared power to impact Man's eternal state. Men are Mystic Despots when they insist that failure to believe what they demand means you will suffer hell.

Combine these elements with the power of Peanut Butter Orthodoxy from the previous chapter, and the combination of religious affections and social inclusion is hard to escape. The greater **our** love for **our** highest value, and the more effective the leaders are at inserting themselves into the equation, the harder it is for people to "Just leave." The reason people stick through bad marriages tends to be the same reasons they stay through bad church interactions: Their personal value is

---

6. Just guess how I know this can be done to a member of a church congregation.

subordinate to some overt despotism, and they are terrified to "just leave."

And this leads nicely to the topic of PDI/CLC/SGM membership and prolonged commitment.

Is becoming a member at PDI/CLC/SGM easy? Are there hoops to crawl through, and buildings to leap, and pastoral interviews to endure? Is the scrutiny intense? Do the pastors take seriously the membership affirmation? Yeah, brethren, and multiply by fifty.

Robin Boisvert likes to make this distinction: "Cults are easy to get into and hard to get out of. Covenant Life Church is hard to get into and easy to get out of." I'm not sure this definition of cult or his portrayal of SGM exodus is accurate.[7] PDI/CLC/SGM leadership takes membership very, very, very, very seriously, applying rigor to determine who is in and who is not. By their own definition, they describe church life as a marriage, a covenant, a commitment. The mother church is called **Covenant** Life Church. Being consistent with the metaphor, marriages are partnerships, a union of equals, are they not? Or are marriages the bond of superior and subordinates?

Islam makes wives property, but Christianity . . . mmmm . . . depending on who is reading what, seems to be about equality. So, we will presume that a good marriage is between equals.

So, the "just leave" dismissal is not as simple as it sounds. There is an entire backstory of personal values and overt spiritual extortions that come into play when making the choice to "just leave." Members have the melody of love sung in one ear and submission, confrontation, and error drummed into the other.

---

7. By the way, it was Robin's "felt need" that prompted the Cult/Covenant Life equation. Why would he feel that necessary? I'll let that question dangle in your mind like a stray hair because that is another conversation.

John Immel

Are these the sweet nothings of equals?

What happens when wives on the bus realize the destination is not what they want?

Oops . . . mixing metaphors here—riding a bus and participating in a group marriage. . . .

Uh . . .

Err . . .

Ehem . . .

What if a member of the marriage riding the bus listens to the song, sees a problem, and seeks to confront? Wouldn't that mean people are free to come question the bus driver, oops, I mean marriage partner?

Don't Make Me Pull Over

Robin Boisvert is a Calvinist. OK, so now it is no mystery that a member of PDI/CLC/SGM is a Calvinist. But back in the day, this was news hot off the pulpit press. It took a few interactions with Robin to get this admission out of him. Anyway, during one conversation, I made a passing comment about doctrinal changes that I'd seen circa 1993-94. He was quick to tell me that C. J. Mahaney had been a Calvinist since 1982.[8] I did not mention Calvin or C.J.; that was all him.

Robin thought I was equating the doctrinal changes with his arrival to CLC, and he was trying to set the record straight. Basically, Robin was letting me know that the motivating doctrinal force was C.J. (At the very least,

---

8. OK, yeah, whatevs. Whatever vague intellectual assent *El Primo Doctrinal Mover and Shaker* had with Calvinism, it didn't come out in his preaching until the doctrinal "refocus." By definition, they would not have needed a "refocus" if Reformed Theology was at all central to their historic preaching. And I'd be interested to know Larry Tomczak's take on that factoid since he preached with C.J. for those years. And Larry is no Calvinist.

Blight in the Vineyard

Robin was establishing a co-conspirator in crim—oops, I mean Calvinism.) This comment is part and parcel of why I insist that the whole team leadership thing is a polite fiction. Implicit to Robin's deflection is the presumption that C.J. is the defining measure of doctrinal content. He didn't mention anyone else or start extolling the virtues of the SGM hive mind. He defaulted to one name as the validating measure of doctrinal emphasis. This is not a surprise, really, because all groups end up defaulting to one doctrinal mover and shaker. It is just the way of human social structure based on specific philosophical assumptions.

But notice at the core of Robin's bus metaphor is the assumption, the implicit **obligation** for everybody to ride quietly. Heaven forefend you make him pull over. He expects mindless obedience, because he believes that he has arrived at Sound Doctrine. People that believe what he believes, therefore, also have Sound Doctrine, and those who disagree with him. . . .

No . . . Unsound Doctrine, Please.

All right, everybody who wants Unsound Doctrine, raise your hand.

What, no takers?

Jedi, this is important. If we don't want Unsound Doctrine, shouldn't we all go where Sound Doctrine is being preached? And isn't the SGM temple CLC where Sound Doctrine is offered up? (And sadly, other churches do not.) Don't they (C.J.) weep big alligator tears as they applaud themselves for what they have found and what they are very careful to preach? (And sadly, other churches do not.)

Aspiring Jedi, this is crucial. If PDI/CLC/SGM has Sound Doctrine (and sadly other churches do not), then if we don't attend SGM, by default, we want unsound doctrine? Remember the equation:

A willingness to pursue God intellectually = the explicit commitment to "Absolute Truth" = sound doctrine = ride the bus quietly = Reformation Theology.

All the preamble about "Impassioned Orthodoxy," all the exhortations to "sound doctrine," all the high-minded appeals to mental reflection is little more than a sales pitch to demand mindless obedience to Reformed Theology. So, this leads to the obvious question: What makes Reformed Theology so special?

It is to this question that we will now turn our attention.

8
That Waskally Critter

Don't think it hasn't been a little slice of heaven ... 'cause it hasn't!

—**Bugs Bunny**

Well, as it turns out, I'm secwetwy evil.

—**Elmer Fudd**

How can I hypnotize you if you don't co-opewate?

—**Elmer Fudd**

I want to make my meaning explicit. My goal requires that I continue the tour around the theological arena. We are hunting down **Orthodoxy**. Get your lightsaber, Elmer. And beware, Bugs Bunny is a formidable foe.

People use the word "orthodoxy" to mean the rightest belief, the most authoritative declaration of human existence. When preachers say orthodoxy, they mean **absolute** TRUTH. When preachers say orthodoxy, they mean **the** Christian truth in accordance with all the historic councils and creeds. That is not an exact translation, but that is how the word is used.

This presumes that the historic councils from 325 onward and the subsequent conclusions were perfect. From the ten-thousand-foot view, all the details blend together like a postmodern painting. Did The Tasmanian Devil toss paint on a canvas when Elmer wasn't looking, or is it a masterpiece by a creative genius? Are these random blobs

John Immel

or profound intentions too great for our small minds to grasp?

Getting answers to these questions requires enormous work, peering into some of the most disturbing evolutions of thought in the Western world, so people don't look too close and let the vague images become inkblot reality.

For lots of reasons that have nothing to do with the Bible, historic groupies seek to keep the details murky, out of focus, and away from the relationship between the finer points. And if that doesn't work and people start pressing into the details, they face self-styled aficionados insisting that the conundrums of historic confusions are really the work of a master whose genius is far beyond our meager abilities. So, you just never mind those questions. Greater minds than yours have wrestled with these outcomes and that should be good enough for you. Just accept Orthodoxy!

This, of course, begs the question: What is Orthodoxy?

Can you find it in a box? Does it come with lox? Does it come with instructions? Is it the obvious conclusion of clear biblical teaching? If the teaching is so dang "clear," why are there so many different denominations with so many different flavors of Christian thought and practice?

OK, wait, here is a thought.

Does that mean true Orthodoxy is Christian **diversity** since it seems to be the universal experience of Christianity?

Did some of you just choke?

Since PDI/CLC/SGM is fussing about Postmodernism and demanding adherence to absolutes that have "stood the test of time," I'm guessing they think Christian diversity is a bad thing.

Hmmm . . .

But what then makes someone orthodox? What **must** we believe to be "authentic"?

Is "Orthodoxy" correct belief about the Trinity? So, what is the correct belief? Can you find explicit teaching about the Trinity in the Bible? Can you find the word in a Strong's Concordance? Nope, it ain't there. Are there a few miles of interpretation, a few miles of Theology that can be done to arrive at the Trinity? Well, if we are Orthodox Roman Catholics accepting the conclusion of the First Nicene Council's importation of entirely Greek philosophical ideas into Christianity, the answer is yes. If we are Jewish Christians committed to "Hear, O Israel! Adonai is our God! Adonai is one! . . ." the answer is no.

"Oh, John. They are Jews and therefore, not 'Christian' Orthodox."

So, are you then saying that Orthodoxy then is about **racial purity**?

Really?

You can smell that historic bigotry from miles. The truth is, untold misery and disaster has been visited on the Church from the casual intellectual dismissal of Jewish thought. But that is definitely another book.

OK. So, what if I believe everything that the early church believed? Does that make me orthodox? How early is early? 35 AD? 60 AD? Or how about 100 AD? How about the Orthodoxy of the Early Church Fathers? These were the guys that came immediately after the original 12 apostles. Polycarp of Smyrna, circa AD 100, possibly knew the Apostle John. Ignatius of Antioch wrote seven letters to various churches as he was being taken to the Imperial Capital to be devoured by beasts. These guys might have had insider knowledge being part of the apostolic succession (or so the theory goes).[1] So, that would make

---

1. The evolutions of thought in early Christianity are vast and tumultuous. I am a fan of Justo L. Gonzalez, *History of Christian Thought*, vol. 1-3 (Nashville: Abingdon Press, 1970). His work is the best combination of scholastic/academic and

John Immel

what they believed more accurate because they were closer to the beginning. So, is Orthodoxy tied to apostolic succession? That is what the Catholics believe.

But, ummm . . . here is an interesting factoid: The doctrine of Christ has a tendency to be confused with the Early Church Fathers.'[2] Or maybe I should say that their Christology didn't necessarily line up with succeeding centuries of Orthodox decree.[3] If we take the lead of the Church Fathers and accept their hazy, undefined relationship between Father God and Jesus, what do we do with the Council in 325 when they declared the doctrine of the Trinity absolutely definitively determined? Which Orthodoxy do we pick?

How do we know **what** defines orthodoxy?

What if I told you that the Nicene Council's quest for absolute, definitive irrefutability took over fifty years? A curious reality if I was a "clear" absolute. What if I told you that the "absolute" view—the current definition of Trinity that everyone who is "anyone" believes now—was nonexistent for most of the preceding two hundred fifty years? What if I told you that the fight was a politically motivated fuss that turned on the Emperor's decree that called opposing positions demented and insane? What if I told you that the shared nature of God and Jesus—was Jesus of the same *homoousios* as the Father—required the

---

readable. His discussion in volume 1 of the Apostolic Fathers' Christology gives sufficient details to understand their specific intellectual challenges while keeping the tides of thought brief. This is a rare gift.

2. H. B. Bumpus, *The Christological Awareness of Clement of Rome and Its Sources* (Cambridge: University Press, 1972).

3. There is nothing easy about reading the Apostolic Fathers; their concerns have hints of what we have come to understand as Bible ideas but their overarching preoccupations are vastly different. For you Greek readers, might I recommend Michael W. Holmes, ed. and trans., *Apostolic Fathers: Greek Texts and English Translations*, 3rd

metaphysical framework of Aristotle and the philosophical instruction of Plotinus Neo-Platonism?[4] What if I told you the word *homoousios* is nowhere in Hebraic Canon or Christian 1st and 2nd century authoritative writings; indeed was expressly condemned for its Gnostic connotations as heretical by a council of Antioch Bishops in 268 AD?[5] What if I told you that the "winning" side of the argument knew full well this was an entirely pagan concept but used it anyway to galvanize ecumenical support for their political position and save their state-paid jobs?

That is a very uncomfortable thought—Orthodoxy by pagan extortion, civil authority, and imperial demagoguery. But just because it is an uncomfortable thought doesn't mean it isn't true. It could be possible that Government force and Ecclesiastical patronage are essential ingredients for orthodoxy. I could have missed that specific chapter in First Orthodoxy 1: 1, but maybe it is in the canon.

For those of you who are committed to the First Nicene Council formulation, here is a question: By importing **non-biblical** concepts into Bible interpretation, into authoritative Christian doctrine, what does that do to your

---

ed. (Grand Rapids: Backer Academic, 2007).

4. Richard Patrick Crosland Hanson, *The Search for the Christian Doctrine of God* (London: Continuum, 1988). See discussion starting p. 856, "The Influences of Philosophy."

5. One of the most exhaustive studies of the Trinitarian fight is Richard Hanson's work cited in note 4. Having said that, it is important to note, as Mr. Hanson observes in his preface, that "Writing a book such as this resembles the attempt to photograph a running stream." Nailing down the elements of this part of Christian history is a huge challenge because modern research into the background material sources and key figures are just now starting to mature out from under the historic threat of governing powers who refused critical review. Hanson's work is a great place to start because it is such a broad attempt to evaluate the scope of the issues from 318 to roughly 400 AD. However, the scholarship continues to emerge, expanding our understanding of the driving forces of Christianity's early intellectual history.

John Immel

"Scripture Alone" interpretive purity?

"No, no, no," you say. "All those details don't matter. No matter the circumstance, no matter how sinful human effort, God led them to the right conclusions. Orthodoxy refers to the general theological conclusions. Orthodoxy is kinda, sorta what God wanted everyone to believe."

Really? Your measure of divine affirmation, of "authentic" Christian doctrine is manifest reality? Because successive generations affirmed the conclusion—arrived at by extortion, civil authority, and intellectual denigration—**that** is what God really wanted everybody to believe? So, it doesn't matter **how** consensus is achieved, it only matters that the historic churches' intellectual record reflects the presumption?

Those are your mental reflections? Wow! Wow! And Wow!

Well, that is definitely the Dave Harvey brand of intellectual consistency. You've learned well.

OK, so you are advocating the Vincent of Lerins theory of Orthodoxy: "that which has been believed everywhere, (*quod ubique*) always (*quod semper*) and by all (*quod ab omnibus*)."

Gimme That Old Time Religion . . .

Now this is where Robin Boisvert rests his beret. He has told me this. Maybe he was quoting good old Vincent; maybe he wasn't. He likes to say that Word of Faith teaching is eccentric or literally not round. He wants to be centrist in his beliefs.

This sounds pretty good, right? Let's all be normative—a noble goal, right? Let's not stray far from the middle. Let's believe what everybody has believed, everywhere, always, and by all: Sound Doctrine by consensus.

But like Thomas Aquinas, I must ask the question, "What is the meaning of your affirmation?"

Do we have our definition? Orthodoxy: that which has been believed everywhere, always, and by all.

Good, because Yoda is going to mess with your mind some more.

Which century is the defining one? When do we start taking our poll?

Is orthodoxy fully reflected in the 1st century? Well, *goyim* have a problem, because for thirty plus years, the Early Church didn't think Gentiles could be given access to the Covenants of Promise without circumcision. That is what everybody believed, everywhere, always, and by all. It wasn't until Paul of Tarsus had a fight with Peter that the consensus of Church thinking began to change. That was **1st** century orthodoxy. Should we keep that century? Or were they just wrong and God had to reveal their error?

Be careful with your answer, because if we throw that century out of the "orthodoxy" equation because **God** has **fixed** their **wrong** consensus, then a contingency of Orthodoxy is **time**. If **time** is the deciding factor in the consensus, then what do we do with the next seventeen centuries when the Church at large believed that Jews were the source of Antichrist, the home of Satanic deception, because they crucified Jesus, because they had been pruned from the tree? From the 1st century onward, this scriptural justification for racial hatred was an "orthodoxy" interpretive conclusion and at the heart of every subsequent Jewish persecution, including the Holocaust. This is what everyone believed, everywhere, and by all.

Before you pooh-pooh my point, remember that by

accepting the Nicene conclusion in its current form, arrived at by its recorded methods, it doesn't matter **how** the consensus is achieved, right? Once the consensus is achieved, Christians have a moral obligation to believe accordingly, right? God shows forth his doctrinal will by the manifestation of reality and the history writers' consensus, right? So this means the persecutions—even the holocaust—was the correct expression of church orthodoxy, right? It can't be wrong, because we believed it for the duration of **time**?

For those of you who see the implicit conundrum, are you ready to go back and rethink Nicene orthodoxy yet?

Is this hitting a little too close to home?

Do you suddenly fear the boogieman of Arianism lurking under your bed, ready to grab your feet, and drag you into hell? Are you feeling the unquenchable urge to clutch a cross to your chest, wrap your neck in garlic, and to shout the word "Heretic," as a talisman to ward off the bad, bad, bad man messing with your mind?

Buwaahahahahahahah

BuwwhahahaHAHAHAHAHAH

BUWAHAHAHAHAHAHAHAHAHAHHAAHAH!!!

>snicker<

OK. I'll let you off the hook this time, Jedi. Maybe we can rationalize the 1st century because the primitive Church didn't have its act together yet. Besides, someone could contend that Gentile access to God's Covenant does not deal with the core issues of Christianity—those being the nature of man, the divinity of Christ, and the death, burial, and resurrection, et cetera. . . .

How Gentile participation in the Covenants of Promise is not a central issue to Christianity, I'll never understand. But all right, for the sake of the discussion, let's look for a defining century where everybody agreed

Blight in the Vineyard

on all things. Let us find that consensus.

We already addressed the 4th century. The very reason for the Nicene Council was because there was no consensus. So contentious was the fight that the Emperor Constantine said this: "Even the barbarians now through me, the true servant of God, know God and have learned to reverence him . . . while [you the bishops], do nothing but that which encourages discord and hatred, and to speak frankly, which leads to the destruction of the Human race." [sic][6]

Shhhhhh! Be vewry, vewry qwuiet. We still haven't sighted Bugs Bunny.

Hmmm . . . what century? OK, I got it, we'll tally up the general belief of the first ten centuries and that should do it. Here is an abbreviated chart highlighting some doctrinal distinctions between the Church in the Greek-speaking East and the Church in the Latin-speaking West. The break between East and West could arguably be called the first major "denominational" split in Christianity.[7]

---

6. H.A. Drake, *Constantine and the Bishops: The Politics of Intolerance* (Baltimore: Johns Hopkins University Press, 2000), 4.

Addressing this same issue of the character of the Trinitarian fight, Charles Freeman notes this in his work, *The Closing of the Western Mind* (New York: Vintage Books, 2002). On page 373, he provides this description of the fight between rival bishops in Ancyra in Galatia that was delivered to a synod in Africa (343 A.D): Houses were burned down and all manner of fighting broke out. Priests were dragged naked to the forum by the Bishop himself . . . he profaned the sacred Host of the Lord by hanging it openly and in public from the necks of the priests, and with horrendous barbarity tore the vestments from holy virgins dedicated to God and Christ, and displayed them naked before the public in the forum, in the middle of the city. And I know preachers that reject Kenneth Copeland teaching because he "Prowls around on stage and looks mean."

7. In the first three centuries after Pentecost, there were no denominations as we would understand the concept.

John Immel
Causes of the East-West Schism Of 1054

Eastern Church
- **Political Rival:** Byzantine Empire
- **Papal Claim:** Rejected subordination of Patriarch of Constantinople to Rome.
- **Theological Development:** Stagnated after Council of Chalcedon.
- **Filioque Controversy:** Declared that the Holy Spirit proceeds from the Father.
- **Iconoclastic Controversy**: Engaged in 120-year dispute over the use of icons in worship. (Statues prohibited.)
- **Language and Culture:** Greek/Oriental
- **Clerical Celibacy**: Lower clergy were permitted to marry.

Western Church
- **Political Rival:** Holy Roman Empire
- **Papal Claim:** Bishop of Rome claimed supremacy over entire church.
- **Theological Development:** Continuous change in response to controversies and expansion.
- **Filioque Controversy:** Declared that the Holy Spirit proceeds from the Father and Son.
- **Iconoclastic Controversy:** Made constant attempts to interfere in Eastern dispute. (Statues

---

Christianity was very loosely organized and had an intellectually diverse tradition that was vast and varied. But that changed dramatically in the 4th century. By roughly A.D. 350, the Church was making a concerted effort to condemn as heresy most every strand of thought not specifically subordinate to Constantine's Bishops and the subsequent "Christian" Emperors. For the next few hundred years, the Church persecuted or killed anyone who would not subordinate.

permitted).
- **Language and Culture:** Latin/Occidental
- **Clerical Celibacy:** All clergy were required to be celibate.[8]

Do you see this list of distinctions? What makes each distinctive, more right, more normative, more about consensus? Did the East have it more right? Did the West? Do you really think that the modern Protestant leaders would fall in line with Western Orthodoxy and its required celibacy? I mean, if they are going to be Orthodox, that is what they should do, right? Western Theology is what brought us Europeans our theological ancestry via the Orthodox Catholic Church. To be Orthodox, shouldn't all those married preachers step down?

I know I am hitting below the belt.

Jedi, I'll let you off the hook this one last time. But what are we going to do about that waskally critter called Orthodoxy?

Wait, I know what we will do. I know. I know. I know. We'll go the 16th century when John Calvin wrote his *Institutes of the Christian Religion*. That's it. That is the century where God spoke to men once and for all. That is the century when God made it possible for everybody to finally read the New Testament rightly. Paul was talking about reading John Calvin's *Institutes* when he said, "Study to show yourself approved, a workman unto God." This is it, the end of all doctrinal disagreement, the beginning of Orthodox consensus. Finally, the church can judge the legitimacy of all other expressions of faith.

Oh, darn. We've got that pesky guy, Jacobus Arminius who just wouldn't get with the program, and Simon

---

8. Based on the book by Robert C. Walton, *Chronological and Background Charts of Church History* (Grand Rapids:

John Immel

Episcopius, and Janus Uytenbogaert, and Hugo Grotius, and the State of Holland, and Michael Servetus and . . .

Wow, this is getting frustrating. And you know what else? I just remembered that Martin Luther and John Calvin were Reformers. Hmmmm. How can you have an original if you RE-form something? I'm just full of these mental reflections.

Anyway, Johnny and Martin were part of the split from the Catholic "Big C" Church, and that has never been fixed. If we are really about "Orthodoxy," does that mean we have to become Catholic "Big C"? I mean, they've been around the longest, and by population, the case could be made that they have had more people join the consensus. Complicated, so very complicated, and all we want to do is achieve the very noble goal of knowing when everybody believes rightly.

Jedi, history is running out. Elmer is going to be outsmarted by Bugs Bunny again. What should we do?

Maybe if we go to our lifetime, we can find consensus. Big laughs, right? What do we do with all the different thinking people in our own century? The Boogieman of Postmodernism is working a dastardly plan. And God has been making people speak in tongues and healing people. And then a bunch of backwoods, uneducated, West Texans start teaching this Faith stuff and telling people to read the promises of God for themselves without any creeds, or any seminary training, or anything. Now that just isn't good for consensus at all. The Subjectivity Beast is going to get us all.

Scandalous!!!!!

"John, you are misstating the issue. Orthodoxy deals with the historic conclusions of 'essential' doctrines; we can lovingly disagree over details, but the list above, are

---

Zondervan, 1986), chart 22.

'nonessentials' and not really things to be burned at the stake over."

Yeah, huh?

I will deal with this essential versus nonessential evasion in more detail in chapter 11. But for now, let me point out that my argument is not against the relative importance of specific Christian doctrines. The issue I **am** spotlighting is the ultimate justification for our interpretive methodology and subsequent conclusions: The validation of TRUTH is that "everyone" has decided that it is TRUTH.

Here is the punch line: This standard is observably false.

First, contrary to a massive propaganda campaign initiated from ages long past and carried on through the 21st century, Church history is a study in doctrinal plurality destroyed by blood and sword.

Second, the "consensus" the perpetrators of the propaganda campaign try to insist exists is really the authority of the state imposing ideology in behalf of civil and imperial social objectives.

Third, the TRUTH exists if no one gets it. If TRUTH is contingent on the greatest numbers of people assenting to its veracity, then a billion Chinese cannot be wrong.

Fourth, "standing the test of time" assumes that the past is an authority, that something is right merely because it is old. Or said another way, it presumes that human tradition has implicit power to define TRUTH. Hence this circular logic: It is TRUTH because we have always believed it; we have always believed it because it is TRUTH. Of course, this is absurd. A flat earth "stood the test of time," but that did not make it TRUTH. The Easter Bunny, Santa Claus, and the day of the sun god Ra (Sunday) have all "stood the test of time," but that does

John Immel

not make them real, or their original traditions synonymous with divine command. As a standard of knowledge, this condemns every generation to continue with the rational failures of their forefathers.

Fifth, this whole house of cards is hilarious in light of Original Sin. Surely, you see the wonderful irony here. As Augustine described in his *Letter to Simplicianus*, man is a lump infused with the guilt of Adam, a corruption so absolute that he is deprived of any rational, moral, or epistemological power. Or in centuries later, man was described as having a "flavor for sin" in his mouth. He is on the back of a horse being led around by the Devil. Man is *non posse non peccare*—Latin for "not able not to sin." This means (is expressly taught) that man's epistemology, his ability to **know** TRUTH, is irreparably flawed so that he is not inclined to understand himself or God. Even our lovable resident mental reflection advocate Dave Harvey said that man can't really be trusted with his doctrinal conclusions. **But** . . . the foundation of Orthodoxy is Man's ability to identify TRUTH by epistemological consensus??!!!!

I got big belly laughs on this one deep down to my toes. Come on, guys, laugh with me; this is wonderfully absurd. Orthodoxy is a rich fiction.

PDI/CLC/SGM is touting Reformed Theology as the intellectual/infallible system of theology. Remember I mentioned as an example John Calvin's *Institutes of the Christian Religion* as an example of Systematic Theology? The foundation of their current doctrine is embedded in Calvin's Systematic—in his specific **Interpretive Methodology**.

Jedi, you can evaluate the claims being made underneath the noble goal. You can now identify the filters PDI/CLC/SGM brings to their Bible reading and

Blight in the Vineyard

how those assumptions shape their assertions. They want people to believe that Paul was telling Timothy to be diligent with a theological system some 1,500 years in the future. Here is a question: If our doctrine is by Scripture Alone, why are we jumping fifteen centuries to start our doctrinal assurance?

Jedi, what do you think? Hmmmmm . . .

Oh, this thinking is fun, fun, fun. "True insight is always preceded by mental reflection." Thank you so much, Mr. Harvey.

"John, are you saying there is no final recitation of TRUTH, no infallible belief system, no way to discern who believes right?"

Actually, I have made no attempt to answer those questions. My goal has been, and remains, to illustrate that the "everyone, everywhere, who is anyone has always believed . . ." orthodoxy is a myth. My goal has been, and remains, to explain the theological arena that the Sovereign Grace Ministries Hair Club for Men dove headlong into two decades ago is much, much larger than they like to pretend. My goal has been, and remains, to introduce people to the tools of Higher Critical Methodology so that they can make an informed assessment of the tides of European "Sound Doctrine." My goal has been, and remains, to expose the intellectual sleights of hand used by a growing number of church leaders to demand intellectual obedience.

"John, you're an Arminian, aren't you?"

Sigh.

Raise the standard of your mental reflections. Get past the narrow, historical indoctrination, and start looking at the broader Arena of Ideas. I know it is tough because self-styled Reformed Theology Puritan groupies refuse to educate. They indoctrinate because they are more interested in the "authority" of historic solidarity than actually equipping you to deal with the Arena's rigor.

But I don't indoctrinate, and I am not interested in historic solidarity, and I don't need authority to beat people into submission. I have provided the tools that enable you to see that the question misses my point like missing the broad side of the barn. It has never been that black and white. It has never been a one or the other issue. They don't tell you the real events of Simon Episcopius and the Synod of Dort because they don't want you to know what it implies about their authority. If you begin to understand what really happened in the Calvinism/Arminianism debate, you would see the fraud of their "orthodox" appeal. More often than not, the "orthodox" view had more to do with civic use of the bonfire, or sword, or the rack, or the dungeon.

The PDI/CLC/SGM Hair Club for Men continues to represent that no conversation exists over the content of Sound Doctrine because it is orthodoxy. But now you can see the progression they use to dominate you:

> **Manipulate your love and your fear + Paul's "watch your life and your doctrine" = Sound Doctrine = a specific theological system = Reformed Theology + academic study = Orthodoxy = anyone demanding authority**

9
Bonfire-Lighting and a Bucket of Water

> A person is to be punished with a just penalty, who ... utters blasphemy, or gravely harms public morals, or rails at or excites hatred of or contempt for religion or the Church.
>
> **—Catholic Canon Law 1369**

> What havoc has been made of books through every century of the Christian era? Where are fifty gospels, condemned as spurious by the bull of Pope Gelasius? Where are the forty wagon-loads of Hebrew manuscripts burned in France, by order of another pope, because suspected of heresy? Remember the 'index expurgatorius,' the inquisition, the stake, the axe, the halter and the guillotine.
>
> **—John Adams**

> It is error alone which needs the support of government. Truth can stand by itself.
>
> **—Thomas Jefferson**

Many "orthodoxy" apologists think I have finally gotten to the nub of self-revelation, having deliberately placed myself in the non-orthodox camp. In doing so, I have located myself outside mainstream Christianity. You're saying "Aha!" or "Eureka!" or "John Calvin!" giving each other high fives heading to the mic and proclaim *El Primo Doctrinal Mover and Shaker* defender of Orthodoxy against a poor disillusioned Arminian (at best) or leading the ouster of a budding heretic before he could do real damage (at worst).

Well, I'm gonna burst your bubble. C. J. Mahaney—*El Primo Doctrinal Mover and Shaker*—never tried to defend anything but his authority. He ignored my arguments, set out to diminish my character, and bought me a book on conflict resolution. He defaulted to the standard SGM deflection of pride and arrogance and the general impropriety of disagreeing with pastoral judgment. One of his minions offered up this gem of intellectual sparing: "John, I'm old enough to be your father, but I don't feel the least bit patronized." That appeal to the Geriatric Enlightenment Club doesn't rank on the polemic[1] so-what meter. No one is right merely because they are old, and wisdom is not the sole domain of the geriatric. Besides, I had read most of their books plus a few dozen more. Additionally, I had produced written evaluations of many doctrinal issues long before I landed in their cushy pastor's office where Robin Boisvert seems to refuse to wear shoes. When I mentioned my reading list or offered my various theses, they were not nearly so interested in mental reflections.

Back in the (Charismatic) day, the average CLC/PDI pastor's academic pursuits were self-driven efforts, which is fine. Learning should be self-driven and some of them read an impressive amount. But they never had to defend their scholasticism against peer or professorial review. If the grades come back wanting, they can wave the magic "I'm a pastor and old enough to be your father" wand. Indeed, they were insulted by the notion that they should

---

1. The art or practice of aggressive debate, attack on or refutation of the opinions or principles of another; a person who writes in support of one opinion, doctrine, or system in opposition to another; one skilled in polemics; a controversialist; a disputant; an argument or controversy.

need to justify their ideas, so they never seriously entertained thoughts opposed to their Puritan agenda.

I understand that many leaders have since gone on to like-minded divinity schools where teachers must sign some variation of Reformed doctrinal solidarity statement. But that is like a budding Word of Faith preacher going to *Rhema* Bible College and pretending that two years of indoctrination has given a broad theological education. It doesn't matter that, unlike *Rhema* graduates, they can discuss all the branches of Systematic theology and rattle off the primary church councils and the names of the historical heretics. The teachers enforce the school's doctrinal statements, not challenge the historic dogma, or seriously try to combat the assumptions. And if the first third of this book has done anything, it should illustrate that the Arena of Ideas and the sub-arena of theology and Church history is a vast place. The notion that the only theological game in town is in the 16th century is riotously funny.

I understand the temptation to reduce my commentary to a rehash of the Calvinist vs. Arminian debate. I understand how that leads a person to dismiss my comments as mere axe grinding. I get that Reformation Theology groupies are committed to the Reformers first, last, and always. As near as I can tell, intellectual solidarity trumps all else. Historical realities are usually irrelevant and biblical verses get hijacked with impunity.

Jedi, all this is understandable . . . but wrong.

So that we can cut to the bonfire-lighting ceremony, I will be blunt. I don't accept the premise that Christians must pay homage to historic academic debates. I cut Antiquity's religious Gordian Knot long before I get to the 16th century, so I have no moral, spiritual, or intellectual obligation to justify myself to dead men's ideas. So, chant orthodoxy all you like. The history of that fiction is on my side.

Pull the façade away from "Orthodoxy" and look into the sources, events, and circumstance that defined it, and you will see a cesspool of ham-fisted intellectual thuggery, political infighting, Christian doctrine paid for by Imperial coin, gross injustice, statist totalitarianism, pagan syncretism, ignoble men with horrifically deviant personalities potentiating over God's Church, and more putrid invective coming from Christian leaders in the name of Christ than any Islamic fatwa.

Modern Orthodoxy defenders think they are advocating a purist intellectual/spiritual pedigree. They like to believe they have grasped the very roots of God's sweetness and light. But the pedigree is Mystic Despotism, and the root is the deep and abiding core of tyranny.

The open, obvious elements of my advocacy are available for any who will actually look. That means rationality is my tool of persuasion. To win this argument, all I have to do is identify people with intellectual integrity, teach critical thinking tools, and educate on the historic record.

This book contains the barest historical overview and one of the few challenges to the moral and ethical foundations to the deep roots of tyranny within Christian history and theology. For many people, this is the first time they have **ever** heard these challenges. Or maybe even worse, the first time they have ever heard there should **be** a challenge. So, it is very easy to take all the new thoughts, all the new ideas, all the conceptual chaos that threatens to make your worldview go tilt, put them in a nice tidy box called heretic, and chalk it up to an undergirding deception. This quest for an easy organization against the chaos, this fear is exactly what I told you **they** manipulate. The fulcrum of your fears is what keeps many from persisting in the very, very hard questions about the foundation and nature of Christianity. It terrifies us to think that we have invested **everything** into something that might be a lie. Or maybe better said: We fear that we will uncover realities that challenge the very foundations of our faith and drive us towards some abyss of apostasy. So we let the polite fictions persist, winking and nodding at our mutual self-enforced ignorance.

The result is that good men do nothing and the evil persists disguised behind the useful lie. As Martin Luther said, "What harm would it do if a man told a good strong lie for the sake of the good and for the Christian church?" And we rationalize by saying, "A lie out of necessity, a useful lie, a helpful lie, such lies would not be against God; he would accept them."[2]

For those of you sitting on the sidelines, unsure but interested, notice this: Who has to approve books? For all of SGM's vaunted appeal to mental reflections and their high-minded assertions to academic excellence, far too many people remain uninformed about the very evolutions

---

2. From Luther to Philip of Hesse who committed bigamy in 1540. Luther counseled that Philip should lie about his conduct because it was for the good of the Christian church.

Preserved Smith, *The Life and Letters of Martin Luther*, 2nd ed. (Boston & New York: Houghton Mifflin, 1914). If you dare, read the entire case of the Bigamy of Philip of Hess, starting on page 377. It isn't pretty.

Luther's advocacy is discussed in Sissela Bok's, *Lying*, 2nd ed. (New York: Vintage Books, 1999).

The source for Bok's book is a German work, *Briefwechsel Landgraf Philips des Grossmuthigen von Hessen mit Bucer*, 3 volumes, published by S. Hirzel in Leipzig from 1880-1891.

For those of you who read German you can find the quote here: http://fig.lib.harvard.edu/fig/?bib=0034660031

John Immel

and conclusions of Orthodoxy. They will point to the vague Boogieman of Postmodernism as some encroaching evil to justify portraying intellectual inquiry as spiritual sedition, all the while advocating mental reflections . . . **their** mental reflections.

To bolster doctrinal foundation:
- Who has to sensor intellectual inquiry?
- Who appeals to authority to validate intellectual content?
- Why is it necessary to use the force of church government to sustain unified thinking?
- Why the endless refrain to avoid ideas not approved by the pastors?
- Why is authority and submission to its edicts so essential to their governance?

For the moment, we will let these remain rhetorical questions, but the underlying theme should be obvious: Why does the TRUTH need a mechanism to insulate its bearers, compel ignorance, and limit information?

This is not a rhetorical question: the TRUTH doesn't.

Under the Reformed Theology Bus

In the early '90s, PDI/CLC did not make their "doctrinal refocus" explicit. They sufficiently danced around the edges of full disclosure so as to not be guilty of lying. But unless pressed, they would not fess up to the doctrinal pedigree. I contend the leadership took this approach because they knew the people in the pews would reject Reformed Theology if they were clear about doctrinal pedigree. To prevent a wholesale revolt, they fed the sheep small bite after small bite, alternately glutting the unwary or driving away the doctrinally savvy. I vividly remember standing in our Care Group leader's kitchen, explaining the content of Calvinism and one dear woman accused me of proselytizing people **away** from the pastors to **become** Calvinist. When I clarified that the doctrines under discussion were not my ideas but what the pastors were teaching, she thought I was lying. She was scandalized by the doctrines and repulsed that the pastors could believe such things. She and her husband promptly started fishing through Bible passages to point out what they saw as errors of **my** thinking.

Oh, the irony in that event.

Many early PDI/CLC abuse stories revolve around people who sought to understand the change from the historically charismatic-ish teaching and found themselves in a bewildering onslaught of character assassination and heavy-handed pastoral intellectual thuggery. PDI/CLC/SGM leaders drove the bus where they wanted and heaven forefend you ask the driver to explain the route. **Now** the doctrinal movers and shakers are open advocates of the Reformed doctrinal elements that serve their purposes. This leadership team is focused on the truths that serve their governmental outcome: to entrench **their** monopoly of force. This is the important part, the dirty little secret behind the true appeal of the Reformed Theology construct: Calvin's synthesis, at its core, is a turnkey academic solution to morally justify a monopoly of ecclesiastical force.

Most people would never know this because they don't understand the rise and development of Reformation ideas. Calvin's synthesis has been reduced to a trite acronym that is easy to remember and therefore, easy to believe. But people are (at best) unaware of the details and (at worst) ignorant of the Protestant doctrinal evolution from Luther to Zwingli, to Calvin, to Beza, to the subsequent synods of Dorchester and Westminster.

John Immel

Generations of Luther to Calvin defenders make the expansive leap that all things Calvin are necessarily all things Bible. Dissenters from Calvin's synthesis get dumped into Arminian camp and treated to some variation of "If you only really **understood** the doctrines, if you were only truly enlightened, you would believe the Bible." These thinkers and doctrinal evolutions get dumped into a monolithic defense of that waskally critter "orthodoxy." And who has the nerve to challenge such a noble "time-tested" manifestation of TRUTH?

If one wants to be a Calvinist, then you are free to be about that. But understand, the conflicts with PDI/CLC/SGM doesn't stem from agreement or disagreement with the hodgepodge of their Impassioned Orthodoxy. Over the last fifteen years, there has been any number of self-styled Reformed Theology aficionados who suffered the same spiritual tyranny perpetrated on people with Arminian bad attitudes. These were people in doctrinal solidarity with PDI/CLC/SGM who ended up in the same place as the budding, deleterious problem children.

It is easy to assume people were thrown under the Reformed Theology bus because they were not sufficiently "orthodox" and then absolve the SGM leadership of their driving skill because the roadkill was in defense of purist Bible teaching. It is easy to render people's objections to the tire tracks running up their back as the mad mutterings of inauthentic Christians. But this reductionism will cause you to miss the real issue: the use of an ideological system in service to government force to run over people.

10
Major Players, Major Thoughts

> I do further promise and declare that I will, when opportunity presents, make and wage relentless war, secretly or openly, against all heretics, Protestants and Liberals, as I am directed to do and to extirpate and exterminate them from the face of the whole earth; and that I will spare neither sex, age nor condition; and that I will hang, waste, boil, flay, strangle and bury alive these infamous heretics; rip up the stomachs and wombs of their women and crush their infants' heads against the wall, in order to annihilate forever their execrable race.
>
> —**Pope Paul III, 1576**

> Christianity persecuted, tortured, and burned. Like a hound it tracked the very scent of heresy. It kindled wars, and nursed furious hatreds and ambitions. . . Man, far from being freed from his natural passions, was plunged into artificial ones quite as violent and much more disappointing.
>
> —**George Santayana**

> In every country and every age, the priest has been hostile to Liberty. He is always in alliance with the despot, abetting his abuses in return for protection to his own.
>
> —**Thomas Jefferson**

Martin Luther's life and doctrine is and isn't necessary to understand because it does and it doesn't have to do with our current discussion.

John Immel

See, here is the rub: There isn't enough space to rehash the details of Lutheran and Calvin Theology. But the general trend of their thoughts, ideas, and doctrines are being held up as the foundation of Orthodoxy of the Impassioned Orthodoxy equation. So, in as much as church leaders fancy themselves Lutheran/Calvin Orthodox—there is that word again—and its corresponding theological heritage, it is necessary to familiarize ourselves to the players and the times that formed the thought.

By most people Martin Luther is considered the leader of the Protestant Reformation. His life becomes important to our discussion in the year 1507 and thereafter; 1507 marks the year he became an ordained Augustinian Priest. And a year later, Luther became professor of Philosophy at the University of Wittenberg. The church door at Wittenberg was Luther's first foray into the Arena of Ideas, where he posted his *Ninety-Five Theses* on October 31, 1517, which was a statement about penance and his protest against selling indulgences. The bulwark of his dissent with the church authorities evolved into the Reformation battle cry: sola gratia, sola fide, sola scriptura—grace alone, faith alone, and scripture alone.

As an academic pursuit, theologians write about men named Luther, and Calvin, and Zwingli, filling up college curriculum like it was God's own gospel. Some of you, dear readers, go to churches that bear the name Lutheran. Some of you attended churches that are the theological heirs of some Lutheran doctrines—Baptists, Presbyterian, et cetera—but most would be hard-pressed to explain what that means.

I submit that the Reformation has no real understanding in modern thought. We may understand

Blight in the Vineyard

that something bad was happening in the Catholic Church and some people called Protestants fixed it. We may have heard that the Catholic Church was selling something called indulgences—money for the absolution of sin. In our contemporary Christian culture—a culture of simplicity and speed—even five hundred years later, that scandal still translates easily in our minds leaving our Christian piety ringing with outrage. But beyond that simple understanding, the people and ideas are fuzzy.

The Catholic Church during the 13th and 14th century was filled with politics, and intrigue, and social evolution. Part of that evolution was the infectious spirit of the Renaissance, which in turn inspired the Papacy to undertake a massive building program, and you know what happens when preachers start building things.

Just to be sure that everybody knows, "catholic" means universal, so Catholic Church means **Universal** Church. That means the everywhere church. That means they considered themselves THE church and everyone else was departing from orthodoxy. That means "Orthodoxy" was what the **Universal** Church believed by everyone, everywhere, by all. To hammer home the mythical Orthodoxy point, I am going to keep poking people in the eye with the historic reality: The Reformers left **Universal** Church Orthodoxy. Whether they really wanted to or not is irrelevant because as we will see shortly, they challenged the very foundations of Orthodoxy.

Therefore, realize that from roughly the 6th century onward, **Universal** Church Orthodoxy was the defining measure of correct church doctrine. Splits were considered departure from Orthodoxy. If you didn't like what the Pope said, well, it sucks to be you. As far as

John Immel

Europe was concerned, the **Universal** Church held the "keys" to people's spiritual lives.

It is important to understand the spiritual capital the **Universal** Church Leadership was spending to maintain their authority. Understand this and it is easy to fathom the abuses they perpetrated on the people.

Please Indulge Me

"Gosh, John, I thought that is what we've been doing."

Ha ha ha . . . very funny. Leave the jokes to the professionals.

I suppose everybody has come up against the apparent paradox: I am a Christian. How then can I keep committing sin? This question has plagued the minds of scholars, and pontificators, and pastors, and so forth for, well, since the beginning, I suppose. My goal here is not to answer the question but to point out how the **Universal** Church dealt with the issue.

How does the Church deal with post-baptismal sins?

The Orthodox—there's that word again—belief was that mortal sins (sins that kill God's friendship) and venial sins (minor faults of disposition and unloving actions) destroy or strain one's relationship with God. **Universal** Church Leadership decided that penalties—penance—was necessary to make up for committing sin. Now, don't get ahead of us and dismiss 1,500 years of church thinking because you don't believe that. Penance has its roots as far back as Tertullian in the 3rd century. And Penance evolved over the course of twelve centuries in various forms. From the humiliation of open public confession to the wearing of sackcloth and ashes, to self-imposed fasting, and finally, to private confession to a "priest of the Lord," that was accompanied with various

Blight in the Vineyard

forms of *poena,* Latin for punishments. Given the **Universal** Church's assumptions, presuppositions, and filters, bishops had reasonable and compelling intellectual foundation for teaching Penance, a doctrine the **Universal** Church denomination still affirms as Orthodoxy because it has stood the test of time.

When Martin Luther raised his hand to say, "No, fellas, I disagree," he was dissenting with an entire body of tradition that stood the test of time for 1,300 years and had a very important theological concern: dealing with known sin. But *Disputation of Doctor Martin Luther on the Power and Efficacy of Indulgences,* also known as the *Ninety-Five Theses,* ultimately implied a much more important argument.

The Nicene Council ultimately caused more doctrinal problems than it fixed precisely because it enforced the "Orthodox" understanding of *homoousios* by the parasitic link between ecclesiastical concerns and imperial authority. For years to come, Church leadership was embroiled in doctrinal fights where the counterarguments were of the "scripture alone" variety. But once the vaunted "Orthodoxy" was defined, any argument that even hinted subversion to longstanding doctrines became heresy and punishable by civil sanction. The Church bishops that came out on top of imperial patronage and civil power fight were desperately afraid of the domino effect, one successful counterargument that opened up greater and greater challenges to their right to rule. Consider the full implication of the scriptures as the property of the state. When Government power is tied to the definition of TRUTH, leaders have no choice but to hold absolute control over its presentation. To sustain control of government, Church leadership must move to find justification that secures Bible interpretation in their private domain. The reason is simple: If one person successfully makes a more purely "Scriptural" counterargument against existing authorities, it follows that those authorities are false and therefore disqualified. So to undercut the implicit "Scripture Alone" counterargument, the Council of Constantinople in 553 confirmed its commitment to judging doctrinal accuracy through this standard:

> . . . the things we have received from the Holy Scriptures **and** from the teachings of the Holy Fathers **and** from the definitions of one and the same faith by four sacred councils.

The four councils referenced are Nicaea in 325, Constantinople in 381, Ephesus in 431, and Chalcedon in 451. Pope Gregory the Great (600 AD), arguably the first Pope of Western Christianity, set the governmental tone in Catholic practice through Europe for the next 800 years by presuming that these councils held equal status with the Gospels. The inevitable conclusion manifest in the formal statements of the Council of Trent (1545–63):

> I accept Sacred Scriptures in the sense in which it has been held, and is held, by the Holy Mother Church, to whom it belongs to judge the true sense and interpretation of the Sacred Scripture, nor will I interpret in any other way than is in accordance with the unanimous agreement of the Fathers.

This was a doctrine that had stood the test of time, affirmed and reconfirmed by ecclesiastical council over and over and over reflecting **the** theological consensus *quod ubique, quod semper, quod ab omnibus*. So, the logic behind indulgences effectively said that if the Pope had the power to interpret scripture and define doctrine, then it stood to "reason" that indulgences were effective

Blight in the Vineyard

because the Pope said so. And the Pope said so because the Church had always believed this.

This Papal tautology gave the Catholic Church blanket intellectual latitude had inspired endless animosity. The Papacy could execute any governmental action and claim immunity by referencing any point of authority. And if one didn't exist, they made them up and pretended that they always existed. The Papacy enjoyed a divine right of despotism and Europe hated or loved their spiritual task master depending on which sword was swinging—Sword of the Spirit or Sword of the State. By the time of Innocent III (1198), the charge of heresy was the same as the charge of treason and gave rise to the first Inquisition. The Fourth Lateran Council (1215) further laid out the criteria for the burning of suspected heretics which was synonymous with alleged political traitors.

Now you can begin to grasp what Luther faced. He stood directly opposed to the impenetrable, circular logic of Orthodox—there's that word again—Papal authority to establish doctrine and impose that doctrine by governmental force.

Here is the real heart and soul of the Reformation conflict: the source, practice, and methodology of Papal Authority. The Reformation's theological battleground was over the use of force married to inspiration, authority, interpretation, and tradition. Said another way, the Reformation was over that dastardly Subjectivity Beast.

Read the following written by Martin Luther:

The Three Walls of the Romanists

> The Romanists have, with great adroitness, drawn three walls round themselves, with which they have hitherto protected themselves,

so that no one could reform them, whereby all Christendom has fallen terribly.

Firstly, if pressed by the temporal power, they have affirmed and maintained that the temporal power has no jurisdiction over them, but, on the contrary, that the spiritual power is above the temporal.

Secondly, if it were proposed to admonish them with the Scriptures, they objected that no one may interpret the Scriptures but the Pope.

Thirdly, if they are threatened with a council, they pretend that no one may call a council but the Pope.[1]

Martin Luther's comments point to the intellectual bulwark that kept the Papacy immune from scrutiny because truth and falsehood were state property.

"Aha!" you say.

Now you are starting to see the situation. By grabbing Bible interpretation out of the hands of the state and giving all men moral access to TRUTH, Martin Luther undermined the power of the State to determine TRUTH. Sola Scriptura was a stake in the heart of Papal authority. Good ol' Martin was fighting the entirely self-enforcing logic in the Authority of Tradition and the Tradition of Authority. And lo and behold, (a little biblical language for you purists) here we are a few centuries later and preachers are making very similar claims, erecting a strikingly similar statist intellectual bulwark to keep their method and practice immune from scrutiny.

---

1. Martin Luther, "Address to the Christian Nobility of the German Nation Respecting the Reformation of the Christian Estate," in *The Harvard Classics*, ed. Charles W. Eliot, (New

Johnny C.

Everybody shake hands and exchange names. John Calvin, this is everybody. Everybody, this is John Calvin. By the way, I like your first name, Mr. Calvin.

Anyway, everybody, John Calvin is a writer. He wrote a few books and burned some people at the stake. Mr. Calvin, we are now talking about some of your thoughts. We won't talk about Michael Servetus right now. I would ask Mr. Calvin to sign autographs for us afterwards, but he's busy striking matches for my S'mores party. Mr. Calvin, we are going to talk about you for a little while and . . . well, I don't want to hurt your feelings, but I . . . uh . . .

Tell you what. I'll say a good thing about you first.

Given Mr. Calvin's tool set—meaning, the existing theological resources available—his current academic assumptions, and the age of thinking in which he lived, his synthesis is the work of genius. Writing a comprehensive intellectual system that gives men historic and philosophical continuity is an amazing human feat. Very few people have accomplished such a thing, and those who have, their names are instantly recognizable to most anyone in the literate western world.

There. I said something nice.

I believe him wrong and his theology, ultimately, a synthesis of philosophical despotism and among the most disastrous bodies of thought perpetrated on man, and a murdering Mystic Despot, but still a genius.

Discussing the details of Calvin's theology isn't necessary. But I do want everyone to be familiar with his contribution. Calvin's *Institutes* (1530) is the formal

---

York: P.F. Collier & Son, 1909–14), vol. 36, part 5.

systematic institutionalization of Platonist/Augustinian syncretism that was refined and conformed to Lutheran thinking and became the doctrinal blueprint for the **Reformed Tradition**.

Remember what I said in the first chapter?

Comprehensive intellectual systems give men idea continuity, which is how we identify stability for our lives. Here are two important principles of human existence:

1. Man abhors chaos.
2. Man needs a coherent body of ideas to govern his actions.

With this principle, with this human drive in mind, you can grasp the potent motivations that Luther set in motion. The Reformation left chaos in Europe; the politics of religion and the religion of politics was in a shambles. Longstanding power structures were destroyed from the root, and nations felt the intense civic and religious turmoil. The very philosophical justification for European governmental systems was left in ruin. Papal authority was the leading force of governmental power for the better part of 1,100 years. The Reformation dealt Papal Authority serious intellectual violence by giving men a unifying reason to justifying wholesale abandonment of the Catholic state. Entire nations, Europe's governing powers, were indebted to Platonist depravity and the hijacked Bible ideas of Augustinian syncretism. This philosophical power base, this coherent body of ideas, undergirded the Divine Right of Kings and the collectivist social contract of the Three Estates that held Europe's populace in tyrannical grip. This is the cohesive worldview that held the European Middle Ages together and justified the Crusades and the Inquisitions. The Reformation delivered a deathblow to this worldview

Blight in the Vineyard

and utterly subverted the Papal monopoly on Mystic Despotism: civic power based on man's spiritual insecurities.

The result was the necessary search to find a new cohesive worldview: Man set out to fill the vacuum to adjust his assumptions about life and the means to proscribe his ideas and actions. The implications of Scripture Alone, coupled with the growing Renaissance affirmation that Man had the ability to grasp his world, implied an ocean of chaos. Church Leaders felt that the very moorings of existence had been severed as they suffered their own postmodern polyglot hell. They resented the "inauthentic" Christian movements and sub-movements that sprung up, advocating their own brand of spiritual truth. The narrow medieval minds were terrified of a secular state: government that was in service to nothing more than the conventions of Men. Church leaders were sure that God was moments away from raining down fire and brimstone because life no longer revolved around Church authority.

Justo L. Gonzalez writes in his book, *A History of Christian Thought*, volume 3, page 70:

> But the forces unleashed by Luther could not be controlled by any one person—certainly not by Luther himself. Thus arose various diverging views . . . At first there seemed to be no pattern to these various views, **for the possible points of divergence were many and therefore, an exhaustive description of Protestant theology in the sixteenth century would require separate discussions of at least two dozen significant theologians."** [emphasis mine]

The bottom line is, in the years after 1517, Christian thought and practice exploded with divergent views and claims and flavors. And the logical criticism by the

John Immel

Universal Church, Mr. Gonzalez mentions on page 102 of the same volume:

> Catholic polemists pointed out that once the dams of ecclesiastical authority were broken, there was no way to prevent the flood of extreme positions, and that the proliferation of sects was therefore a logical consequence of the Reformation.

John F. MacArthur should write a book called Reformation Chaos. (Oh, what a knee slapper!)

The doctrinal chaos that spread like "wildfire" (a little Pentecostal language there for all the Holy Rollers amongst us) and men like John Calvin set out to find a logic that brought everything into control. Everybody had a creed, or a statement of faith, or a yardstick of authentic Christian expression. We would go buggy if I tried to describe it all.

Buggy is a good theological word, isn't it?

Anyway, for the next few decades, everybody set out to beat back the Subjectivity Beast. No one really succeeded . . . until Calvin . . . sort of.

For many Reformers, the overarching intellectual hurdle was "How can we have a moral justification to separate ourselves from Orthodoxy by the power of 'Scripture Alone,' and eliminate all comers to the interpretive throne?"

Calvin went back to the two-thousand-year-old playbook, the ancient foundation for despots: Platonism. Plato disqualified man's existence by disqualifying man's ability to grasp existence. Plato taught a form of human depravity, which logically preceded a governing elite who ruled the unenlightened. Augustine co-opted Irenaeus of Lyons' concept called Original Sin and took Plato's philosophy (Plotinus Neo-Platonism) and comprehensively integrated it into Christian doctrine

Blight in the Vineyard

circa 430. The concept of depravity is what the **Universal** Church used to enforce its brand of Dictated Good for the next 1,000 years. From Augustine to Luther, from Luther to Zwingli, and eventually to Calvin, the predicates of Plato's depravity were re-instituted. This stood in direct contrast to St. Thomas Aquinas' teaching that inspired the subsequent Age of Reason. Aristotle via Aquinas reintroduced reason and logic back into the minds of men. The undergirding assumption was that rational and logical men had the ability to grasp the world in which they lived. This was the philosophical source of freedom sweeping through Europe. This assumption of individual rational self-appointment was the very concept that made Luther's initial dissent viable. Men throughout Europe had an expectation of ability. So the battle cry Sola Scriptura, Sola Fide, Sola Gratia was a potent counter to the Universal Church's insistence that they held the keys to everyone's earthly lives and eternal salvation. Notice that every part of the declaration undermines the Metaphysical and Epistemological foundations of Catholic despotism.

But here is the tragedy: Martin Luther and John Calvin abandoned the very ideas that made the original arguments possible. Or maybe better said, they never realized how important rational self-appointment was to the underlying force of the objection. Depravity is a readymade disqualifier. You can't know the truth for yourself because your very nature corrupts the ability to grasp truth. Your very nature is shot through with disqualifying drives and desires. Once a man accepts this premise, "Scripture Alone" is mere pretense to a new dictatorial governing body. Authority is the arbitrator of GOOD because they are appointed by God. You need someone to dictate GOOD because you will not do GOOD.

John Immel

Alakazam! Poof! Christianity is right back in the threshold of Mystic Despotism that had kept it in bondage under the **Universal** Church.

Calvin's *Institutes of the Christian Religion* are not compelling because they are true, but because they offer an ironclad philosophical consistency. His logic goes to the heart of man's willingness to venture ideas. Calvin seeks to destroy man's willingness to inquire by destroying confidence in his ability to inquire. For all of Calvin's prolific writerliness, the sum of his case is "If you don't believe what I'm saying, you are deceived." From this "intellectual" foundation, the rest of his arguments are swings of an unopposed hammer. Anyone who resists his assault is disqualified **because** they defend themselves.

Calvin was the most successful of his peers at offering a cohesive worldview. The comprehensive nature of *Institutes* aided its movement into the public mind, but its cultural value was the moral clarity for despotism. He was quick to carry his theology into the civic world, joining William Farel in governing the city-state of Geneva. In Europe, through the late 1500s, there was only microscopic distinction between church authority and civic authority. And Calvin was not shy about using his civic/religious authority to drive his political opponents from the playing field.

Rulers and governors, kings and queens, saw the value of his synthesis to pacify a populace—while refusing Papal obeisance—as opposed to the theology of Menno Simons'[2] philosophical passivism. Even with a casual familiarity of European history, one can see this outworking in the Church of England. In England we have the merging of Calvin's ideas with the sword of

---

2. Founder of the Mennonites.

state. Mere decades from the publication of Calvin's synthesis of Mystic Despotism, the Church found itself in the same tyrannical place as Pre-Reformation Catholicism: Christian doctrine dictated by governmental authority and enforced by the point of a sword or the flaming stake.

Now that gives you a spiritual warm fuzzy, doesn't it?

I'll bet about now your jaw is close to the floor. You've only heard the warm, fuzzy version of Church history and the accolades heaped upon the great Reformer of Geneva. You've only ever heard him spoken of in reverent tones and extolled as a great champion of spiritual truth. I told you the details made the picture look very different, and this is hardly everything that could be brought to light. At 10,000 feet everything looks seamless, neat, and tidy. The roads look straight and neatly cut through the countryside. But put your feet on the road and everything slams into harsh, jagged, rough, twisted relief.

I bet that for many of you who have suffered under authoritarian groups, the picture of your interaction is coming into focus. As you make your way to the center of the vortex and take an emotionless look at the swirling ideological tumult, everything starts to make sense. You are seeing that it is no accident: How they act and what they preach has very specific goals.

What did Jesus say about Trees and Fruit?

Notes

11
Convenient Calvinists

The Truth will make you free.

—Jesus

A man has free choice to the extent that he is rational.

—Thomas Aquinas

The United States of America have exhibited, perhaps, the first example of governments erected on the simple principles of nature; and if men are now sufficiently enlightened to disabuse themselves of artifice, imposture, hypocrisy, and superstition, they will consider this event as an era in their history. Although the detail of the formation of the American governments is at present little known or regarded either in Europe or in America, it may hereafter become an object of curiosity. It will never be pretended that any persons employed in that service had interviews with the gods, or were in any degree under the influence of Heaven, more than those at work upon ships or houses, or laboring in merchandise or agriculture; it will forever be acknowledged that these governments were contrived merely by the use of reason and the senses. . . .

—John Adams

No matter what the glossy brochure says about the affection for Reformation Theology, the leaders of PDI/CLC/SGM are not really adherents to the Lutheran Reformed Tradition. For you current members, when was

John Immel

the last time you went to confession? Or saw an infant baptism, not a baby **dedication**? I could go on, but it would be more fun if you, dear Jedi, did some research on Orthodox—there is that word again—Lutheran Reformed practice and see what a true pure Reformed Tradition church looks like and then tell me if PDI/CLC/SGM is really a Reformed Church.

And neither are those within the Hair Club for Men classic Calvinists. Well, there really is no such thing as a "classic" Calvinist. A mere fifty years after Johnny C's *Institutes* was written, the intellectual heirs were rethinking and reworking his "orthodox" synthesis in response to effective criticism.

Anyway, what is often called *American* Calvinism is really a misnomer. The form of Calvinism that arrived in the New World was a separatist sub-movement among the dozens and dozens Reformation doctrinal developments. From Calvin's *Christian Institutes* come the systematic construct that has been carried on and refined by men, including Bucer (Strasbourg), Knox (Scotland), Beza (Switzerland), and the Puritanism of England. The Puritans are the people who packed into boats and landed on Plymouth Rock, but they are at no point American as we would understand that concept in 1620 and the years following. The ideological framework of the American Republic was still a future event yet to be conceived in all its social, political, and religious freedom brilliance. The uniquely American concept of freedom of religion that you and I take as a foundation principle of life came roughly eighty years after the Salem witch trials and was steeped in the diametrically opposed philosophical thought that arose from the Enlightenment. Until the years following the American Revolution, the religious preoccupations of Colonial Calvinism were a persisting manifestation of medieval European Christianity.

The ideological framework of colonial Calvinism developed under the influences of Cotton Mather, John Owen, and Jonathan Edwards who sought yet again to blend Augustinianism and religious enthusiasm into civic structure.[1] The leading Puritans were not innovative thinkers (as some apologists like to pretend) but rather purist defenders of the most virulent form of Reformation thought. By intention, the Puritans sought to contrast themselves from the Church of England and broader European Reformation. This elitist determination is at the root of the Puritan involvement in the English civil war and their stated objective to establish God's rule in the New World when the European goal didn't work out so well.

The impact of these Puritan leaders on colonial religious life is summarized by the following articles of religion:

- "Sinners in the hands of an angry God" is the lingering metaphysical worldview etched on the minds of men declaring God as a vindictive sovereign.
- Whatever God's benevolence might theoretically

---

1. The scope of this discussion comes from a distillation of the following works in their individual treatment of the social religious developments of "American" Calvinism.

James Ward Smith and A. Leland Jamison, eds., *The Shaping of American Religion* (Princeton: Princeton University Press, 1961).

Alan Heimert, *Religion and the American Mind* (Cambridge: Harvard University Press, 1966).

Lefferts A. Loetscher, *The Broadening Church: A Study of Theological Issues in the Presbyterian Church Since 1869* (Philadelphia: University of Pennsylvania Press, 1954).

John T. McNeill, *The History and Character of Calvinism* (New York: Oxford University Press, 1954).

Leonard J. Trinterud, *The Forming of an American Tradition* (Philadelphia: Westminster Press, 1949).

Justo L. Gonzalez, *A History of Christian Thought* (Nashville: Abingdon Press, 1970), vol. 3.

represent, ultimately, this worldview makes Him wrathful and damning; terror is the only appropriate reaction to divine awareness.
- Man's depravity requires authoritarian governance to stand between himself and his lascivious impulses.
- Pride in human ability is man's leading vice and the outworking of wretched deception.
- Salvation is the miracle of being approved access to Heaven. This otherworld utopia is granted or denied according to God's mysterious plan.
- The unintelligible nature of God's intentions—in the feeble minds of men—makes Him capricious and malicious to every failing of human existence.
- Men are pilgrims through this worldly realm, a hostile empire fraught with all manner of evil; Man is a depraved creature entirely ill-suited in the bewildering environs and specifically prone to sinful self-destruction.
- The boons of wealth and health are gifts. Therefore, man is merely a steward charged with a divine trust. The elect are then qualified to dispose of their brothers as the collective sees fit. Stewards of God's appointment rule those siblings granted to their control.

Because the roots of American Calvinist tradition are deeply embedded in the medieval-minded European Puritans, the modern groupies tend to exist as an uneasy hybrid movement unable to reconcile two polar opposite worldviews. Their enduring affection for the Puritan thinkers places them at metaphysical odds with the world of religious toleration and the rational, independent, rugged individualism that is the direct product of the

Blight in the Vineyard

Enlightenment and its subsequent Age of Reason. Yet without the philosophical foundation of the American Revolution and its implicit religious freedom, they could not exist.

People tend to assume that critics of Calvin Orthodoxy are by default committed to the Jacobus Arminius "heresy." And most people don't even bother trying to reconcile the differences. It is no accident that this conversation ends at the same place: treading down the well-worn path of dead men's ideas and the endless scripture-stacking of contextual-less Bible verses. Unraveling this Gordian Knot is like trying to trim thorns off a bush inside the thicket: hot, painful, tedious work of no apparent value.

The historic debate of all things Calvin vs. Arminian has some huge failings. Unfortunately, the juggernaut of historical orthodoxy—there is that word again—and those people in solidarity with its tyranny to dead men's ideas prevent the faint of heart and mind from effective dissent. To unravel this scholastic Gordian Knot requires cutting the convenience away from those adopting historical positions that frame Christian thinking.

To that end, let us discuss Convenient Calvinists.

This is the title I give folks who tweak the content of Reformed Theology to mean pretty much whatever they want it to mean or more precisely, they tweak Calvin's synthesis of Bible ideas to satisfy their particular spiritual *feng shui*. They play fast and loose with the doctrines summed up in the T.U.L.I.P.[2] acronym, accepting or rejecting the parts and pieces of the construct depending on the day or the argument.

Semi-Pelagian. . . Semi-Calvinist. . . what's the diff?

---

2. Total Depravity, Unconditional Election, Limited Atonement, Irresistible Grace, Perseverance of the Saints.

John Immel

>snicker<

This is why the discussion of the mythical creature called Orthodoxy is so crucial. When Preachers pound the pulpit in the name of Orthodoxy, they are really saying final Authority of Tradition. They are staking a claim to **the** standard of theological judgment. They are seeking to demagogue the definition of Absolute Truth. This empowers them to dismiss any interpretation that deviates and demand that people justify "un-authentic" Christian thinking for daring to depart from what everyone, who is anyone, has always believed. This gives Orthodoxy proponents enormous power because they can frame every conversation while bearing no responsibility for the argumentative outcomes. They parrot the historic doctrines and pretend that is the same as "scriptural" truth. It is wonderfully convenient to claim authority founded on consensus with no responsibility to the failures of what came before in the name of orthodoxy, or what comes next in the name of orthodoxy.

Conversely, rejecting this parroted definition brings the implied criticism: To disagree with me is to disagree with orthodoxy, which is to disagree with minds greater than yours, which is to disagree with time-tested truths, which is to disagree with the Bible, which is to disagree with God—Heretic!

Most people succumb to the pressure and in an endless effort to show their non-heretic status, they revisit the historic councils, and default to the conclusions as if they were the only right ones in pursuit of enough academic credibility to engage the scripture debates.

And herein is the problem. This has nothing to do with scripture as such. While people do wrangle over Bible

---

Discussed in more detail on page 123 and following.

Blight in the Vineyard

verses, they are really wrangling over the power to compel a specific understanding. Do you remember Dave Harvey's summation to his article, *Avoiding the Snare of Subjectivity*? It was an innocuous sentence, but it reveals the true heart and soul of this discussion. "It comes down to an issue of authority."

What does?

TRUTH comes down to an issue of authority. Authority determines truth because truth is the property of the Church, which is really the property of leadership. And when leadership marries the force of Government, we have Truth as property of the State.

Some of you, dear readers, have been spoiling for a fight since I took aim in your beloved authority. The first line on your Amazon review: "But where is the Bible in your book?!! Where is the scripture??!!" As if no idea is authorized unless it has a verse to back it up. And this is **exactly** the point I am making. The endless quest for authority is **exactly** the issue at hand. I could have spent as many pages exegeting Bible verses and illustrating some different interpretive methods to show many fallacies of the medieval European Puritan assertions. But at the end of the day, the people who don't like my conclusions would boo and hiss and throw popcorn. Then they would stack up their Bible verses and demand a justification for deviating from **their** interpretive understanding driven by their presumed authority to dictate meaning.

It doesn't matter what verses one quotes or stacks together, because at the root of this conversation is a presumed authority to define the meaning of scripture. This is why most people—those who choose to wade into this thornbush-trimming exercise—work so hard to gain credibility by showing themselves in historic solidarity with the ancient debates. They are looking to share in the traditional authority. But to gain credibility means to adopt the assumption of the debates. Those assumptions are deeply embedded in the interpretive methodology handed down from intellectual father to intellectual son until we have a monkey see monkey do orthodoxy: We believe this just because this is the way we've always believed.

Here is the dirty little secret of Orthodoxy: The Bible does not drive orthodox belief.

Orthodoxy = Interpretive **methods** based on specific **historic assumptions** married to **government force**.

Let me say this again with an illustration. Many attempts were made at Universal Church reform before good ol' Martin. But until the Orthodox interpretive **method** changed, the Pope's understanding remained the standard for all biblical discussion because the Pope was in charge of **meaning**. And the meaning was enforced by government force. So, in as much as reformers were compelled to concede the Pope's authority to define meaning, they could not escape Papal conclusions, which meant they could not escape the doctrinal outcomes.

This is exactly the same situation. British Colonial Calvinist groupies are posing as historic papists swaggering around as the meaning police. And in many ways, this situation is worse. The Papacy was confined to one denomination and to an ironclad authoritarian structure, which places some limitations on the nature and scope of tyranny. But all C. J. Mahaney and the PDI/CLC/SGM bunch had to do was start saying, "We are Orthodox. Submit to our authority! Submit to our authority!" Alakazam! Poof! Instant doctrinal justification. Now all comers to the interpretive throne need to justify themselves against their Convenient

Calvinist standards.

There is no greater irony and no more ridiculous reality than a bunch of twenty-something kids thumbing their nose at denominational authority structures to justify preaching and then twenty years later claim for themselves the rights of dictatorial authority based on "Orthodoxy."[3]

Virtually no man at the crest of the PDI to SGM evolution in their drug-induced haze could have qualified for seminary propaganda into Sound Doctrine, let alone leverage the denominational authority to a bid for ministry. And those who abandoned the Catholic Church to clap their hands would have been required to enter the priesthood to "submit to the authority" of the Universal Church's prescriptions. But that mental reflection does not seem to deter the rich intellectual fraud, and PDI/CLC/SGM exploits the need to justify non-hereticness with impunity as if they are the end-all-be-all arbitrators of doctrinal precision.

And here is the problem. Conceding the historic interpretive methods condemns all counterarguments to the flaws and failures deep within the doctrine. By conceding their right to measure accuracy, people set up the historic interpretation as the default standard, which really elevates historic assumptions, presuppositions, and filters to the status of "scripture" which is the overt

---

3. This ridiculousness applies to all independent churches that got their start during the deliberate exodus from the mainline denominations and after twenty years and mega church status demand submission for their second and third generation preachers. The lever of their power is the implied reward of being granted a church. This is little more than Christian Feudalism: men compensated with minor kingdoms (church plants) for paternal fealty. It is a marvel how far we have all been sucked down the path of Charismatic Papacy, considering the history of the independent church movement is easily within most short-term memory.

John Immel

assertion of the Council of Trent and the beloved tenet of Papacy.

Ding! Ding! Ding! Ding!

Those are the bells that should be going off in your mind as you remember back to the beginning of the book. As you recollect Dave Harvey's article discussed in the second chapter, I suspect that a gasket is blowing in your head.

Remember what he said?

> But do we readily accept the testimony of Scripture itself that the foundation of the Bible is . . . the church? "If I am delayed," Paul wrote to Timothy, "you will know how people ought to conduct themselves in God's household, which is the church of the living God, the pillar and foundation of the truth" (1 Ti 3:15)

> Paradoxically, although truth is indeed the foundation of the church (Eph 2:20), the church is also the foundation for truth. . . .truth must be anchored and applied within the local church.

Again, mentally reflect on Dave's comment. This is the central doctrine of **Papacy**! Dave is making the very claim of the Catholic Church that scripture interpretation, that TRUTH, is the property of the **Church**, which is code for the property of leadership! Which begs the question, if you are going to concede the premise of Papal decree, how can you depart from orthodoxy at any point? And I mean the **original** Catholic Orthodoxy!

That point is guaranteed to cause wailing and gnashing of teeth. Puritan Protestants don't like being told they are in scriptural failure. They like to pick and choose which parts of the Bible that satisfy their separatist and divisive spirit.

Uh . . .

Errr . . .

Blight in the Vineyard

Ehem . . .

Anyway, most thinking Bible readers quickly see Bible passages not easily contained by Calvin's wire brush. But challenging those failures is impossible because by accepting the interpretive methods, one has accepted the ideas that created the conclusions. And I am not talking about resident Arminians; I am talking about self-styled Reformation Theology aficionados who trip over the implications of their own body of thought. In seeking to reconcile the logical failings by offering up separate interpretive methods, people are met with Calvinist groupies chanting Orthodoxy, Orthodoxy, Orthodoxy who believe they've played the ultimate "biblical" trump card. In their mind, this sums up the total of Christianity. Nothing else is "scriptural," which is really code for "We don't reasonably consider anything that isn't orthodox." They flaunt their intellectual stubbornness like a badge of qualification, emulating the obstinate spirit of their intellectual forefather:

> This is my reply to you and to him. It is not my purpose to quarrel with the Jews, nor to learn from them how they interpret or understand Scripture; I know all of that very well already.[4]

And if the obstinate song doesn't bully people away and get the Puritan groupies off the argumentative hook, they sing the Essential vs. Nonessential song. The rationalization offered is that certain doctrines are core to Christian teaching and are worth going to the stake for, but others, *"Que sera sera.* We can quibble over some vain theological exactness, but in the end, it is all just a

---

4. Martin Luther, *On the Jews and Their Lies*, 1543, trans. Martin H. Bertram (Philadelphia: Fortress Press & Augsburg Fortress, 1971) vol. 47, part 1, 3rd paragraph. http://www.humanitas- international.org/ showcase/ chronography/documents/luther-jews.htm

John Immel

great mystery. So, let us treat each other with LOOOOOVE and grace."

This gets argumentative traction because it is wrapped in two vague truisms and one hazy moral absolute. The first truism: Christianity has some leading themes (which it does). The second truism: There are mysteries in reality. (Duh . . . Man is not omniscient.) The hazy moral absolute = being unloving is a sin. But "unloving" is a tyrannically subjective accusation. All a lily-livered pansy has to do in an argument is decide if they feel unloved and shed big alligator tears because John is a big meaner.

Let us evaluate the chorus of the Essential vs. Nonessential song. Notice, **Essential** pretends that some ideas stand in a vacuum, unconnected, and superior by default. Now notice that **Nonessential** presumes the authority to pronounce ideas trivial, a matter of opinion, and therefore, subordinate to (someone's) lofty consideration.

Essential? To What? To Whom? In every context? In what context? How can you measure intellectual importance in a vacuum?

Nonessential? Based on whose judgment? Defined by what interpretive authority? These are but a few questions that really determine the specific value of a doctrine.

Here is the reality. The Essential vs. Nonessential song is really just another gambit at presumed authority; they want the freedom to invent doctrinal hierarchies as it serves their agenda with no obligation to consistency, logic, or outcome. And most importantly, they do not want the obligation to submit to someone else's authority.

Convenient Calvinists don't really believe that some

Blight in the Vineyard

doctrines are negotiable when **they** are pressing a doctrinal point. They know that ideas do not stand in a vacuum. By definition, the leading interpretive Bible method that dominated the last 600 years of Christian interpretation, Systematic Theology, is based on using Bible verses from book to book, as if all Bible verses are inseparably linked and then stacked together to build doctrines. Treating Bible verses like Legos is central to their ability to manufacture doctrines into a whole cohesive philosophical statement. So, when they start chanting Nonessential, they are really saying that they can declare some Legos superior. This gives them power to play with their toys all by themselves. And who are you to demand submission to any counter understanding?

So, when you hear Convenient Calvinists singing, "Can't we just all get along over Non-essential doctrines?" Know this: They want to take their Legos and go home. They have run out of scriptures to stack, and in their mind, the argument is over because to disagree with them is a function of deception. So, why waste time picking fly poop out of the pepper?

Alakazam! Poof! Status quo sustained, spiritual tyranny persists. Never once were the Reformed Theology groupies and self-styled Puritan aficionados made responsible for their intellectual passivity, logical sleights of hand, and their impiety.

They get all the benefit of authority but none of the responsibility of their authoritarian outcomes—historic or present. They can make claims to "Orthodoxy" and somehow, magically, all historic Church governmental atrocity and contemporary ministerial failures are due to the vagaries of "we are all just sinners." Yet people who challenge "Orthodoxy" are immediately responsible for every sin and debauchery known to human existence because they think wrong things. Everybody else's bad ideas, bad doctrine, bad theology is directly responsible for bad actions. But **their** ideas cannot possibly be at the core of their bad actions. Human failures are not "Orthodoxy" failures but rather the inevitable outcomes of depraved humanity. The truths stand apart, eternal, and affirmed by the universal depravity of Man—actions he is condemned to fulfill, independent of intention, action or desire.

This is why I call them Convenient Calvinists. They get authority, power, and absolution all in one magic word.

This is the theology algebra being offered:

> **PDI/CLC/SGM = Reformation Theology = Orthodoxy = Authority of Tradition = What everybody, who is anybody, has always rightly believed = Paul's "Sound Doctrine" = Scripture.**

But now we know that the equation is false. We know that Orthodoxy part of the equation is wrong because it does not equal some monolithic centrist belief structure. Orthodoxy cannot be the product of epistemological[5] consensus. Orthodoxy is not the distilled utterings of God's sweetness and light that a select few super righteous souls defended by their great minds, excellent character, and spiritual commitment. The ugly truth behind the curtain is that orthodoxy equals nothing more than a narrow ecclesiastical antagonism sustained by threat of eternal damnation or government violence. Said another way, orthodoxy is really political correctness

---

5. For a review, I defined epistemology in chapter 4.

manufactured by emperors with a bunch of church boy bullies in their back pocket.

So, if we take the false claim to Orthodoxy out of the equation, it looks like this:

PDI/CLC/SGM =
> **Reformation Theology =**
>> **Scripture.**

That equation looks convenient, doesn't it? Suddenly, the SGM assertion that all things them equals scripture seems presumptuous.

Jedi, don't you love these mental reflections?

Notes

12
Three Walls of the Modern Day Romanists

> A wise man associating with the vicious becomes an idiot; a dog traveling with good men becomes a rational being.
>
> **—Arabian Proverb**

> There are a thousand hacking at the branches of evil to one who is striking at the root.
>
> **—Henry David Thoreau**

> Men never do evil so completely and cheerfully as when they do it from religious conviction.
>
> **—Blaise Pascal**

Calvin's governmental despotism is founded on an unequivocal Pervasive Depravity because it is the ultimate *ad hominem* argument.[1] This implicit argument to the Man doctrine is utterly consistent with Augustine and Luther "Orthodoxy." But it didn't take but roughly 100 years before there was a referendum on the correct presentation of Calvin. By the Synod of Dordrecht (1618), his intellectual heirs were toning down Calvin's synthesis in direct response to the successful criticism.

---

1. ad ho·mi·nem/ad hämənəm/adverb
   a. (of an argument or reaction) arising from or appealing to the emotions and not reason or logic.
   b. Attacking an opponent's motives or character rather than the policy or position they maintain.

John Immel

Pervasive Depravity of the Calvin/Beza kind became the Total Inability of the Canon of Dort kind: a hedge on Calvin's absolute. And here is one of many manifestations of the malleable nature of orthodoxy, the ongoing evolution of thought that gets portrayed as absolute.

Indeed, it took Luther the better part of thirty years, through numerous debates with leading Catholic defenders demanding a coherent response for deviating from Universal Church Orthodoxy, to get his doctrine ironed out. The doctrinal content behind the faith alone, grace alone, scripture alone marquee did not spring fully formed from good ol' Martin's head. It developed over time, a curious reality if it is a "clear" biblical teaching.

In the modern day, a new Reformed Theology movement has been fueled by writers like (but not limited to) John Piper, Jerry Bridges, R. C. Sproul, and that oldie but a Calvinist treaty by John Bunyan. These twentieth generation dogmatic heirs have repackaged the scholastic presentation, and redefined the unpalatable parts of Puritan doctrine. They have worked to sanitize the leading Protestant thinkers—Luther, Zwingli, Calvin, Beza, Mather, Owen, and Edwards—into Reformation saints that cannot be challenged.

Subsequent generations of Calvinists thinkers have played fast and loose with the T.U.L.I.P. mnemonic. Usurpers to Orthodoxy throne like to defend the human possession of character by saying things like: "Calvinists believe that man can do no salvific[2] good, but that doesn't mean he can't **do** good." This makes it possible for (their) character to be a qualification for ministry. A character, that without fail, they hold the yardstick, and define.

---

2. Salvific means salvation. Salvific Good means good works that earn your salvation.

Blight in the Vineyard

Convenient Calvinists are easy to spot because in natural habitat they say something like: "I'm a two-and-a-half-point Calvinist," which really means they see a couple doctrinal points reflected in scripture but the rest . . . not so much.

When confronted with the content of strict Calvin or Luther teaching—after the convenience is stripped away—they usually trot out this blithe dismissal: "I'm not really a Calvinist, but I do believe in man's total salvation inability," as if denying Calvin makes the doctrinal implications different. The distinction has all the merit of saying: "I'm not a Marxist, but rather a communist who believes the government should administrate your substance." This useless comment is really an intellectual sleight of hand designed to open some wiggle in the argumentative room by playing with word meaning.

Depending on the day or the argument, Orthodoxy takes on whatever shape necessary. Point out the logical implications of "orthodox" thought and a Convenient Calvinist starts hedging and nudging the definitions. Or worse, they hijack the interpretive evolutions of John Wesley (circa 1750) and Charles Finney (circa 1850) and act like Calvinism has always believed that too. Curiously enough, if you point out the source of their thought is Charles Finney, they start frothing at the mouth about wolves in sheep's clothing and begin demagoguing the interpretive standard. All things Calvin are all things Bible, and how dare you challenge that assumption. And if this doesn't scare the doctrinal challenger into submission, they default to: "Piffle, we can think for ourselves and disagree over nonessentials. And who cares anyway? It's all just a great mystery, and we are sinners who struggle to understand. And as a Pan

John Immel

Theologian, it will all just pan out in the end."

But that whatever-will-be-will-be attitude vanishes when challenged in their authority to arbitrate scripture. Immediately, they start chanting Orthodoxy, Orthodoxy, Orthodoxy! But orthodoxy, by definition, defies any attempt to redefine. Orthodoxy demands intellectual obeisance to dead men's ideas. There is **no** wiggle room in this.

I am going to hammer this home.

How exactly do you get to pick and choose which parts of "orthodox" thinking you want to accept? By definition, orthodoxy is exactly what we **must** believe because . . . well, because everybody else has believed it.

Pervasive Depravity means that Man can do **no** good, ever, any place, any time. This **is** the effective declaration of Augustine, Luther, and Calvin and only willful blindness (and a host of hedging and definition-nudging) to historical documentation can account for any other understanding. Reformation Theology of the Luther, Zwingli, Calvin, and Beza kind held, advocated, and taught that definition of Pervasive Depravity. Yet, you will hear Convenient Calvinists utter many equivocations, all the while making the endlessly disturbing rant about orthodoxy and heresy as if Catholic Orthodoxy is a quaint aberration.

Convenient Calvinists are some of the first to get on the heresy bandwagon, condemn speaking in tongues as a scary subjective practice, mock healing ministries, and sniff at prosperity-preaching for its lack of "orthodox" precision. And the *hutesium et clamor*[3] never stops. If there is even a hint of sexual misconduct and the preacher does not teach Pervasive Depravity, he is a false prophet and false teacher of the first order. But if

---

3. Latin for hue and cry.

he does preach that he's a wretched old sinner, well, then you need to forgive and just move on, because there can be no question about the truth of his doctrine. This rational license is the heart and soul of PDI/CLC/SGM's profound manipulations perpetrated in the name of Orthodoxy.

The modern Puritan Romanists have, with great adroitness, drawn walls round themselves. Up till now, these walls have protected them so that no one could hold them responsible for tyranny, whereby people have fallen terribly.

> First: If it were proposed to admonish them with the Scriptures, they objected that no one but Reformed Theologians (sort of) may stand in the stead of God, for it is the job of appointed leadership to correct leadership.

> Second: If pressed with external scrutiny, they insist that such conversation can only be motivated by bitterness, gossip, and slander which disqualifies the critic and frees them to summarily refuse review from anyone not submitted to their authority.

> Third: All obvious manifestation of tyranny are attributed to the vagaries of human sinfulness, the humble efforts of good but failed intentions, and justified by comparison to other churches.

Notes

13
The Growing Protestant Sainthood

> God creates out of nothing. Wonderful you say. Yes, to be sure, but he does what is still more wonderful: he makes saints out of sinners.
>
> **—Sören Kierkegaard**

> Develop a built-in b^!!$#!t detector.
>
> **—Ernest Hemingway**

> Single acts of tyranny may be ascribed to the accidental opinion of a day; but a series of oppressions, begun at a distinguished period and pursued unalterably through every change of ministers, too plainly proves a deliberate, systematic plan of reducing [a people] to slavery.
>
> **—Thomas Jefferson**

Since mere mortals cannot be saints, they cannot be born like you and me. They need rich soil to sprout their flawless roots and flourish magically before our eyes. The best blend of dirt and fertilizer is what makes all things grow. Protestant Saints are no different. The soil of the seedbed is the mad pursuit of **Sound** Doctrine.

What is meant by Sound?

In context, the preoccupation over soundness is an effort to define an absolute, to find an immovable assurance. By insisting that the doctrine discussed are the **final** presentation of all pure, righteous, and perfect Christian theology, men are defining **soundness** as an unquestionable, unerring, and unassailable given. Or said another way, they pretend that there are no successful counterarguments because the ideas are so utterly, internally, compellingly irrefutable.

As we mentally reflect on this sound, compelling, utterly consistent irrefutability, it will soon become clear why this doctrine relies so heavily on authority to intimidate and bully. Without this power, the muddy, loose, moving, pliant "logic" drains through the fingers like a . . .

T.U.L.I.P. in Mud

A synod is like a big meeting of *El Primo Doctrinal Movers and Shakers*, confined to a small geographic location, like maybe the size of Montgomery County, Maryland. The Synod of Dort created this acronym about fifty years after Johnny C's death. It isn't Calvin "Orthodox," but since people who are Calvinists lead with the elements of this mnemonic, so it is worth review.

T = Total Depravity: This means that Adam's sin fills all humanity through sex. Absolute evil resides in us all. We are rotten to the core. We are worms that have floated to the surface during the rainstorm of life, fit only to have God step on us. From the little crumb-cruncher that looks like an angel to the white haired-sage that speaks pearls of wisdom, people are totally evil, inclined only to do wickedness. "Man is on a horse, led around by the devil." Man is fully and entirely depraved. There is no good in him and neither can he seek GOOD.

U = Unconditional Election: This means those who are picked for God's grace are golden. He has a sovereign purpose in their salvation. If you are not picked, you ain't got a prayer. All of your loved ones that ain't invited to the party are going to where it's warm and smoky. Why? Because God wanted it that way? Why? Because He did and who are you to ask?

L = Limited Atonement: The logic goes that Jesus' blood did not atone for all men because it is obvious that all men are not saved and God could not possibly squander such a precious gift.

I = Irresistible Grace: This goes hand in hand with **Limited Atonement**. The logic says that since the blood of Jesus only atones for a few elect, those he does call will respond, because his grace is irresistible. You cannot help but to conform to His righteous actions because your change is a manifestation of His saving Grace.

P = Perseverance of the Saints: This is the foundation of once saved, always saved. No matter what the elect do, they will always achieve the destination: salvation. No matter your temporal "unsaved" action, you will at some point start acting like you are saved by God's appointment and Sovereign dictate. He imputes to you the GOOD actions your total depravity can never achieve and thereby persevere in election.

OK, that sums up the mnemonic. Now I have to address one more theme that runs through the doctrinal overtones in PDI/CLC/SGM. Actually, this is more than an overtone; they named their organization in solidarity with this theological theme. So it is most certainly central to the SGM worldview.

Sovereignty: "God sovereignly put us together," or "This is a sovereign work of God," and other comments of this ilk are distributed around in conversations like so much chaff. The word is intended to define an event, or action, as God's purpose and thereby part of a grander authority. If it was all God and none of man, then who can argue with the outcome, right? The emphasis on

John Immel

Sovereignty is designed to do two things: place God out of the inquiry of man and make all circumstance the product of God's providence. This means that reality, the content of a man's life, is an ironclad expression of God's intent.

I am curious. Which one of these doctrines is Nonessential?

>snicker<

Many complex explanations of this mnemonic exist but the real function of T.U.L.I.P. and the emphasis on Sovereignty is very simple. The goal is to universally disqualify Man and entrench governing power in a predestined leadership.

The elements of T.U.L.I.P. work in concert to undermine man and give moral justification for the ultimate governmental trump card. Notice that the doctrines juxtapose Man before a dictatorial Sovereign. This eliminates human objection, any human challenge to the meaning of right and truth, and destroys any moral certainty to change the world for man's individual betterment.

Let me make this personal. You were born to your lot in life. The very fact that you didn't pick your parents and the culture that shapes your helpless psyche is part of the broader reality that you have no real free will. God places you in milieu for His own purpose. Some people are created vessels of grace. Others are created vessels of destruction. Why would He do this? Who are you to even ask? God also appointed those who rule, the governing powers get their authority from His appointment. If they do evil, it is by sovereign appointment to fulfill His great mysterious purpose, which is really GOOD anyway. If they do GOOD, it is because God does the GOOD that they perform.

Blight in the Vineyard

This is why Protestant Saints **love** predestination. It is the unbendable foundation of a caste system and they are at the top of the pyramid.

Then Add Fertilizer

We all know what fertilizer is, right? Well, if you are going to pile it on, make it thick and deep because the volume makes it harder to escape. The depth and breadth of this compost pile is what makes it impossible to flee.

For nomination to Sainthood, the Catholic Church requires an exhaustive investigation into the life of a candidate and then adds two verifiable miracles. And oh, you have to be dead to achieve canonization. Posthumous sainthood is one of the ways the Catholic Church advances or enforces the power to teach evolutions in doctrine. If a mere mortal taught it in life but the ideas need authority to proclaim as gospel, what better way than by the power of the sainthood? Saints, of course, are mere men . . . but not really. They are superior kinds of men . . . but not exactly. Protestants have the same sainthood for the same reasons, just absent the miracles and death requirements. Protestant sainthood comes from Predestination.

The spiritual peasantry, the barbarian church masses, *der* **Unter***menschen* are appointed their lot in life and violate divine will by seeking change. Any effort at self-change and any attempt towards self-improvement is a manifestation of corrupt self-will defying nature in pursuit of impossibility. This makes all ambition spiritual treason. Objections to unwanted circumstance, no matter how unjust, are railing against God's manifest intent.

Conversely, the ruling class, the Oligarchs, the First Among Equals, *der* **Uber***menschen,* are an expression of

God's specific will. Whatever benefits of their office, their station and their charge might bring them, that gift is trivial gift in light of the crushing burdens of higher judgment. So, they accept their appointment to governance, humbly embracing the responsibility of dictating God's revelation. Because their office is the product of supernatural appointment, they are absolved of treasonous ambition and transformed into mere "servants" of a higher reality. They love to imply that they are innocent bystanders in God's cosmic mystery. God held a celestial draft and **somehow** they got saddled with the stewardship of His revelation.

Far be it from them to claim authority, the revelation is the authority, and they are mere humble servants to the revelation. To avoid even the appearance of self-service, they will make an appeal to altruism. The sacrificial riff goes something like this: "I resisted all I could for my own great selfish and self-willed reasons. But in the end, God in his great wisdom saw fit to break me down, deliver me from myself, and I took my place serving as His steward of His great GOOD."

If one were inclined to actually evaluate the altruistic rot, the first question should be how a mere mortal can **choose** to "resist" God's Sovereign power? The second question should be, how can a Pervasively Depraved man ever be "selfless?" But you just never mind the unsoundness in their deep-felt, utterly qualifying altruistic marketing and packaging. Just judge them on their good intentions. And oh, you just never mind that man cannot even have "good intentions." Just submit to their authority and be done with it.

Alakazam! Poof! They are in charge.

This mindset has roots in Christian doctrine as far back as Gregory of Nazianzus in 380 AD. His theological orations were predicated on this very idea: that only a select few, who had been specifically elected and subsequently vetted in their actions and peerage, were qualified to grace the deep ideas of theology. (Gregory's argument is an open reference to Plato's governmental philosophy.) This demagoguery was his leading weapon in overcoming his intellectual and political adversaries. This evil concept has reared its head throughout history as men, the Saints, *der* **Ubermenschen**, the Oligarchs, the First Among Equals, pretend they are uniquely qualified to stand in the Stead of God.

When confronted with error, *der* **Ubermenschen** act as if only those predestined, only those appointed to the same stewardship, only those of theological solidarity, those of the Protestant Sainthood, are qualified to supply correction. Those who are not appointed cannot offer effective criticism because they are corrupt. Their nature disqualifies their ability to make effective judgments and any doctrinal alternative is necessarily the product of divine sanction manifest as satanic deception.

Man cannot know the depth of his sin because he is corrupt in every necessary way to know, grasp, pursue, act, or will toward truth. Said another way: Man is insane. Since man can only do evil, he needs someone to save him from himself. He needs leadership to grab his throat and hold him "accountable" to righteous actions. And what is this righteous action? Curiously enough, the definition of **righteous** seems to change depending on who was in charge.

Over time, men realized these doctrinal assumptions vested enormous power in one man, so they went searching for a rationale that subverted individual tyrants while at no point evaluating the doctrines that created the rich soil that made the dictators grow. As I said before, the ideas cannot be at the core of bad actions. Human failures are not orthodoxy failures but rather the inevitable outcomes of depraved humanity. The truths stand apart, eternal, and affirmed by the universal depravity Man.

For most of post-Christian world history, man has been chasing his tail trying to tweak church government structure to find means to restrain the tyranny. This tail-chasing gave rise to the concept of shared governing authority. The evolutions of this specific thought are not useful to this conversation, but we have all heard the modern version. Preachers speak sagely of Apostolic **Teams**: men bound in fraternity, called, appointed, predestined to the task of governing God's Church and shepherd men's souls. These ministry **teams** justify their existence by saying they provide checks and balances to sinful natures. Leadership is given a greater measure—whatever that means—so leadership is kinda sorta exempt from the insanity because they are in a group. Mere mortals transformed into something . . . else. Alakazam Poof! Sainthood!

People have heard the concept of checks and balances as a hedge against man's sinful nature for so long that we take this justification for Church leadership group authority as sound reasoning. We all recognize the value of social mechanism to curtail individual interest and the sweeping powers of government—a.k.a. force—over a people. Man figured out long ago that the Attilas and the Alexanders of the world were a plague. We all fear the man who, by the sheer force of his muscle and sword, can compel anyone and everyone to his whim. And we equally fear the mob, the majority, the masses tyrannizing the individual by their collective will. Political science is the long slog through millennia, learning how to create an effective and lasting social harmony. In terms of world history, the concept of Check and Balance first emerged in Greco/Roman political thought but was comparatively short-lived. The concept has reemerged through the Western world in fits and starts with intermittent practical success and finally found real power in the American representative Republic as constructed by the Founding Fathers who, interestingly enough, put absolute barriers between civil power and religious authority. They learned the lessons of history well.

Man, of course, needs a means to negotiate his individual interests with other individuals and his culture as a whole. Only two methods of such negotiation exist: ideas or force. Checks and balances are concepts of reason but when man descends to force, he is no longer negotiating.

And here is the problem: When groups of Protestant Saints, leading with the ideas embedded within T.U.L.I.P. and Sovereignty, offer "checks and balances" as a rationalization for their right to rule, their qualification to dictate, they are relying on your willingness to let them get away with a profound intellectual sleight of hand. The loose logic says that man's nature is utterly corrupt, so no **individual** may be perfect and therefore worthy of ruling, but a **group** somehow offers a composite righteousness that sets them apart.

The group is special, insulated from error by their group-ness and are therefore qualified to dictate. These Protestant Saints demand the right to demagogue conformity to an already arbitrated standard of GOOD. They are the check and they are the balance, so you just never mind the problems of leadership and believe what they tell you.

John Immel

This rational larceny allows Demagogues of Dictated Good to get away with three piles of fertilizer—oops, three intellectual evasions.

First pile of fertilizer: This makes the means of grace locality and proximity; because a bunch of them commune in the same space, they do morality and righteousness and spirituality better. So the circular logic goes like this: Their inclusion in the group vets their unique character and their matchless moral fiber vets their inclusion in the group. Alakazam! Poof! They are qualified to wield force to compel specific ideas.

And here is the fraud: The folks in the asylum are not less insane because a thousand crazy people live in the same geographic location. Nor is the insanity refined into rationality by the force of numbers. Riddle me this. If everyone in the asylum is crazy, how can they know what sane looks like? What is the magic elixir that sanitizes the group's nature but somehow leaves an individual's nature pervasively depraved?

"No, no, no," you say. "The individuals bring their various strengths to offset others' weakness; this offers checks and balances."

Yeah, this is a rich fiction. Pervasive Depravity destroys the concept of moral or ethical strength. And this very assertion shows forth the intellectual fraud underlying the doctrine. A single apple placed in a bushel with his brothers does not magically become a bunch of bananas. T.U.L.I.P.'s fragrant doctrine demands **one** understanding of man's **nature**! Therefore, the group *homoousios* must maintain the substance of the individual's *homoousios*.[1]

---

1. That is hilarious. *Homoousios* is the Neo-Platonist concept that was grafted into Christian theology that made the **nature** of God the Father and the **nature** of Jesus the Son effectively the same divine substance and the foundation of

Uhhh . . .

Errr . . .

Sorry, I did not want to resist the inside joke. Let me rewrite that last sentence for general consumption. For the doctrine to be utterly, internally, compellingly, irrefutability sound, the group nature should maintain the substance of the individual's nature. There is no wiggle room in this.

Second pile of fertilizer: The glossy brochure says that shared leadership's reason for existence is to steward revelation, right? God spoke by hot fax from Heaven to some men who were uniquely superior to all other men, and they wrote down what He said for *der Untermenschen*. And then other uniquely superior men, Protestant Saints (but not as qualified as the first bunch) are now charged with defending this writing from the spiritual barbarians, right? (And as far as Christians are concerned, the revelation, the Bible, is the GOOD, right?) So riddle me this: If the group's job is to be a steward of **revelation**, be a steward of GOOD, what is the need for check and balance? By doctrinal standard, leaders are not equipped to **determine** GOOD because the hot fax from heaven already came. The collective leadership's job is to **deliver** GOOD.

Let us mentally reflect some more, because it is important to understand the evasion. If the revelation is GOOD, what then are we checking? The accuracy of the revelation? Or the accuracy of the Protestant Saints? The accuracy of the revelation does not need checked. The group is incapable of checking itself because they are mutually insane and the spiritual peasantry is disqualified to check.

---

what has come to be known as the Trinity. Hahaha . . . Get the irony?

John Immel

What is left?

Now notice this: Checking implies the ability to curtail some kind of action. But the shared leadership holds the monopoly on governmental force. Who has the authority—God appointed force—to **stop** the action? By definition, if another group of Protestant Saints had the authority to check, wouldn't it be **their** decree being dictated?

Here is the third pile of fertilizer: If Authority **dictates** GOOD, what are we balancing?

In context, balancing needs an objective standard that can be measured. Balancing requires the ability to weigh both sides of a rational, moral, or spiritual teeter-tooter. How did man see the need to offset one side of the teeter-totter with more weight? Man is Pervasively Depraved, inflicted with the blinding, deafening, utterly corrupting self-will. His every action is shot through with sin. How can he even see the need for corrective action? (Remember, this exact argument is how they justify why **you** need **them**.)

The answer is he cannot, because he is corrupt and thereby forever unbalanced; **how can he balance**? Man is blind because he has eyes. Man is deaf because he has ears. Man is mute because he has a mouth. Man is depraved because he has self-interest.

And this is precisely why this ideology trends towards authoritarianism, despotism, and—trip far enough down this path—bloodshed. These three evasions empower a group that is, by definition, **insulated** from any corrective judgment or action or force. They are set up as unquestionable and unquestioning authorities in service to what no man can ever really know. As I have often said: Be arrogant if you must. Be ignorant if you must. But don't be arrogant and ignorant. Unquestionable

Blight in the Vineyard

authorities is dangerous enough, men so sure of their authority that their blinding arrogance brooks no challenge. But the second part of this dynamic is by far the more insidious. When men don't even question the cause and effect of their actions or ideas, they can never correct their course. When they are convinced that what they know is all they will ever need to know. Every appeal to knowledge and truth are mere pretense to their self-enforcing governing mandate. Think Copernicus. Think Galileo. The second part of this dynamic is what has placed Christian leaders on opposite sides of almost every advance of human understanding and makes them the poster children for enforced ignorance. They are Protestant Saints entirely divorced from the very forces they insist qualification to control.

Taken to its logical conclusion, the doctrine says that whatever action Authority demands is GOOD. There is no just or unjust action as long as the actions are in obedience, in service to the authority's stewardship of the revelation. So, authority commits no unjust action, and those who act on authority's orders cannot commit sin.

"Oh, John. That is absurd. No one believes that."

You are correct. It is absurd, yet a long list of people do believe this. Augustine made this very argument to rationalize using violence as an exercise of "divine love." The loose logic presented said that just as God used punishment as an expression of love, by extension, so too could the Holy Mother Church use force as an expression of love to save sinners from everlasting Hell Fire. This is Augie's way of saying "Church discipline is a privilege." The Church's function became to grab people by the throat and save them from themselves because they are insane. This was **the** justification for the slaughter and pillaging of Jews, and Donatists,[2] and pagans, and a host of "heretics" for ages to come. It became the Church's responsibility to stand between people's bad ideas and actions and their path to hell, a truly absurd job if God appoints people to eternal damnation. But who's quibbling over soundness when we get to burn people in the name of God? And besides, the ideas cannot be at fault. We are all just poor sinners trying to defend against Arminians with bad attitudes.

---

2. Donatists were a Christian movement in North Africa in the 4th and 5th century that was named after Donatus Magnus. They advocated that the church should be pure and the clergy must be qualified to hold office, which primarily included refusing to succumb to persecutions by offering sacrifices to other gods or surrendering the early churches' sacred texts. These bishops were known as *traditors*. Donatists contended that sacraments, like baptism, from sellout bishops were invalid. The Donatist movement persisted through the time of Augustine and seems to have been wiped out only after the African Muslim invasion in the 7th and 8th century.

14
I Wouldn't Go That Far

> If we are going to save America and evangelize the world, we cannot accommodate secular philosophies that are diametrically opposed to Christian truth.
>
> —Jerry Falwell

> The Church has through the centuries, understood that ideas are really more dangerous than other weapons. Their use should be restricted.
>
> —Francis J. Lally

> Nobody has the right to worship on this planet any other God than Jehovah. And therefore the state does not have the responsibility to defend anybody's pseudo-right to worship an idol.
>
> —Joseph Morecraft[1]

Some will be tempted to pooh-pooh the previous chapter's point because—somehow—the American Church

---

1. I assumed that most other quotes were from recognizable people. These three quotes go to my central point in this chapter and are illustrative of the very issue I'm seeking to combat. I made the assumption that these people were not immediately recognizable. References in order.
- Jerry Falwell: "Moral Majority Report," September, 1984.
- Francis J. Lally: American Roman Catholic Monsignor. Interview with Mike Wallace, 1958.
- Rev. Joseph Morecraft: Chalcedon Presbyterian Church, "Biblical Role of Civil Government" speech delivered on August 21, 1993 at the Biblical Worldview and Christian Education Conference.

John Immel

is immune from conducting itself in the despicable manner of European Christianity or you think it waaaaaay outrageous that I put bonfires and PDI/CLC/SGM in the same book. But the issue is not American Christianity or SGM specifically. The issue is the premise. Once an argument concedes the foundational assumption, everything else is a fight over degree. While there are no bonfires on Muncaster Mill Road to defend their brand of "Sound Doctrine," PDI/CLC/SGM is the poster child of the progression. The driving personalities and preoccupations of the leadership make their practice a study of justified Mystic Despotism.

"John, that is disgraceful. This is the Slippery Slope logical fallacy. What those people did way back then doesn't matter. This isn't the same thing at all. No one goes that far today. . . ."

Well, true they may not stand in the pulpit and shout "Authority commits no Injustice! All hail the People's State of Heaven!" but they manufacture arguments that serve this exact rationalized conclusion. Depending on the day, or the doctrinal fight, or the blogosphere outrage, they rotate between the Divine Right of Protestant Saints to demand submission to authority at all cost or absolve despotic outcomes in the name of, "We are not like other churches, but when we are, woe is us. We are all just sinners."

But this raises a point that needs to be addressed: the slippery slope of Christian Despotism. Just so everyone knows the Slippery Slope is a generalized logical fallacy. The form of the argument follows this equation: A, B, and C event occurred. Therefore, X, Y, and Z are inevitable. The weakness of the argument is that it presumes a series of unproved cause and effect outcomes and ignores the potential of a mediating middle or an outside

Blight in the Vineyard

balancing force.

One example would be: If we legalize pot, then there will be a worldwide shortage of potato chips. Or here is another: If we give everyone freedom, people become a law unto themselves and anarchy will reign.

OK, here is the crucial distinction between the Slippery Slope and the central theme of my evaluation.

First, Leadership has already said that it is their unique place to define the nature of TRUTH. They have staked a claim to the foundation of every argument. If they own TRUTH, it means they have arrived at the slope's bottom.

Second, the doctrines require a moral/rational deference, placing spiritual second-class citizens in a place of mandated intellectual submission. Man's ethical requirement is obedience to the Protestant Saints who have a specific power—somehow—to enforce their collective understanding.

This "one-two punch" knocks people head first down the slope and destroys any ladder to climb back up. OK, so I mixed metaphors and idioms in that last sentence, but the point is made. **They** control all "rational" conclusions because **they** control the moral authority to define all outcomes. What stops the Protestant Saints from lighting bonfires?

This is why I say that anytime an argument concedes the premise, the only thing left to discuss is How Much? In this case, the premise is Protestant Saints—that is leaders or governing authorities—own the definition of TRUTH.

The next time you are having a fight with someone, pause and ask yourself this question: Is this an either/or argument or a how much argument? The first argument is a fight over principles. The second is an argument over

John Immel
degree.

Here is an example:

Charles is passionate about his Mowie Wowie and expects those under his oversight to smoke a nickel bag of the most wholesome ganja on earth.

Joseph says, no, that community over there, we are not like those people. And to prove it he raises the bar: In the name of South American Gold gods, a dime bag, or bust!

The argument grows so heated over who has the purest brand of cannabis; they duel at twenty paces with Twinkies and Doritos.

Cheech and Chong say, "Can't we just get along?" because they want to end the junk food Armageddon. They try to stop Charles and Joseph's munchies melee by suggesting a middle position: a 7-cent bag of Mowie American Wowie Gold so everyone can love one another— Kum-by-yah, Kum-by-yah.

Joseph is scandalized that his hippy lettuce would be mixed with such abomination. "Sadly, other people are not watching their lives and their toking. As a steward of Mary Jane Orthodoxy, I must defend against the postmodern corruptions. Sola Dime, Sola Gold, Sola . . . uh . . . I think someone is watching me."

And Charles says: "Yo Pal! I'm cool man. I'm cool! I don't go that far. My grass is so pure, you only need half the chronic to find heaven. My happy leaf is all a man will ever need. Our oversight teams will defend against the nine enemies of Cannabis Sativa. As the good book says, 'Many are called but few are smoking.'"

In the fight above, we have all the classic problems: Charles and Joseph argue over the either/or of their pot superiority. While it looked like a mediating position, Cheech and Chong could not stop the fight because they

Blight in the Vineyard

never addressed the underlying premise. The issue was not the purity of the weed, or the amount to be inhaled, or a mediated middle ground. The fight was over the authority to dictate an outcome. They never challenged the **principle** that fueled the fight. The only way to undercut this whole fight is for John to challenge Charles and Joseph by saying, "No, you do not have the **authority** to compel anyone to smoke pot, so you can put down the Doritos and step away from the Twinkies."

I added this nostalgia trip for the '60s retreads' reading pleasure. Since I've never smoked anything, I had to look the particulars up online. But hey, never let it be said that I can't be all things to all men.

Does this mini exercise seem absurd? Try applying this same test to the doctrines of submission and authority. Remember what I said in the section called the Arena of Ideas? Remember that I said your philosophy will shade your ethics? The underlying metaphysical assumption says that man is selfish and self-destructive and therefore needs to submit to authority, whose job is to keep people faithful to purist doctrine. Pure doctrine is the source of righteous actions. Since church leaders are currently limited in their use of violence, self-subordination is held out as the ethical ideal, and men are encouraged to conform to whatever authority demands.

This seems sort of right. We have all had our run-in with the "authority" (Mom) who is not as limited in the use of violence. She can swat a know-it-all fifteen-year-old in the head when he refuses to listen. In context, self-subordination seems like a great idea. But this loose logic gets extended to categorize all men as adolescent Homer Simpson ax murderers on the verge of creating utter destruction but for the Grace of Marge. The Grace

John Immel

of Marge is, of course, nagging Protestant Saints harassing people in their inevitable life of . . . doh?! And if Marge's nagging doesn't get Homer's attention, how much more pain does God cause if Man doesn't do what His stewards say?

As a brief aside, I find the following glaring reality fascinating. Man is selfish and unruly "by nature," but man will obey "authority" in the face of horrendous atrocity.

The world is full of examples where men waited patiently while their compatriots were one by one shot in the head (or crashed planes into towers). The ratio of victim to killer were 10 to 1 (or more) and they stayed still merely because they were told to. And this is not unique to small groups of people. Entire nations have come to a tyrannical standstill while a small percentage of the population destroys the masses in the name of Authority—Germany, Russia, China, Cuba, Cambodia. The list of nations whose populace obeyed authority while that same authority stacked bodies like cord wood, is as long as history itself.

I contend that the terror over ax-murdering adolescent Homer Simpson's refusing to submit to authority is utterly misplaced. The real terror should be over men failing to be more like Bart and Lisa Simpson—a cross between a lovable prankster and self-appointed social activist. Tyranny prevails because millions of respectful, "selfless," compliant men and women refuse to resist the edicts of "authority" on a mad dash to despotism.

"But, John, that is just a few sinful men who did evil. The idea of submission and authority is good in the hands of the right people. They just perverted a biblical, godly idea and took it too far. . . ."

Blight in the Vineyard

Well, if people can take an idea **too far**, then one must check the premise of the idea. And this is the point. Once an argument concedes the principle, the only thing left to discuss is how much: So if the saints are conceding the foundation of the evil sinner's ideas, what defense is there?

Let us take a deeper look into the undergirding assumption of our Christian understanding. The single most influential thinker for Western Christianity is Saint Augustine. Most all of our modern doctrines have been shaped by him and were passed down through his intellectual heirs.

From Augustine's *Confessions*, he summarizes man's state as follows. Man is deformed, squalid, tainted with ulcers and sores. Augustine characterized man's existence thus: a hellish, rotted life, his mind is helpless, and his body lust-ridden. He advocated that such a creature's only moral existence is renunciation: the abandon of reason and the subordination of self-value. Humility is only achieved when man fully grasps his utter worthlessness. Humility is expressed in an entire abandon of any pleasure. As Augustine said, "God did not leave any part of life which should be free and find itself room to desire the enjoyment of something else."

The measure of self-subordination is absolute. Augustine put it this way, "And all that you asked of me was that I deny my own will and accept yours." This, of course, echoes Jesus' words in the Garden: "Not my will but yours be done."

There is no more sickening reality that Jesus' declaration has become the lever of the greatest tyranny. But as Augustine framed the implication of man's nature and the subsequent moral standard of self-resignation, it is the logical conclusion.

John Immel

How can man resist a gun to the head when he can claim no self-value? By moral decree, the bullet has more value than life. How can men justify a right to fight against those who would do harm when their lives are hellish cesspools of torment of less value than a hunk of metal? Women carry the very enemy of God in their womb. If God chooses to destroy His enemies by the hands of genocidal maniacs, who are we to question?

And we do not question, nor do we resist.

Through the ages, tyrants have gotten more power with Jesus' words in the Garden of Gethsemane than any other seven words. The preachers did the work for them by teaching that all men are subordinate to God's will. And God's will is manifest as whatever **is**. Whatever **is** reflects "authority's" right of action to enforce God's mysterious purpose. Alakazam! Poof! Any man pretending "authority" is empowered in the minds of the Church to do as he wills. This is why the Church has stood mute or impotent in the face of untold carnage.

Notice the inescapable prison. Supernaturally, man is told that the sum of circumstance is God's specific intent. In his makeup, Man is an ill-suited buffoon who cannot know the world in which he lives. Ethically, he is told that self-subordination, the sacrifice of his rational mind is the highest moral action.

How does this creature resist anything?

Do you see the progression from the metaphysical to the epistemological, to the ethical? Are you beginning to see how deep the roots of this issue go? Are you beginning to see why all philosophy is not vain? How ideas go together is how Man functions in the world. Are you beginning to see how effectively the chains of tyranny have been forged?

The reason I picked PDI/CLC/SGM as my anecdote is

the contrast between their starting place in the Charismatic renewal and their current efforts to paint themselves as all things Orthodoxy Christianity. In the Renewal movements, men could find the call and will of God by self-appointed action. The early PDI/CLC leadership exploited this freedom to start their ministerial existence. But then they decided they didn't like the chaos that surrounds such spiritual freedom and sought a means to centralize power in their own hands, and thereby self-consecrate their own authentic Christian governing authority. They dove headfirst into this body of thought that produces unswerving tyranny. So, it is no accident that their current conduct is fully consistent with the ideology. This comprehensive philosophical system harnesses all of the elements of man's affections and fears. Or maybe better said, this system is refined to fully exploit Man's nature in service to authoritarianism. That is what makes Reformed Theology so dang appealing to so many closet despots. And once they come out of the closet, who can restrain the tyranny?

There are plenty of variations on this system, advocated by many men in the pulpit of all denominational stripes and pedigrees, but here is the bottom line. The express purpose of these doctrines is to make man's highest existence utter servility.

When you hear a balding, quick-witted, winsome man standing behind a plexiglass podium speaking of submission and authority, self-sacrifice, and humility, you struggle to picture him as a despot cut from the cloth of Stalin, and Pol Pot, and Mao. He sits with you in the painful hours and prays over you when the world looks dark. How could this man contribute to the tyrants of the world? There are no mass graves under the chancel. He

John Immel doesn't go that far!

You cannot conceptualize this because you have never paid attention to the similarities in the philosophical statements between your balding Sunday preacher and the list of Marxist malcontents above. Mass graves are the leaf on the very end of the ideological tree. The roots of the tree go deep into the bedrock of a specific assumption about human existence. When the premise says that man must subordinate and authority is responsible to enforce the standard of authentic moral existence, how do you counter the atheist Bolshevik assertion when Christians concede the premise? **This is the bottom of the slope.** The only difference is who is in charge of the governmental conclusion. If it is the atheists, the force of government is used to sacrifice everyone to the communist collective. In church context, Protestant Saints use the force of government to achieve their vision of heavenly utopia.

Today, the balding humorous, winsome preacher demands you participate in the local church. The implicit assumption is that some part of your life is not yours to dispose of as you see fit. And besides, Sunday church attendance is in the Bible after all. Tomorrow, he demands that all God-robbers tithe. This implicit assumption is that the heartbeats you used to create wealth is not yours to dispose of as you see fit. They are God funds, but the preacher is empowered to collect on God's behalf. And besides, it is in the Bible after all. The day after that, he preaches about his authority to tell you what the Bible says. The implicit assumption is that your mind is not yours to command and requires your subordination to his conclusions. The day after that, he tells you that the he is uniquely elected to make the Massachusetts Bay Colony the foundation of a godly nation, and the devil has risen up Witches in our midst, and we must not suffer them to live. And besides, it is in the Bible after all.

It doesn't matter what passages he reads or what the Bible actually says. He is utterly free to make up his doctrine by whatever intellectual sleight of hand that suits his purpose. And when confronted, he condemns the conclusions with the same Pervasive Depravity metaphysic, with the Leadership owns TRUTH epistemology, and with the submission to authority ethic. You don't own your mind! You don't own you! How dare you!

And now our pot-smoker metaphor has come full circle. Every argument that concedes the premise is really a fight about **how much**. The doctrines that morally demand your rational obedience in the small things are the same arguments that will compel you to concede authority's dictates and the Burning at the Stake things.

Notes

15
Predestined Eugenics

> It is necessary for the welfare of the nation that men's lives be based on the principles of the Bible. No man, educated or uneducated, can afford to be ignorant of the Bible.
>
> —Theodore Roosevelt

> I wish very much that the wrong people could be prevented entirely from breeding; and when the evil nature of these people is sufficiently flagrant, this should be done. Criminals should be sterilized and feebleminded persons forbidden to leave offspring behind them. . . .
>
> —Theodore Roosevelt[1]

> . . . the right of holding slaves is clearly established in the Holy Scriptures, both by precept and example. . . . Had the holding of slaves been a moral evil, it cannot be supposed that the inspired Apostles, . . . would have tolerated it for a moment in the Christian Church. In proving this subject justifiable by Scriptural authority [Luke 12:47], its morality is also proved; for the Divine Law never sanctions immoral actions.
>
> —Richard Furman, Baptist State Convention, letter to South Carolina Governor, 1822

Injustice, oppression, and exploitation, all assume **individual** rights. These concepts measure the breach of a person's boundaries. These concepts are calculated

John Immel

against the fullest definition of freedom as man pursues his intentions and is restrained or brutalized in that process. Or said another way, man is individually sovereign disposing his life as he sees fit and unjust forces harm him in that pursuit. Without sovereign individuality as the moral starting place, injustice, oppression, and exploitation are absurd ethical criticisms. If a man does not own himself, then he is the property of some other entity—individual or civil—without right or recourse.

Historically, man has been property of the state. The theocracies of Christendom, Islam, Kali, Ra, Moloch and a host of others, have insisted that Man's life is disposed at "God's" discretion with **no** remedy, because whatever happened to man is the product of divine will as His stewards execute his purpose in the earth. In Europe, the effects of these assumptions are most readily seen through the Dark Ages. Humanity has lived the elements of Platonist/Augustinian ideas for the larger percentage of Western history. Government philosophy assumed the Divine Right of Kings and the Church advocated the social structure of the Three Estates where 90 percent of the population was born into serfdom. Serfdom is of course caste slavery. The caste system of the Three Estates is effectively Christian Eugenics, justified by the doctrinal assumptions of Predestination. And notice that instead of Heaven on Earth, all is right with the world; every man in harmony with peace, love, and cosmic church-ness, Kum-by-yah, Kum-by-yah. The Medieval world was characterized by mass slavery, famines, want, lack, death, war and destruction—all justified by Authority's right of action in a predestined society.

I was not being inflammatory with the class division

---

1. See discussion on page 175.

of people: *Untermenschen* and *Ubermenschen*. I was laying out the logical ranks based on the assumption of Predestination combined with the doctrine of Pervasive Depravity. This is why Dictators love predestination (a.k.a. determinism). They need an ironclad justification for their rule and an ironclad rationalization for your subordination. You are a lesser creature because God created you that way (or naturally selected) and are therefore disqualified in every sense to object to their superiority, their governance, their law, their police power, their punitive power.

Even a casual reading of history illustrates in every age where Predestination/Determinism is evangelized, it is an auxiliary doctrine to justify a class society divided between those above and those below—those who rule and those who are enslaved.[2] This doctrine is a key element in the moral justification of genocide: the Jews, the "savages" of Australia, Africa, South America, and North America. In every instance, the people in the mass graves were not real people. They were pre-ordained vessels of

---

2. The quote at the chapter beginning was from *The Works of Theodore Roosevelt*, National ed. vol. 12 (New York: Charles Scribner's Sons, 1926), 201. Teddy's essay titled "Twisted Eugenics" is a scathing review of an unnamed professor's article in the Atlantic Monthly, July, 1913. The unnamed professor made the dubious case that "militarism" should be abandoned in service to eugenics. Meaning, the best and brightest fight wars, the indolent and cowardly remain at home and make babies. Ergo, wars are immoral because it genetically ensures racial inferiority. Teddy is fully outraged by the assertion, but not by the social engineering and social control implicit to the professor's case. As he says in his own words, "Eugenics is an excellent thing . . ." Teddy's fury is over the denunciation of militarism. He said: "My concern is with the United States, where militarism is absolutely negligible factor from the standpoint of eugenics." Consider the scope: an American president utterly persuaded of his Christianity fully defending, fully advocating eugenics in service to racial health and moral duty.

destruction, and God smiles his approval for eradicating them from the Earth.

The intellectual progression starts with a seemingly harmless truism: "The sheep are stupid and need a shepherd." The sheep metaphor is in the Holy book after all, so who is going to argue with the implications of human stupidity? Besides, it seems true-ish because some people appear determined to make horrifically bad decisions and others are utterly oblivious about their relationship to the world. And still other people cannot handle the ideological chaos from the postmodern polyglot hell. They lust for someone, anyone, to impose order. "I'm really smart, so **I** see true wisdom. But would someone **make** these other nincompoops believe the right thing so I can find security?!"

Ask and you shall receive. Some man inevitably rides in on his high horse to save the day, to give a moral justification why some men **should** have the power to order everyone's mind. Men with the same agenda as Alexander Strauch institutionalize "the sheep are stupid and need a shepherd" concept into modern spiritual doctrine with books that pretend at being full treatments of "scriptural" government.[3] They mask the cruel

---

3. Alexander Strauch predicates his entire evaluation of "Biblical Eldership" with the concept of what I call Mass Incompetence. He takes enormous liberty with the Bible's use of the sheep/shepherd metaphor to justify a uniquely separate group of men that he calls "First Among Equals." His full treatment can be found in his book, *Biblical Eldership: An Urgent Call to Restore Biblical Church Leadership* (Colorado: Lewis and Roth, 1995), 18.

I wrote a brief evaluation of this premise for SpiritualTyranny.com. in an article called Pass the Mint Jelly. In every expression of tyranny, the arguments used to advance and execute tyranny exploit five concepts: Incompetent Masses, Universal Guilt, Dictated Good, Abolition of Ambition, and Collective Conformity. Strauch's book is a study in the conclusion of doctrinal Mass Incompetence.

Blight in the Vineyard

presumption with sanctimony: The baby sheep just need some compassionate men to shower their delicate minds with love and sanitize the big bad ideas from their cribs. "We just care deeply for all the lost souls. Our efforts are just compassion. Our intentions are just rainbows, sweetness, and light. Coo coo coo. Here is your Binky."

But pull the good-intentioned, altruistic, paternalistic mask away and the vicious, evil premise is revealed for anyone with the courage to see. Everyone else is too stupid to know the truth because "God" condemned them to their wretched animal state. And "God" appointed a few truly enlightened **men** to be in charge of the herd **animals**. The men teaching the doctrines are always the ones whom "God" appointed in charge of the pitiful beasts. Alakazam! Poof! Let the shearing and butchering begin. And to make sure that all the wool and mutton comes into the store house, the class society needs organized from central planning—to the Glory of God—of course. Who can argue with the Glory of God? Can there be a higher spiritual goal? It is in the Holy book after all.

When the sheep figure out that the shepherd only defends against the wolf because **He** wants the same wool and mutton. When it dawns on his herd animal mind that he will be eaten either way, he finally stands up like a man and argues against the definition of "God's Glory" equaling being served for dinner. In that moment, the howl from the wolves and the shepherds is the same: "How dare the infidel challenge our right to 'godly government'!" When it becomes obvious that the infidel just won't get with the program and submit to their rule, der *Ubermenschen* goes to war for one purpose: Eliminate the "rebellious"! Eradicate the enemy of God!

It is baby steps down this intellectual path to

destruction because once an argument concedes the premise, every other conversation is about how much:

> Step 1: Man is an inarguable **Predestined** Enemy of God who subverts the faithful sheep with bad ideas and sexual decadence.
>
> Step 2: God appoints some men to be **Predestined** Vessels of Destruction.
>
> Step 3: Therefore, God appoints unquestionable **Predestined** Leadership, who **must** have the force of government to defend the faithful sheep from bad people doing bad things with body parts.
>
> Step 4: The result is unquestionable **Predestined** Leadership destroying the **Predestined** Vessels of Destruction in the name of God and righteousness.[4]

This is the path of historic tyranny trod to the world's mass graves.

What was the solution? The answer is: the utter philosophical shift from predestined collectivism to free-willed individualism. You will have to remember the long political evolution that won increasing victories for justice, freedom, and protection for **individuals**. The assumption of freedom requires that man own himself. This evolution produced the *Magna Carta*, eventually the philosophy of John Locke, and the political thought of Thomas Paine, and

---

4. Heaven forbid that these **predestined** leaders get it in their head that their very righteous governmental efforts are in service to the apocalyptic return of the Messiah or the millennial reign of Christ. The moment **predestined** leaders thinks they are essential to purify the world for the return of Christ, make EVERY effort to get them out of power. If you fail, the blood runs thick and deep. Do not doubt me here. History is full of examples of this very dynamic. And American Christianity is ripe for a repeat performance.

Blight in the Vineyard

ultimately, the U.S. Constitution. Notice the contrast of the governmental assumptions historically illustrated in full relief: Man does not own himself (Dark Ages) or man fully owns himself (United States of America).

When you hear men evangelizing predestination, no matter how often they pay lip service to defending some godly principle, or scriptural doctrine, or eternal security, know that the real motive is insidious. Pay close attention to their theory of governance. Listen to them long enough and you will realize they are advocating some form of class society where a select few are free to dispose of the many as they see fit. The sole function of such a teaching is to justify social engineering. No other reason exists to advance the doctrine of predestination.

Again, let me make this personal. If you stay submitted to your predestined place under PDI/CLC/SGM authority, it is because God facilitates your perseverance. If you do not, the logic goes:

- This doctrine is the hard truth. Those who stay **persevere** in the truth, thereby affirming the doctrine.
- Not everyone will receive the hard truth, because they have itching ears and God has not revealed this truth to everybody.

So, if you left PDI/CLC/SGM, you did so because you were **not perseverant**, thereby affirming the doctrine. Ergo, those who leave were not authentic believers. You ever owned yourself, so you did not own your decision. **Their** conduct is **irrelevant** because their authority is secured by Divine Mandate. Your conduct is *relevant* because it illustrated God's manifest predestination.

Notes

16
Peerless Passion

Nothing great in the world has been accomplished without passion.

—G. W. F. Hegel

The greatest dangers to liberty lurk in the insidious encroachment by men of zeal, well meaning but without understanding.

—Louis D. Brandeis

Great ambition is the passion of a great character. Those endowed with it may perform very good or very bad acts. All depends on the principles which direct them.

—Napoleon Bonaparte

**Impassioned Orthodoxy =
PDI/CLC/SGM Passion + Orthodoxy**

OK, one more tour around the evolutions of Christian thought. It will be fun.

Now we have to talk about the Passion part of the Impassioned Orthodoxy PDI/CLC/SGM marketing and packaging. What it describes is very revealing.

Hey, did some of you know that many of the SGM leadership came into the kingdom through ministries of Faith? Robin Boisvert told me that he used to listen to Kenneth Hagin all the time.

Circa 1960 people bolted mainline denominations

because the churches were stodgy and socially irrelevant. Suddenly the music part of church was lively like a Beatles rock concert because people wanted to be passionate about Jesus. Rumor had it that other preachers were healing people, and there was this funny tongue-talking thing. So, informal groups started to clap hands and play music with guitars and drums, sing songs without hymnals, and dance about. This got added to healing, and miracles, and tongue-talking. Alakazam! Poof! The Charismatic Movement.

The children of the charismatic renewal movements tend to sniff at "mainline" churches insisting that they are mere "religion," where as independent churches teach a "relationship with Jesus." If they dare walk into a mainline church, after the service, they decry the staid quietness and wrinkle their nose at the liturgy and the architecture that defines the sanctuary. Never once do they realize that what they saw was a slice of living history, a practice that often has its roots in well-developed theology over 1,000 years old that is designed to communicate very complex ideas to an illiterate mass. Neither do they realize that the roots of the practice started pretty much exactly like their church started. Most "mainline churches" started the way of all denominations: a magnetic speaker with a message that connects with a contemporary audience and the force of his personality carries his ideas deep into the public mind. This person-to-public dynamic has been central to most every revival (as we would define the term) from John the Baptist, to Azuza Street, to Brownsville, Florida. However, the failing underneath personality-driven movements is that they tend to be short on a full thought systems. Second-generation preachers emulate their predecessor, but by the third generation, the

Blight in the Vineyard

question is inevitably: "So . . . what's next?" And the quest for a cohesive idea structure begins, which leads to the inevitable rise of the denomination.

Of course, most men do not want to reinvent the wheel, so the ideologues seek out fully developed theologies. In light of America's "me too" philosophical and theological obsession, our path to denominationalism means that after the "renewal" movement passes the third generation, preachers find their comprehensive systems in Divinity Schools fully committed to European thought. Even if the schools muster some courage to depart on "Nonessentials," they have no academic courage to challenge the core assumptions. Who is going to challenge the Protestant Sacred Cow of Reformed Theology or Platonist/Augustinianism at the very center of historic Christianity? Whatever the founders of each movement preached, the trend towards repeating denominational assumptions is almost irresistible.

So, no matter how many renewal/revival movements have risen up in American Piety over the last hundred plus years, at the end of the day, the ideological power of the philosophical system wins by attrition. Whatever freedom-producing ideas were introduced into the public mind in the first generation inevitably disappears by the third generation because the message lacked a fully developed philosophy that could compete with the European ideological despotism. This means that from the top down—from the intellectual crown down to the average pulpit pounder—American Christian thought has been shaped by European ideologues.

Conversely, the fuel for most American renewal movements have been a steady stream of populist uprisings led by men with little or no formal, that is, divinity school or seminary training. But while they would often preach doctrines counter to the European roots, their congregations very often held a Scofield Bible in their lap. They would preach about the healing power of Jesus or the gift of tongues, or casting out demons on Sunday morning often oblivious to the European philosophical commentary in the margins contradicting their proclamation. For decades (circa 1920 forward) the most widely read version of the Bible in America had a Calvinist commentary just under the verses. The result: No matter what the preacher said, his audience held in their lap the broad ideological commentary advocated by university traditions. Long after the preacher left town, the people were "feeding" on the thought system printed in the book. Until the late 1960s, average Christians never knew there was any other Bible interpretive methodology that could account for other interpretive conclusions. That changed with the advent of mass broadcast media. (More about this in a moment.)

Deep within the Reformation Theology construct is Dispensational theology. This theology says that God doesn't do miracles, heal, and cause speaking in tongues because apostles were the conduit, and they are dead. Dispensationalism has its roots as far back as Augustine and was the Protestant Orthodox position for centuries. The essential logic goes: Jesus did miracles because of his Deity. His Deity is the highest expression of his authority. Jesus appointed unique stewards of that authority to carry out His dictated will. Their conferred authority was expressed in the working of miracles, the bestowing of supernatural gifts, and the writing of scripture. God has divided history into specific dispensations and this miracle period existed for an express purpose of establishing the Gospel, which established the Church and ended when those specific stewards died.

The direct relationship between authority and gifts is the important part in the broader Calvinist Orthodoxy. **Here is the Pandora's Box that everyone is trying to keep closed:** If a man has the **authority** to work miracles, cast out demons, and heal the sick, does that also mean he has the **authority** to write scripture and bind men to their dictates?

Catholics don't have this specific problem because they uphold apostolic succession from Peter. The authority to heal is embedded in the authority of the *Pontifex Maximus*. The sacrament of healing still resides within Catholic doctrine because they can solve the (authority = gifts) x (authority = scripture) x (authority = governance) equation since the Catholic Church affirms the Papal responsibility to preside over the meaning of scripture. Ergo, they have the authority to heal, work miracles, et cetera, et cetera.

The Reformers could not appeal to an apostolic succession without the accusation of some serious interpretive hypocrisy. To preempt this equation, they resurrected Augustine's "scripture" justification for miracle and gift cessation. If they just don't exist anymore, then it doesn't matter. Alakazam! Poof! No more worry about who can write scripture and human agency is eradicated.

Let me flip this around so you can see it from the other side and maybe begin to grasp why this issue is central and important to PDI/SGM's claims to Impassioned Orthodoxy.

What if healing, gifts, tongues, and miracles are not the product of authority?

What if the gifts are not dictated by divine pre-ordination?

John Immel

If miracles are not stewarded by *der **Ubermenschen**—*better kinds of men in God's service—then where do they come from? The only thing left to source such an outcome is human agency, or at the very least, a co-operative relationship between God and Man.

Now watch the dominoes tumble.

First Domino: If Man can take action to get something from God, this ability destroys the T in T.U.L.I.P. The moment human volition enters the God and Man equation, it means that Man cannot be **totally depraved**—he does not suffer **total inability**—because some part of him can will and **do** and **seek** GOOD.

Next Domino: Because men obtain this something from God but men do not all receive the same things, this implies conditions to man's participation in the Covenants of Promise.

Next Domino: Therefore, election is contingent on human agency, which means that all comers to the conditions can access God's grace (God's gifts).

Next Domino: Therefore, Atonement must be comprehensive, which means that **Grace is Prevalent**.

Next Domino: Therefore, Perseverance in the Faith is the product of man's accumulated good action, a.k.a. character.

Next Domino: If man must use volition as a key element of his sanctification, man does not suffer bondage of the will.

Human agency in God's salvation plan? Scandalous!!

What does that say about Sovereignty?

Next Domino: The answer is that the nature of God's sovereignty has nothing to do with dictatorial, deterministic power. Moment-to-moment manifestations of reality are not specifically reflective of divine intent.

Next Domino: Man is not standing before a dictatorial

sovereign where circumstance is the product of divine determinism. So, man is not **morally** compelled to accept the beggarly elements of this world.

Next Domino: Therefore, man is free to overcome death and improve his life by eliminating suffering. Ambition is a correct expression of human conduct and the moral clarity to pursue anything that empowers and liberates life.

Last Domino: Because man possesses GOOD, he is also responsible to GOOD. Or said another way, because GOOD is within his grasp to define, acquire, and act in accordance, he is without excuse. His life requires moral self-appointment which is the foundation of self-governance.

This last domino is the most damaging to Mystic Despots. If authority and TRUTH and government force are not tied together, they do not rule by fiat. It was this counter-argumentative progression that the Catholic Church feared for hundreds of years. One "Scripture Alone" argument that led to another that led to another that successfully invalidated their moral justification to own the monopoly of force. The moral justification for self-governance—distributed abroad in the minds of men—is the tyrant's nightmare.

This tumbling domino trail gained real momentum in Christian thinking through the late 1700s in Europe and took root in America just prior to the American Revolution. Human competence, religious freedom, a cooperative understanding of Grace—the rejection of predestination—gained a broad social acceptance and led directly to the decision to resist British tyranny. Eventually, these doctrinal predicates filled the Christian worldview and emerged in American 20th century piety. I know I skipped a lot of evolutions and

John Immel

tides of thought, but as generalizations go, this is the philosophical progression that occurred to create the charis-costal mindset that permeates the world today.

The existence of modern day miracles, miracle workers, and manifest spiritual gifts is a stake in the heart of the Reformed doctrine. If you can **choose** to speak in tongues, if you can **choose** to be healed, if you can **choose** to raise the dead, if you can **choose** to work miracles and demonstrate Dispensationalism false, then what else exists in the modern age? Apostles? Prophets? And if they exist, do they have the power to write scripture and bind us all to their dictates? Listen to the modern day hardcore Reformed Theology Orthodoxy advocates; those people who are detractors of the Charismatic worldview, and notice this is core of their fuss.

Now let me draw this back to our specific conversation. Hit rewind and take a new look at the PDI to SGM evolution, from their early days to the present.

Once upon a time, PDI/CLC/SGM spoke in tongues with regularity (I was present for their own mini Toronto outpouring with laughing and rolling on the ground and all the other charismatic chaos type stuff), preached healing, had prophecies from the mic, and called themselves Apostles and Prophets. Well, the prophet title gives them some consternation, but they called their leadership teams Apostolic Teams for forever and a month and presumed all the authority that title implies. And, of course, SGM Central Planning has world-class contemporary music. The combination of charismatic-ish beliefs and the modern feel of Sunday worship is the Passion part of the Impassioned Orthodoxy glossy brochure. This is what PDI/CLC/SGM love to present to the world and what attracts so many people to their particular brand of Christianity.

But here is the problem: None of the Impassioned/Charismatic part of this equation is Orthodox. And this includes everyone's favorite contemporary music and instrument. Not even thirty years ago, the fight over bringing a piano or guitar into church was as contentious as tongues based on the same assertions of Orthodoxy and human depravity. So, forget saying that tongues and healing are devilish spiritual counterfeit but the instruments of music and the contemporary style obvious scriptural expressions. If you go to a church where much more than a voice is raised in worship, you owe a great debt to those who resisted orthodoxy and its implicit denigration of most outward forms of worship.

To drive this point home, virtually no one who is anyone, anywhere, anytime in the last 500 years has believed that apostles still exist or that God is supplying a steady manifestation of healing, miracles, and tongues through free will and human agency.

What is the definition of Orthodoxy again?

The acceptance of spiritual gifts worldwide is largely attributed to the **deliberate** abandoning of Reformed Orthodoxy and its implicit Dispensationalism at the turn of the 20th century. Preachers like John Alexander Dowie, and John G. Lake, among many others laid the ideological foundation for men like William J. Seymour and the subsequent Azusa Street revival that sparked the Pentecostal, Full Gospel denominations. This broad doctrinal movement gave rise to Oral Roberts.

Oral stands unique in Christian history, arguably having the single greatest impact in transforming American—if not the world—understanding of God's use of spiritual gifts through his sweeping revivals from the

John Immel

late '40s to the early '70s and pioneering efforts of mass broadcast media. For the first time in history, a man could speak to tens of thousands. For the first time in history, the revival leader could leave town and his words did not leave with him. For the first time, the interpretive assumptions within the Scofield bible did not win out by attrition. Mass media made it possible for people to continue listening to ideas that ran utterly counter to the Reformation "Orthodoxy" that produced the staid, quiet, dull, boring, hope-crushing, and freedom-destroying doctrines. Oral's leading message rang clear and potent into the people's mind: "God is a GOOD God." The message insisted that GOOD meant God's purpose was to deliver man from suffering, from lack, from want, from the beggarly elements of the world: He would heal the whole man. For the first time, GOOD meant LIFE and Liberty in the here and now for man to enjoy. For the first time, people could see the contrast between those who were seminary educated and those who were empowered to unapologetically proclaim a message of life. It was not long until those seminaries were aptly named cemeteries.

In America the evolutions of these thoughts start roughly at the turn of the 20th century and culminate with the birth of the "Pentecostal" revivals. These revivals developed into many separate movements and flavors that inevitably trended towards the denominationalism described above. Fast forward roughly twenty years, Oral's message and evangelization spearheaded the resurgence of the early 20th century "Pentecostal" doctrines. This was the seed that was to sprout into American piety through the '70s that has been generally called the Charismatic Renewal. I combine the historic doctrinal trend from Pentecostal to

Blight in the Vineyard

the Charismatic movement into this coined term, Charis-costal, because the Pentecostal and Charismatic doctrinal assumptions and biblical worldview tends to be similar but not identical. Charismatic refers to the Greek word *charismata*, which is the root of our word *charisma*. The Greek root translates to "things given" and is used to define spiritual gifts, i.e., tongues, miracles, healing.

One branch of the Charis-costal resurgence was The Jesus movement that rose in post-Vietnam America that grabbed most drug-induced '60s retreads and pulled them from the brink of permanent pharmacological vacation. I'm pretty sure that includes some of the primary doctrinal movers and shakers at SGM. But even if the catalyst movement isn't exactly right, the catalyst vacation is. And here is the important part of this historical exercise. **All** of these tides and movements and evolutions of Christian thought are essential for fledgling TAG/GOB/PDI to manifest. They could not possibly exist in their current Impassioned Orthodoxy snootiness without the heroic efforts of those who resisted "orthodoxy" generations before they were born.

PDI/CLC/SGM got its start from the liberty implicit to the above doctrinal evolution but then opted to abandon those ideas in pursuit of absolute irrefutability, utterly unassailable *El Primo* doctrine. To hedge their bets, they fancy that they are the best of both worlds—the best of the Charismatic and the best of the Orthodox. They believed they represented an apostolic calling and hedge that title by referring to their leadership structure as Apostolic "teams" because no one had the nerve to wear that title individually. I guess they have dropped the apostle thing of late, but they tacked that on to their ministry for decades. I told you they were very good at rewriting their history. But the reality is for the better

John Immel

part of twenty years, they were about as non-Dispensationalist as a church can get. Which means they were about as non "orthodox" as a church can be.

So, what do you do when you are embarrassed by your parents? What do most kids do when they get too cool for school? If you are SGM, you push away or embrace whatever charismatic/orthodox belief that fits *El Primo Doctrinal Mover and Shaker's* apostolic feng shui.

Sovereign Grace Magazine July/August 1998, in an article titled *A matter of Sound Doctrine: Have Tongues Ceased?* by Brian Wasko (Brian was a youth pastor at the time at Southside Church in Virginia Beach.), he wrote a feel good article about the success of one of his own: Craig Cabaniss, then senior pastor at San Diego's Grace Church.

Craig Cabaniss participated in a debate at Westminster Theological Seminary with a Dr. Gaffin about the doctrine of tongues.

The article starts:

> One area of doctrine in which PDI departs from additional Reformed teaching involves the continued existence and exercise of particular spiritual gifts. (Page 5)

OK, they've got orthodoxy and they've got this pesky tongue-talking "experience." What to do?

Brian summarizes the debate:

> Craig's presentation had two primary goals. First, **to distance himself from the usual charismatic position** by affirming his belief in the sufficiency of Scripture and the importance of doctrine. He stated, "I do not value the subjective over the objective, experience over doctrine, or Toronto and

Blight in the Vineyard

Pensacola over Wittenberg and Geneva." (Page 5.)[1]

The last time I checked, Toronto and Pensacola had nothing to do with the doctrinal reality of speaking in tongues. That was Pentecost. And that would be Bible.

But notice this curious denigration. Brownsville and Toronto are irrelevant to any conversation about Bible ideas. This is classic PDI/SGM subterfuge: create a false equation to justify existing belief structure. Whatever Charismatic doctrinal failures might exist, whatever subjectivity might lurk in Renewal movement church practice, what does that have to do with the **fact** of tongues being a biblical Christian expression? If you value the "objective," then the sum of the doctrinal conversation is read the technological manifestation of a printed Bible, specifically Acts, and then talk in tongues until your jaws hurt.[2] Both things are objective, everything else is posturing.

Anyway, what is Mr. Cabaniss saying? What is Geneva? Geneva was the home of good old Johnny C. And what does Craig Cabaniss admits to? Wanting to distance himself from the usual Charismatic position?

---

1. Toronto and Pensacola refer to spiritual outpourings through the late 1990s and early 2000s. Wittenberg is the home of Martin Luther, and Geneva is the home of John Calvin.

2. The fact that the tongues detractors do not have *a priori* understanding of the language is irrelevant. The fact that someone does not have a priori understanding of Spanish, Tagalog, or Hindi does not discount the existence of the language nor the specific manifestation of someone speaking the language.

    a pri·o·ri —adjective
- a. from a general law to a particular instance; valid independently of observation.
- b. existing in the mind prior to and independent of experience, as a faculty or character trait.
- c. not based on prior study or examination; non-

John Immel

Translation?

"Don't hold it against us that we still have those pesky charismatic ideas in our head. We really are smart. We PDI/SGM folk are smart and those Brownsville charismatics aren't. We PDI/SGM folk value our brains; those Brownsville people are being led by the Subjectivity Beast. We PDI/SGM folk are enlightened. Those silly, simple-minded Toronto Outpouring souls aren't.

Love us because we are Orthodox. We really, really are. Our parents are really embarrassing. They are just not sophisticated enough to be truly enlightened."

This makes me laugh.

This is a prime example of why modern day church organizations exist in a hybrid state precariously standing between two opposite worldviews. They get their start from the freedom implicit to the renewal message. **Freedom** is what makes it possible for a bunch of pot smokers avoid going to seminary and start a church. But then—hypocrisy of hypocrisy—when they realize that freedom means **everyone** and the Arena of Ideas is a tough place to live, they suddenly want the moral authority to force rational subordination. When they realize they can't compete with ideas, they go looking for an ethical justification for dictatorial authority.

It doesn't matter that they acquire authority in the name of good intentions: to beat back chaos, and protecting the poor, poor sheep. This, of course, sounds noble and righteous, and to argue against such things must be the product of deception, but the result is an inevitable institutional schizophrenia that gives way to ever increasing levels of Mystic Despotism. Because once a church leadership concedes the premise within the

---

analytic: an a priori judgment.

Blight in the Vineyard

European doctrines, every other conversation is about how much.

They Want Your Mind

In every age where the Church has suffered an identity crisis, it has insisted it should be the undisputed leader of cultural definition and all things not church-approved are unsanitary interloping filth. Circa 1850 the European Church had the exact same problem. The Church seemed impotent in the face of the cultural tides of social and scientific thought. Contemporary philosophers had proclaimed that God was dead. Advances in human understanding through the 1930s led to Man solving the problems that had historically been chalked up to the vagueness of divine blessing or divine wrath: depending on the day or the social climate. Theologians fussed over Modernity, which is to say they fussed over the fact that men thought for themselves and solved their own problems. The Church was reeling from its own irrelevance and openly pining for the nostalgic age of kings and knights and the grander days of Monarchy in "benevolent" cohabitation with the Church. Major, well-respected theologians like, Gerhard Kittel, Paul Althaus, and Emanuel Hirsch added their voices to the effort to return to the ages past when the Church held the appropriate place in "civil" society, a curious advocacy considering the endless destruction that medieval culture perpetrated in the name of God and King. Much like the modern voices of religious conservatism, they insisted that if people would just believed right things, a moment of utter Christian clarity and prevailing cultural acceptance would emerge.[3]

---

3. Robert P. Ericksen, *Theologians Under Hitler* (New

John Immel

Historically, Christians have assumed that cultural breakdown is a problem from without. So, we have approached the solution with two methods. Retreat into highly xenophobic enclaves ruled by doctrinal absolutists who burn Harry Potter books because the gremlins of bad will bite them in the keester if they are in the same room with subversive, devilish instruments of darkness.

Or, the church has sought governmental power to impose broad cultural standards. The logic is that God is King of the world and his Church is the Queen. If everyone would just submit to His rule, via the Glorious Church, all would be hunky-dory. The reason people believe bad stuff is because they won't let the very righteous, very pious, very qualified Stewards of Good revelation dictate the cultural standard. It's everybody else's fault for not submitting to our authority.

When Augustine finalized the merging of Platonism into Christianity—the most dramatic manifestation of syncretism ever—and that hybrid was infused with the force of the Roman state, the face of Christianity changed forever.[4] To be sure, the face of the Western world

---

Haven: Yale University Press, 1987). Curiously, Ericksen concedes that the fight against "modernity" is a justifiable circumstance, a reasonable foe to combat. These thinkers who contributed so dramatically to the theological underpinnings of the National Socialists just "went too far" in their zeal for a righteous goal. Never once does he notice that the very foe they combated was the very source of freedom they ended up conceding to a tyrant.

4. Not that Augustine was alone in merging Christianity with Platonism. The trend towards merging Platonism with Judeo-Christian concepts has its start with men like Philo and Marcion. The trend toward interpreting the Hebrew Scriptures arguably found its fullest expression in Philo (20 BC-50 AD). He was a Jewish theologian/philosopher who worked to harmonize Greek thought with Judaism and was influential in developing the Christian concept of *Logos*. Marcion was a leading Christian thinker in the early 2nd century (85-160 AD). He said that the God of the Old Testament was a

changed forever. The profoundly resilient, creative minds of the Greco/Roman world that had produced so many advances of human understanding almost ceased in the West under the weight of those two formidable powers.

From roughly 450 AD forward in Western Christianity, the leading expectation was exactly Dave Harvey's assertion from chapter 3: The church owns all TRUTH. The church leaders' job is to play idea cop. Every subsequent theological issue is in service to man's intellectual subordination to Church authority. The outcome is obvious: We stopped persuading the world and started dictating the world. Actually, it is worse than that. We stopped even thinking we had to persuade, that we had to offer a better body of ideas and a better qualitative life.

The contemporary Christian terror over Postmodernism is rooted in one glaring fear: the inability to compete in the Arena of Ideas.

Truly, there is nothing new under the sun. The tides and evolutions of thought have once again washed over the minds of men, and the Church is doing what it has always done—seeking to destroy what it refuses to understand. Her leadership is bothered that they even have to respond to what they consider to be unarguable. Her implicit assumption is she stands unique, supreme, by the sheer force of advocating "biblical" authority.

And here is the problem. Force and Authority are ultimately the same thing: the power to compel an outcome. So, the issue is not over right and wrong; the issue is over a subsequent justification for force. It does

---

demiurge or a subordinate God. This is a direct use of Plato's concept in the *Timaeus*. It is no small irony that he (his conclusions) was condemned as a heretic in later centuries, but Christianity ended up keeping the source of his specific ideological foundation: Plato.

not matter if the Bible is the authority if no force exists to compel an outcome. So, the inevitable conclusion of this argument is: Who can beat people into submission?

Jesus sent his disciples into the world "wise as serpents but harmless as doves." But somehow Christians have invaded the world "as harmful as serpents and as rationally vacant as doves." The Mystic Despots always want one thing: your mind. If they can rule this, they can rule everything else. It is to this first crucial salvo into tyranny that we will now turn our attention.

17
Intellectual Beachhead

Reason is the Devil's greatest whore; by nature and manner of being she is a noxious whore; she is a prostitute, the Devil's appointed whore; whore eaten by scab and leprosy who ought to be trodden under foot and destroyed, she and her wisdom . . . Throw dung in her face to make her ugly. She is and she ought to be drowned in baptism. . . . She would deserve, the wretch, to be banished to the filthiest place in the house, to the closets.

—Martin Luther

People gave ear to an upstart astrologer [Copernicus] who strove to show that the earth revolves, not the heavens or the firmament, the sun and the moon. Whoever wishes to appear clever must devise some new system, which of all systems is of course the very best. This fool wishes to reverse the entire science of astronomy; but sacred scripture tells us [Joshua 10:13] that Joshua commanded the sun to stand still, and not the earth.

—Martin Luther[1]

We should always be disposed to believe that which appears to us to be white is really black, if the hierarchy of the church so decides.

—St. Ignatius Loyola

---

1. References in order: Martin Luther
   • Erlangen Edition, vol. 16, pp. 142-148
   • "Works," vol. 22, c. 1543

John Immel

Funny thing: If I challenge Augustine, people shrug and chalk it up to some vague historical wrangling. But if I take on Calvin, suddenly I'm engaging in an unwarranted attack on pure righteous Bible faith. The irony in this distinction is that Johnny C. got his ideas from Brother Augie. Johnny made some adjustments but the bulk of his thought is directly sourced from Augustine's syntheses almost a millennium prior. This reaction has everything to do with the fact that virtually no average pew-sitter in the modern age considers themselves Augustinian, but lots of people consider themselves Calvinist. I talked about this very phenomenon in the early chapters: the co-relationship between our ideas and our identity. People are wedded to their ideas because those ideas are a reflection of their identity. So people's reaction to what follows will be a study in the defense of personal value, but the results won't be too surprising because the counter-criticisms tend to be consistent. When I challenge the content of historic Calvinism, one of the five stock responses I get is, "John, if only you really understood . . . you would see. . ."

Arminians . . . take note.

This is Calvin-lite. The argument that good ol' Johnny C. offered repeatedly in *The Institutes of the Christian Religion* followed this formula: Bible = truth. Calvin ideas = Bible. Deception = blindness to truth.

That was it. Time after time, as Johnny set out to expand his polity synthesis when seeking to overcome an implicit failing, he erected the straw man of depraved understanding to trump the objection. It is no accident that historic groupies emulate the same methodology. "If you only understood . . . you would see . . ." is a toned down version of the same *ad hominem* argument. It is a polite hedge against saying: "John, you are deceived."

See, here is the curious juxtaposition. If there was ever

Blight in the Vineyard

an anti-intellectual body of doctrine, Calvinism is it. Calvin laid the Protestant systematic metaphysical foundation to disqualify every part of man by making his nature = depravity and then make depravity = total epistemological inability.

Calvin is the father disqualifying objectors by destroying their ability to trust their judgments. Johnny C. sought to take everything out of human purview and create a cosmos where everything is determined by forces that are never impacted by human input. Such determinism renders man an ill-suited animal in a bewilderingly hostile environment. He was seeking to make Man utterly incompetent. Man is hopeless to master the most basic functions of his life because he is morally corrupt to will and to do GOOD. I contend this was done for the express purpose of producing a compliant body politic and most importantly, to set the foundation for select men who would dictate the GOOD. He was seeking an ironclad justification for Christian despots. Johnny C's synthesis was designed to elevate a few oligarchs over the many.

By Johnny C. definition, there is no human agency in God's salvific plan. By definition, man's depravity removes any ability to will or assent or sovereign action. Therefore, the content of a man's thinking has nothing to do with his eternal state.

Unconditional Election determines . . . well . . . everything. Human thinking determines nothing. It matters not whether man's thinking is right or wrong, the Doctrine of Election determines man's eternal location. Game over. Or maybe better said, there is no game because there is nothing to understand.

So, having "Sound Doctrine" as a Calvinist is . . . irrelevant. It doesn't matter what I believe. If I'm picked, it's all good. If I'm not picked . . . it sucks to be me.

John Immel

But Calvinists are, curiously, some of the leading academic proselytizers, among the most aggressive scholastic advocates. In the tired, worn-out scripture-stacking debates with unsavvy Arminians, it is always the Arminian who apologize for the conflict, the muddy argumentation, and surrender the intellectual arena. (Guys, quit doing that. You lose because you keep letting them define the debate.)

But to memory, I've never heard a Calvinist initiate the same. And I have had this conversation a lot. Indeed they tend to relish when an intellectual opponent concedes the field because they believe it a manifestation of their superior "biblical" arguments.

Press Calvinist aficionados long enough on the logical extensions of their doctrines and their answers start sounding exactly the same.

Why Evangelize? "Because God commands it."

Why Pray? "Because God commands it."

Why worship? "Because God commands it."

But that is logically inconsistent. "Because it is all great mystery. It's all a great mystery. It's all a great mystery. And who are you, oh Man, to even ask about things of God's wisdom?"

"Because God commands it" is not a conclusion of reason but a dictate of dogma.

How curious it is that Calvinists are the most rabid "intellectuals" but yet their own conclusions mitigate the value of any intellectual inquiry not already ascribed by Orthodoxy. How telling it is that Calvinists only advocate rational inquiry among an elite few who stand in the Stead of God but condemn rational pursuit by the uninitiated and purge opposing views from the approved book list. How revealing it is that the resurgence of Patriarchy in American Christianity is almost synonymous with the revival

Blight in the Vineyard

Calvinistic dogma. Congregations relegate those with two X chromosomes to intellectual third class citizens who must submit to their intellectual, second-class husbands whose doctrine is approved by first class Protestant Saints.

Driving this close to PDI/CLC/SGM home, with consistency, this bunch dismisses female objection to pastoral mistreatment with the wave of the "You are a woman not in submission to a man" wand. It doesn't matter that she is a master's level university graduate, has read every book on the "approved book" list, written effective evaluations of the doctrinal content, or has an IQ in excess of 150; she is disqualified because she is a woman. Her rational skills and abilities, no matter how well developed, are not proof against deception. The proof against error is a chromosome.

How is that for a bold, "rational" argument?

PDI/CLC/SGM relentlessly divide and conquer married couples by demanding men to participate in the Sound Doctrine fraternity by pitting them against the intellectual and spiritual "deficiencies" of their wives. "Does your wife need some theological instruction?" Which is code for: "How come you let your wife speak ideas that we don't approve?" Which is really code for: "Be a man. Put that woman of yours in her place! How dare she think theological thoughts unapproved by us—oops . . . you!?"

How many women are accepted to Pastors College? Whether they take up a pastoral position or not, can they pursue their love of theology? How often does teaching come from the pulpit **encouraging** fathers to keep their daughters at home, **encourage** them to prepare for married life, **encourage** them to have a "quiver full" of babies, **encourage** young women to focus on domestic development instead of say . . . college? How many implicit messages come from leadership to defer individual thinking by

John Immel

adopting approved thinking? How many books are ever openly read that are not on the approved book list? What are the chances that this book will be acceptable reading for the average SGM pew-sitter?

These anecdotes above are the logical extension of Calvin's anti-rational, anti-ability synthesis. Accepting second- and third-class intellectual/spiritual citizens is inevitable when TRUTH is dictated by Authority. It doesn't matter how polite and gracious and winsome they are when they say it; the attitude and corresponding practice is the foreseeable outcome.

Yet in spite of Calvin's **anti**-rationalism, Puritan groupies are quick to accuse their critics of deception—never superior argumentation—when it is their doctrine under scrutiny. This is precisely how the Hair Club for Men responds to women. This is precisely how they respond to any that take them to task for their impiety.

See, the only way "Sound Doctrine" matters is if correct **individual** thinking leads to an end. In other words, unless a man can make a choice to think specific thoughts, and correct thinking leads to specific conclusions, and specific conclusions lead to salvation, thinking is irrelevant.

Again, I will make this very personal. I often hear SGM defenders say that that open, frank criticism turns unbelieving children away from God and his Gospel. So, please, suck up the offense and let sweetness and light shine through so the children can "decide which way to go." I am always amazed the members can make this declaration with a straight face. They don't actually listen to what comes out of the pulpit, or they are listening and are parroting a glaring inconsistency.

Unconditional Election is quite plain: There is no such thing as children **deciding** to choose God. There is no intellectual process that will lead them to the right answers.

Blight in the Vineyard

The current state of their soul is appointed. If they do not believe, God has not granted them grace to repent. It won't matter whether they hear a steady diet of perfect doctrine, theological sunshine, and interpersonal sweetness. Their unbeliever-ness has nothing to do with the controversy openly discussed in this book, or on blog sites, or in a bar. **Your kids are going to where it is warm and smoky because God wants it that way.**

Is this hitting too close to home? Is this suddenly too real?

It is easy to make a theoretical assent to grand doctrinal proclamations. If this remains some vague academic abstraction to satisfy a confessional statement, it is tolerable. But it is entirely another thing to realize that your kids are going to Hell and burn and burn and burn and scream and scream and scream just because a capricious God decided to send them there. You watch them every day and know that their despicable behavior is predetermined. The wreckage of their life is God-**intended**. Their eternal torment is a function of His goodness, Kum-by-yah, Kum-by-yah.

And here is the despair you desperately try to ward off with all manner of hedging and evasion. You have no rational right to object. Period. Your mind is separated from your faith. You are compelled to believe because the very nature of your election is a product of what God put within you. Your mind is not yours.

The destructive power of this premise cannot be understated. To be sure, Immanuel Kant, roughly 200 years after Calvin's *Institutes*, formalized these very assumptions in his work, *Critique of Pure Reason*, to deliberately separate man from his mind and his mind from reality. And the modern age is living the disaster birthed from that philosophical assertion by factors to the nth power.

John Immel

Most every modern governmental atrocity can be traced back to twin destroyers of Kant's anti-rational doctrine and Altruism's destructive ethic. This ideology has so co-opted our contemporary minds that preachers teach Kantian philosophy like it is God's own Gospel, never once realizing they are teaching the single most destructive philosophy of the modern age. Combined with Platonist/Augustinian depravity, Kant's altruistic moral demand creates an almost unassailable fortress sanctifying **any** governmental destruction.

All Things Bible = All things Calvin

And no, this is not an introduction to Venn Diagrams.

Almost immediately on the heels of my above commentary, the zealots grab their leather-bound NIV and start fishing through verses armed and ready to do battle, very sure that their peerless passion will win the day. They are animated, agitated, and want to make sure I know I'm misstating the "Calvinist" position. What they say next is a variation of what follows:

Mr. Gillette (a blog forum alias) from www.sgmsurvivors.com/forum had this to say in response to a similar critique. He wasn't animated or agitated, but he did voice the standard response to my comments.

John:

I really enjoy your posts and you seem like you would be a lot of fun to hang out with.

Just for clarification:

A Calvinist doesn't believe that man is incapable of any good, just that there is no

good that man can do that would merit salvation, or that can please God. (Heb 11:6)

A Calvinist does believe that man, in his natural state (without God) is sinful, because scripture tells us clearly that he is a slave to sin, he is still "in Adam."

Now having said all that, I too have some serious problems with this whole "indwelling sin" thing. It seems to me to be nothing more than a tool SG uses to beat people over the head with. Here are a few of the problems I see with that: . . .

It's not nice.

It is not the method Paul uses.

It doesn't sanctify us.

Where I think SG goes terribly wrong is that they preach exactly the same message to those who are in Adam (non-Christians) as they do to those who are in Christ (Christians). Paul never does this! The whole basis that Paul uses for us to fight our sin is to remind us of who we are in Christ. That those who are in *Christ* are now dead to sin. How shall we who died to sin still live in it? -Romans 6:2b

Another problem I see with SG is that when they talk about the cross, the only thing they seem to be thinking of is substitutionary atonement. Don't get me wrong, that is HUGE! But the cross was more than that.

--Mr. G

Mr. G had some good things to say about me. That is why I quoted him, of course.
Ehem . . .

John Immel

But beyond the cool things he said, I want to draw your attention to the bolded points. The above is Convenient Calvinist thinking. Far too many Convenient Calvinists make the bizarre, intellectual leap that all things Bible are necessarily all things Calvin and all things Calvin are all things Bible. In other words, the Venn Diagram would be the same circle.

I want to expand this point because this is the crux of the historical arguments.

Calvinists get away with this intellectual hedge with far too much regularity, as if concepts like Pervasive Depravity or Limited Atonement or "The Fall of Man" are self-evident from within a specific passage and to argue the cut and paste doctrinal conclusion is to argue against scripture. This kind of Bible demagoguery is flat wrong.

Quoting a passage out of Romans requires a discussion of Pauline Theology circa 60 AD, its relationship to contemporary Jewish thought, and the intellectual challenges faced by new Christian sect in the Roman world. Quoting a passage out of Jeremiah requires a broad discussion of Jewish Theology circa 600 BCE. But quoting verses from each book, cutting and pasting them into a cohesive statement is rational larceny.

It seems strange that I should have to point this out, but it is necessary understanding for all arguments over the **meaning** of scripture. The Bible is an anthology, a collection of various types of literature from different ages and writers. The documents therein were written to specific audiences with specific assumptions about their world by men (or women) with very specific concerns. Those original documents were subsequently edited by people who added or subtracted as their audience needed clarification, or as they sought to solve the problems relevant to their circumstance. This makes people very uncomfortable, but that does not change the demonstrable reality. The anthology spans roughly 3,000 years and has numerous forms and variations. The compilation contains Yahweh's thoughts to man, man's thoughts to Yahweh, and a host of thoughts that may or may not have anything to do with anything. Taking those documents and presuming their substance is by default the same as a systematic theology written 1,500 years after Jesus' life is eisegesis[2] of the worst sort.

The appropriate response to Bible-quoting Calvinists is "All things Calvin are not specifically all things biblical. If we are going to talk Calvinism, stacking Bible quotes are off limits."

We can have a conversation about Pauline Theology and its induction into canon. But if you are going to advocate a Calvinist perspective, you need to identify Calvin's comments to support your position. If we are going to quote Paul, or John, or Matthew, or any of the Prophets, then the issue is **their** theology.

And trust me; this is a very different conversation.

But that conversation never happens because Calvinists don't want this limitation because it severely undercuts their implicit appeal to authority. The appeal to authority of "orthodoxy" is an overt effort to apply the authority of scripture to themselves. As I have already said: Orthodoxy is a magic word.

Arguing with dead men from the 16th century is easy. No man has a moral, spiritual, or intellectual obligation to dead men's ideas, and there is no greater tyranny than to advocate such a thing. So, refusing to accept this presumption changes the entire debate.

Few people have ever read Luther's *Disputations on the*

---

2. The practice of reading and understanding **into** a Bible text.

John Immel

Power and Efficacy of Indulgences or his *Bondage of the Will*. Fewer still have ever read Calvin's *Institutes*. I have yet to meet a Convenient Calvinist who can accurately place the progression of Reformation Theology in the broader evolution of Christian thought or synthesize its implications in 2,000 years of Church history. And almost no one in Protestant Christianity has the onions to say they were wrong.

I have never heard Convenient Calvinists even mention the Covenants of Promise, the Evangelization of the Anointing, or the Ministry of Reconciliation. Raise these concepts in a conversation and they think you're speaking Hebrew at best or some vain philosophy beneath their purist "Christ and Christ Crucified" self-declared superiority. So, it is no mystery that they don't know where Calvin's ideas originate or the subsequent doctrinal developments that made Calvin's governmental despotism arise.

The idea that man can do GOOD but not salvific GOOD is an evolution of thought that came after some years reviewing the Luther version of Reformation Theology and eventually took shape in subsequent historical revivals that led to the emergence of new denominations or splits of historic Lutheran sects. The central argument of Luther's *Disputations on the Power and Efficacy of Indulgences* revolved around the *Bondage of the Will*. Luther rejected the idea that Man could do **any good ever**. Luther's letter, *Bondage of the Will*, written to Erasmus of Rotterdam, details the fundamental inability of Man to will and therefore act out any GOOD. Calvin, of course, concurred with Luther.

Just so you know, I'm not making these distinctions up. Since I am talking about Calvin, I'm going to show a location for some of his ideas. Johnny C. opens chapter 3 of his *Institutes* with this:

CHAPTER 3
EVERY THING PROCEEDING FROM THE CORRUPT NATURE OF MAN DAMNABLE

> The principal matters in this chapter are—I. A recapitulation of the former chapter, proving, from passages of Scriptures that the intellect and will of man are so corrupted, that no integrity, no knowledge or fear of God, can now be found in him, sect. 1 and 2. II. Objections to this doctrine, from the virtues which shone in some of the heathen, refuted, sect. 3 and 4. III. What kind of will remains in man, the slave of sin, sect. 5. The remedy and cure, sect. 6. IV. The opinion of Neo-Pelagian sophists concerning the preparation and efficacy of the will, and also concerning perseverance and co-operating grace, refuted, both by reason and Scripture, sect. 7–12. V. Some passages from Augustine confirming the truth of this doctrine, sect. 13 and 14.

Calvin wrote in an outline format. Each chapter opened with a general thesis and followed with a sub-point outline. Chapter 3 had fourteen sections. It would be tedious to rehash all fourteen points, and the source is easily found online so you can check it at your leisure. I will note three sections that summarize my assertion. There is plenty more, of course. He goes on to argue at length each point below with its own discourse.

> 4. Objection still urged, that the virtuous and vicious among the heathen must be put upon the same level, or the virtuous prove that human nature, properly cultivated, is not devoid of virtue. **Answer, that these are not ordinary properties of human nature, but special gifts of God.** These gifts defiled by ambition, and hence the actions proceeding from them, however esteemed by man, have no merit with God.

John Immel

> 6. Conversion to God constitutes the remedy or soundness of the human will. **This not only begun, but continued and completed; the beginning, continuance, and completion, being ascribed entirely to God.** This proved by Ezekiel's description of the stony heart, and from other passages of Scripture.
>
> 9. Answer to second Objection continued. That good will is merely of grace proved by the prayers of saints. Three axioms 1. **God does not prepare man's heart, so that he can afterwards do some good of himself, but every desire of rectitude, every inclination to study, and every effort to pursue it, is from Him.** 2. This desire, study, and effort, do not stop short, but continue to effect. 3. This progress is constant. The believer perseveres to the end. A third Objection, and three answers to it.

The bolded stuff is my emphasis. Uh . . . you were telling me that Calvinists believe that people can do some good? That after Jesus and the New Birth, all is well, and man has access to an uncorrupted nature that can lay claim to GOOD and subsequently, character?

Hmm . . . interesting.

Well, while some readers stew on this information looking for a way out, I am going to continue my relentless campaign to expose the assumptions, presuppositions, and filters that have been hidden by the outrageous demagoguery that all things PDI/CLC/SGM are all things moral

.

18
Wreckage of Moral Clarity

> Shyness has a strange element of narcissism, a belief that how we look, how we perform, is truly important to other people.
>
> —Andre Dubus

> All men can see these tactics whereby I conquer, but what none can see is the strategy out of which victory is evolved.
>
> —Sun Tzu

"I cannot tell a lie. It was I who chopped down the cherry tree." If the sources on the web are to be believed, one Mason Weems wrote Washington's biography and created this story to illustrate George's great moral makeup. See, here is the *problemo*. If one accepts Original Sin, subsequently Pervasive Depravity, subsequently Indwelling Sin, there is no such thing.

Some of you are ready to rattle off scriptures that say we will have/bear GOOD fruit and that we should have character. And this is precisely what I am talking about with the assumption that all things Bible are necessarily all things Calvin. Those scriptures are not a refutation of my commentary but a reflection of Matthew, Mark, Luke, John, and Paul theology.

If you are a John Calvin groupie, you believe that man is *non posse non peccare*; man is not able not to sin; man is on the back of horse led around by the devil. Man always has a taste for sin in his mouth. Man can do no GOOD. Everything proceeding from the corrupt nature of man is damnable. You preach nothing but "Christ and him crucified." This is the sum of God's Gospel and nothing else matters in light of eternity. The reason you continue to preach the crucifixion and take up your cross is because man will always be a sinner. His motives are shot through with sin, so what GOOD you do is really God in action because your actions are filled with depravity. Sanctification is really the bottomless effort to peel back the depravity layers and confess your faults.

Question: Character is GOOD, right? Or better said, character is accumulated GOOD actions, right?

Uh, if you are a Johnny C. groupie, how can man make a claim to the accumulation of His GOOD action? By definition, character would be God's exclusive creation as He merits, you demonstrate. For those of you who were paying attention in the previous chapter, this would be from point 6 in Calvin's *Institutes*. We just read that, right? Only God can claim possession of those actions. Again, that would be either the "I" in Irresistible Grace or the "P" in the Perseverance of the Saints. Again, for those of you paying attention in the last chapter, you remember, part 9, sub point 2 and 3, right?

How then can character be a qualification for anything?

If you can make a claim to character, you are ultimately saying you can control the good that you do; that by the power of your choice, you can execute GOOD actions. Hence, **your nature** is the reason for your good action.

Beep, wrong answer!

I invite you to re-read the opening paragraph of Calvin's chapter 3: He is expressly rejecting this "Neo-Pelagian sophist" point. In other words, Calvin considered those who believed that man could do GOOD after the new

Blight in the Vineyard

birth as part of a resurgence of the heretical Pelagian sect. So, all you heretics out there, if you presume the Pervasive Depravity metaphysic (subsequently Indwelling Sin), how can character ever be attributed to men? The only good you do, **ever**, is what God put in you. There is no appeal to a longstanding body of action that demonstrates qualification.

Calvin's assertions destroy moral development. To accept Calvin's premise is to say that Man is forever morally bankrupt. He can never do GOOD, because if he could, he would then no longer need God's grace. So, to say that character is a qualification for ministry is a myth. But like Bigfoot sightings, that doesn't mean the Neo-Pelagian SGM "sound doctrine" movers and shakers don't make the claim.

Here is how the SGM logic goes:
1. We are men of such great character. (Everyone oooohhhh and aaahhhh.)
2. Our humility is profound. (Everyone oooohhhh and aaahhhh.)
3. Here is what humility looks like. (They show everybody the SGM yardstick.)
4. See how we demonstrate our humility? (SGM leaders imitate the proscribed actions on the yardstick.)
5. For this great character, we are qualified to have authority. (Everybody nods because they've all been shown the yardstick.)
6. The authority we possess is to shepherd your soul. (Why, of course. They are men of great character after all.)
7. Follow us as we follow Christ. (Gosh . . . how easy is that?)

John Immel

They claim to be worthy of your deference by the power of their great moral development, as displayed by their longstanding action—a.k.a. character.

But John Calvin chopped down the cherry tree. John Calvin institutionalized the Augustinian Pervasive Depravity into post-Reformation Christian thinking. John Calvin eliminated the idea that personal actions can ever define a person as GOOD. John Calvin destroyed the idea of moral growth, and if moral growth is impossible, then character as a qualification for leadership is a myth.

Moral Narcissism

One of the most formative events in PDI/CLC/SGM history was the ouster of Larry Tomczak, cofounder of the PDI movement, marking an absolute shift in structure and ideological commitment.

In ages past, PDI demonstrated a long track record of kicking people to the curb if they failed to measure up to whatever standard they were defying people to jump over at the moment. Maybe those evictions were warranted; maybe they were not. But the bottom line for most anyone within leadership, job security was always a question. But one would think that being a cofounder would come with an understood exemption.

Oh well, I guess not.

Anyway, Larry Tomczak left PDI. Well, depending on who is telling the story, maybe he was booted. In the July 2000 of Charisma Magazine, Larry offers this commentary: "I came to a defining moment where I felt I no longer fit with the direction some of the other men were going with the ministry—doctrinally and directionally." Two years prior (1998) to this article, Larry self-published *What Do You Believe?* Mr. Tomczak comes out, in his own mitigating way, decisively opposed to Reformed Theology. (Mitigating/decisive: It is an "apostolic" paradox. Just enjoy the conundrum.)

This stands in direct contradiction to the letter that PDI circulated about Mr. Tomczak.

Here is a summary of the PDI letter:

> On October 15, 1997 Larry stepped down from his position in the Atlanta Church because of "patterns of sinful behavior which, on the basis of Scripture, disqualified him from serving in ministry." After four months of "necessary and redemptive disciplinary" sabbatical, Larry considered himself qualified to return to senior pastorate. The Leadership Team of PDI and the three men of the local Atlanta Church would not agree with ". . . Larry's assessment of himself. . ." because ". . . for a man simply cannot trust his own assessment of himself or determine unilaterally when he returns to ministry once he has been disqualified.[1]

These words tell us lots and lots about the prevailing assumptions within the ministry. We won't be covering all of the details of their squabble, but rather focusing on the underlying fraud perpetrated by all players.

In this section, I want you to witness the power of wrecking moral clarity. What follows is a potent object lesson.

PDI said in one of their letters concerning Larry:

> (Please understand that throughout this process specific details have been withheld because they involve sins that have been confessed to appropriate leaders within the Atlanta Church and the PDI leadership team. It has always been

---

[1]. The quotes within the paragraph are excerpted from a letter PDI circulated in October of 1997. This letter can be found in the www.scribd.com/sgmwikileaks section 3 in the subhead dealing with the blackmail of Larry Tomczak.

John Immel
> our desire to be merciful, and there is presently no justifiable reason for revealing any further details regarding these sins.)

The function of this paragraph is to end further conversation. SGM doesn't want to discuss the details of Larry's ouster so they pretend mercy by enforcing silence. What is the justification for their silence? Larry has **confessed**; we are satisfied. So, let us all hold our tongues about details.

I want you to see this: They are advocating silence because they were satisfied. They were justifying an information blackout about one of their organizational founders because they affirmed his conformity to **their** redemptive proscriptions. The PDI/SGM equation is: Sin + Confession + Leadership + no ministry = Appropriate Response = redemptive work.

So, let me ask this: Does this seem right? Does this seem like the correct standard of action? A man commits sin, confesses, and must step away from ministry for his actions? Just to be clear that we have our standards correct: A man confesses his sin to the appropriate leaders; the sin disqualifies him from ministry. The "redemptive" sabbatical is at the discretion of the confirming authority, because a man cannot know himself.

You sure you want this as the standard? SGM, is this really what you are committed to enforcing?

Yeah, huh?

This is too easy.

Note on his blog on February 4, 2008, Vicar Charles Joseph took Bill Belichick to task over some innocuous conduct at the Super Bowl in an article titled *Reflections of Super Bowl XLII.*[2]

---

2. Http://www.sovereigngraceministries.com/Blog/

Blight in the Vineyard

This article is evidence that the hive mind is no guarantee against avoiding error. Or maybe better said, team leadership does not assure the "safety of a multitude of councilors." If there was actual critical evaluation going on within the SGM hallowed halls, this article would never, should never, have seen the light of day. When a man presumes the power to manufacture motive (for a man he never met) and doctrine (to condemn him for actions that could have a half dozen explanations) in one article, the gears of "accountability" are a wonderful fiction.

I dealt with C.J.'s willingness to manufacture doctrine in an article on www.spiritualtyranny.com titled *Bill Belichick and Other Lessons in Silliness*.

Now I will point out the utter fraud underlying the whole article and illustrate the power behind wrecking moral clarity.

In *El Primo Doctrinal Mover and Shaker's* own words:

> Bill Belichick is not the worst sinner I know. **I am the worst sinner I know**. For I am most familiar with the countless sins I have committed against God, the countless times I have responded in a similar way as Mr. Belichick when I have encountered the test of adversity. Though it doesn't appear Bill Belichick is a humble man, I know I am not a humble man.

The next time you hear a church leader say "I'm the worst sinner I know . . ." ask him to define his peer group. If he's hanging around with Genghis Khan, Joseph Stalin, and Pol Pot, then maybe he's got an interesting story to tell. And if his peer group is Pope Benedict XVI, Billy Graham, and Mother Teresa, the finest advice is . . . run.

On its face, "I am the **worst** sinner I know . . ." is a comparative statement devoid of any real context or

post/Reflections-on-Super-Bowl-XLII.aspx. [April 08]

substance. It assumes a hierarchy of evil by saying "worst," but then pretends that all sin is functionally the same disqualifying wickedness compared to all men. So, in one sentence the greatest tyrant, with the highest body count, and a wrecker of nations, is on moral par with the average preacher who has noticed a few too many boobies in his lifetime, or the little kid who steals a coveted pack of gum.

Maybe "I am the worst sinner I **know**," could be a declaration of self-awareness, an effort to impress those from without by affirming intimacy with an internal evil. (A curious **self**-awareness in light of Pervasive Depravity since man can **never** know the depth of his own sin.) But while such self-abasing, self-deprecating comments seem like a righteous thing that preachers should say, this explanation is not really any better. The statement reveals a stunning moral narcissism: an intentional subjective shortsightedness that requires a man to ignore the larger world around him and refuse a sense of proportion in the actions of other men.

Is C.J. going to honestly say that he is unaware of Mao Zedong, John Gotti, and a host of other public enemies? What private life must one have to put it on the same moral footing as Caligula, or Diocletian, or Antiochus Epiphanes? What kind of secret genocidal, homicidal, pedophilic, sexual degenerate must this man be to make such a claim?

Did my argument finally get real enough to penetrate the stupor that must be on men's minds when Christian leaders utter such nonsense?

At **best**, the leader is parroting "vain philosophy," giving little thought to the true implications.

At **best**, the leader is afflicted with a case of Moral Narcissism: a disease that creates hierarchies of evil with inexplicit ethics designed to turn natural tendencies into the greatest moral depravity, and virtues to vice.

These are the best case scenarios.

And here is the worst case: This preamble is a high-minded sleight of hand to seduce men into collective moral fraud.

That is right, collective fraud.

Is the fraud not obvious? Larry confessed. C.J. confessed to being the worst sinner he knows. By self-admission, his sin is worse than Larry's. Larry's sin is disqualifying. C.J.'s sin must be disqualifying. Larry had to step down for a redemptive sabbatical. By definition, C.J. should step down for the same redemptive sabbatical. Larry could not return unilaterally because he cannot know himself. C.J. should not be able to unilaterally return; his judgment being equally flawed.

C.J. is lying about so many things but two are obvious. He is lying about being the worst sinner or he lied about the proscription for Larry. So, which lie disqualifies him?

If someone truly is the worst sinner, meaning he is committing sins of wanton destruction, one expression of humility would be to self-evaluate his behavior and confess his error. But here is the issue: Would this man of actionable moral failing become the poster child for "humble" leadership?

Don't be absurd. Forget the genocidal pedophile destroying nations. We don't even tolerate the smallest failing in leaders that offend our most delicate sensibilities—sex with the church secretary, molesting altar boys, building the PTL club with the emotional extortion of old ladies. If a leader confesses actual sin, actual guilt, we put a scarlet letter around his neck and drive him from the pulpit soonest. But to our shame, if a leader confesses theoretical sin, theoretical guilt, that

John Immel

places his actions on the same moral par with Genghis Khan, we oooh and aaahhhh and applaud his manifest humility, diving head first into the moralistic sleight of hand.

One we call humility. The other we call hypocrisy. What is the difference? One guy is being honest.

Ethics are the product of a specific set of values that sustain and preserve life. Law is the cultural agreed upon standards of value. Guilt is the unjustified violation of another individual. Justice is the manifestation of proportional recompense for that violation. Real guilt can **only** be ascribed to specific failings of ethics or law.

We all know this and act accordingly.

We all resist the accusation of guilt when we know we are innocent. We are hard-wired to demand justification for the innocent. We do it so implicitly that it is strange that I should even have to point it out. But a preacher can trot out some pretentious humility and we all wilt under the theoretical guilt.

This is philosophy in action. This is a full-on demonstration of the power of integrated ideas. These seven words, "I am the greatest sinner I know," are the distilled essence of our current American Christian worldview. So potent are those ideas that it never occurs to us to evaluate the wreckage of our moral clarity.

The crowbar prying us apart:
- Humility = self-abasement
- Humility = qualification
- Humility = leadership

The more self-deprecating a man is, the more we attribute humility to his moral makeup. The more humility we grant, the more qualification we assume. The more qualification we take for granted, the more uncritical we are of what comes out of his mouth.

And here is the disaster: True humility has nothing to do with self-effacing, self-deprecating, self-denying, anti-self commentary. We inherited all that rot from philosophical sons of Calvin: Immanuel Kant and Auguste Comte. They fully systemized the moral disaster of Altruism into the modern mind. True humility **requires** a rigorous honest personal assessment that includes vices and **virtues**. By the Calvinist/Kantian definition, this is impossible. Under the current moral worldview, man can posses no moral or ethical strength. The result is the renunciation of any real virtue—real ability, real value, real achievement—and the destruction of moral proportion.

Think of it this way. How can you measure an inch if you are required to denounce **your** ability to count tick marks on a yardstick? How can you measure an inch, if the yardstick is compelled to sell out its increments and measure everything equally?

Regularly, we see this underlying cultural philosophy on TV. Pick a sport. The greatest athlete of that sport by any observable measure is prohibited in polite company from overtly saying he is the best. Our cultural morality demands that he renounce any claim to his own greatness and pretend that some deep-seated depravity disqualifies on every level. This seems trivial but somehow appropriate because we have been spoon-fed the Calvin/Kantian ethic for so long that we refuse to conceive anything else. And besides it is very, very hard to feel sorry for some athletically superior millionaire. So who really cares what inequity this might represent?

But the issue is not the athlete or his undisputed achievement. The issue is the destruction of objective measure by disallowing those with ability to advance a

John Immel

higher standard. The more able a man, the more disqualified he becomes to advocate his ability. This has seeped into every crevasse of our religious, social, and political life.

Listen to our social arguments and the greatest public villains are those of the greatest power to create wealth, those with the clearest claims to personal value, those with the greatest mastery of ethics. The inevitable conclusion of this logic makes the most degenerate, incompetent, useless man the standard.

Just so everyone can see this is not a mere abstraction, let me make this personal. How many preachers—men who have a high school education and **maybe** spent two years at some Bible college listening to the indoctrination *du jour*—decide to start a K through 12 school? Somehow the path to a thousand church attendees magically qualifies him to demand that the professional educators in his congregation quit their jobs, accept a pittance for compensation, and subordinate their professional understanding to his edicts. The church leader decides that the professional ability of career educators, demonstrated by decades of experience, is secondary to his authority and vision. Market value and professional expertise are verboten conversations up against a mythical humility and subordination to the most scholastically, educationally ignorant man in the room.

Do you want to know why American culture is in such shambles? This is it. If **all** action is functionally depraved, then no standard of ethics exists. Man can lay no claim to his ability. He is compelled to denounce the very parts of his existence that give the highest pleasure: work, achievement, self-satisfaction, and moral clarity. Since this makes **righteous pleasure**[3] an oxymoron, what is left

---

3. These ideas are not just a contemporary aberration to

Blight in the Vineyard

but to participate in every debauchery humanity can invent? Everyone is just a wretched old sinner anyway. Eat, drink, stupefy your mind, for tomorrow the Christian God kills us all and sorts us as He sees fit. Or maybe it is the Muslim God who kills us all and sorts them out. What is the difference? At the end of the day, we are all judged by forces beyond our abilities.

Now back to the function behind C.J.'s moral narcissism. This entire posturing preamble to criticizing football Bill is pretense to some serious moral fraud, fraud, fraud, fraud, fraud. C.J. has no intention of acting consistently with his proclamations. He knows full well that he considers some sins greater than others. He knows full well that he does not count his sins among the

---

Christian doctrine. Note Luther's comments on the deception of *righteous pleasure*:

"Meanwhile, however, he does not observe his heart, does not note the reason why he is leading such a fine, good life, that he is merely covering the old hypocrite in his heart with such a beautiful life. . . . "For if he looked at himself right, at his own heart, he would discover that he is doing all these things with dislike and out of compulsion; that he fears hell or seeks heaven, if not also far more insignificant matters, namely, honor, goods, heath; and that he is motivated by the fear of shame or harm or diseases. . . . . "The face of Moses is, therefore, covered for him, that is, he does not recognize the meaning of the Law—**that it wasn't to be fulfilled with joyful, free, cheerful will. Just so an unchaste person, when asked why he commits the act, can only answer: Because of the pleasure I find in it. For he commits it for the sake of neither reward nor punishment, does not proposes to gain anything by it or to escape any evil through it.**

"Such pleasure the Law would also find in us, so that when you ask a chaste person why he is chaste, he should say: Not for the sake of heaven or hell, not for the sake of honor or shame, but simply because it appears to me to be very find, and I heartily approve of it even if it were not commanded." (Emphasis mine)

The Walch Edition of Luther's Works dates from 1740-1753 and is sometimes referred to as the St. Louis version, (1885 - 1910). The section above is taken from 11:81ff.

greater—disqualifying—failings. The sole function of his moral narcissism is to vet his superior self-assessment compared to other men (who fail to stare at their own bellybutton with sufficient intensity—Bill Belichick, Larry Tomczak, Charles Schmidt) so he can manufacture whatever doctrine he chooses. C.J. knows full well that he considers his conduct a manifestation of character, of his longstanding capacity to do GOOD. C.J. knows full well that he considers that moral superiority a qualification for his governing authority. And more importantly, if he were such a wretched, genocidal, homicidal, pedophilic sexual degenerate—that is if he were really the **worst** sinner—men demanding "accountability" to **any** ethical standard would have deposed him long ago. The fact that there is no formal letter circulated by PDI/CLC/SGM for C.J.'s patterns of sinful behavior illustrates the fraud of the moral demagoguery.

The only reason *El Primo Doctrinal Mover and Shaker* gets away with this schizophrenia is because his moral narcissism seduces us to mindless non-mental non-reflection. We lay down our minds and tolerate absurdities. And this is the evil goal of the whole charade. Make no mistake. His moral narcissism is in service to this end: He wants people to accept **their** theoretical fallibility by emulating **his** theoretical guilt. The words are platitudes and worse than lies because it is moral navel-gazing designed to perpetrate a powerful manipulation: to get you to defer critical evaluation to accept any moral assertion, which is exactly how C.J. used the above preamble in the original article.

And herein is the wreckage of moral clarity. Think of the enormous power this gives a man. He **manufactures** anything into the highest moral failing and in the very next moment can **do** anything and be guilty of no disqualifying action because "he's just the worst sinner he knows." This one-two punch is the power to disqualify any virtue and trivialize any vice. This ultimately destroys all human value. Here is the practical result: There is no objective standard because there is no attainable virtue. This is the root of moral relativism and the flip side of the antinomian coin.

This is exactly how all authoritarians justify slaughter on one hand and condemn men to hell for the most trivial manifestation of "sinful attitude" on the other. This is how leaders play down the actions of a child molester, (because he can admit to being the greatest sinner) but condemn the parents of the molested child because they were unforgiving. This is how the most incompetent people in church remain in charge. Performance, ability, and measuring objective outcomes are all subordinate to being able to parrot self-sacrificing, self-deprecating rot. People are not rewarded equal to their competence (or incompetence) but rather granted authority based on a public confessional statement. This elevates the achievement of doctrinal precision over the lives of men. This is how we can make the pursuit of doctrine a greater value than human life and let the invalid lay on the mat because to heal him would violate Torah. This is how Man ignores that the "Sabbath was created for man, not man for the Sabbath." This is exactly how the church strains at gnats and swallows camels. It wrecks all ethical standards by wrecking man.

And when "authorities" can manufacture all moral standards, they have . . .

Absolute Control

I want to revisit the PDI letter summary to drill down on the power of wrecking moral clarity. I now want to

John Immel

show how much power this gives leadership.

Note this again from above:

> The Leadership team of PDI and the three men of the local Atlanta Church would not agree with "... **Larry's assessment of himself . . .**" because "... **for a man simply cannot trust his own assessment of himself or determine unilaterally when he returns to ministry once he has been disqualified.**"

Mentally reflect on the bolded sentence. Consider everything that we have discussed. Think about the doctrine of Pervasive Depravity—absolute self-blinding, self-deceiving evil resides within us all. Remember chapter 4 and the discussion on assumptions, presuppositions, and filters and the implicit power of ideas to shade the meaning of ideas and events. The bolded summation above is potent object lesson for the power of filters to define the judgment brought to bear on Larry Tomczak.

Uh, for those of you who have been paying attention, when can a man trust his self-assessment?

This question is rhetorical and shows forth the fraud of the assertion. Calvinism's foundational allegation is that a man cannot know his sinful heart. At no point can a man trust his self-assessment. The very need to submit, to join the group, to be part of the larger Christian collective is so that environment holds man, compels man to good action. By definition, there is no sabbatical long enough to reinstate a man's self-assessment, which means that SGM's motive for keeping Larry on ice had other ends.

What were those ends? Well, some fifteen years after the event, the truth has emerged and the function was to shut Larry down. We will address the details in a moment. But before we do, let's pretend that the SGM WikiLeaks had never happened. Let us pretend that there was no extortion and the function of the extortion was to keep

Larry from speaking out against the emerging Calvinist doctrine.

You don't need to see his identification.

These are not the droids you want.

You can go about your business.

Move along.

. . .

. . .

. . .

See, the Jedi mind trick works.

Let us review so we can get a scope of the doctrinal and moral manipulation.

Character is longstanding good action, right?

The only reason **time** would have any relevance is if a man could lay claim to longstanding body of good action to demonstrate his character. Jedi, mentally reflect. How is this possible? How can man ever lay claim to what is undisputedly God's Sovereign appointment?

By doctrinal necessity, man can never lay claim to doing GOOD. In Calvin's own words, ". . . everything from the heart of man is damnable. . . ." Therefore, at no point can man claim control of his good actions. Good action is the sole purview of Sovereign appointment. This is the P in T.U.L.I.P. This is the P in Perseverance of the Saints. But to say that man has character is to say that he has control over GOOD action. If he has control over GOOD action, he must have Free Will to act on the GOOD that he knows. Yet under the Reformed Theology standard, we must extract human agency from the redemptive/sanctification equation.

What then does Man do in the redemptive process?

The proper distinction between Law and Gospel says that the sum of Man's role is appropriate despair over an **awareness** of Sin.[4] Or said better, Sin awareness is

---

4. Of course, everyone knows to what I am referring, right?

inspired by the condemning of Law that produces despair. The Gospel is God's sovereign imputation of Grace that inspires an awareness that manifests as confession.

Listen to what is really at the core of Mystic Despotism teaching. No matter how often modern shills try to introduce the concepts of freedom, and "grace," and pleasure, and human change into their teaching, no matter how often they pretend that there is something beyond the academic understanding of depravity, they must default to these underlying proclamations:

- "Don't sin."
- "You're a sinner."
- "You should be visibly moved by the cross."
- "Confess your sin."
- "Don't sin."
- "You are a sinner."
- "You should be visibly moved by the cross."
- "Confess your sin."

There is nothing else to the sanctified life but this endless inescapable vortex.

Strictly speaking, confession is the sum of "righteous" human action. And even that action is facilitated by faith. Faith is wholly and entirely imputed by God. Therefore, the sum of human agency, the sum of human "redemptive" action is opening your mouth and hope that God fills it with a confession. That is it. Perseverance in His righteous

---

Martin Luther, in his Sermon On Galatians (1532), said you might not be a Christian if you don't. "This difference between the Law and the Gospel is the height of knowledge in Christendom. Every person and all persons who assume or glory in the name of Christian should know and be able to state this difference. If this ability is lacking, one cannot tell a Christian from a heathen or a Jew; of such supreme importance is this differentiation. This is why St. Paul so strongly insists on a clean-cut and proper differentiating of

standards is the gift of Grace appointed upon Election. If you fail to persist, it sucks to be you, because it means you were not really picked.

I am going to hammer this home: The T in T.U.L.I.P. means there is no human agency in righteous conduct. The doctrines are quick to condemn an individual's actions as morally bankrupt and therefore disqualified to do GOOD, but somehow that does not extend to those in leadership. But human "salvific" action is still **human** even if the man committing the action has Pastor in front of his name. So if there is no human agency in God's plan, this would include a church leader's human agency to affect change on behalf of someone else. That is orthodoxy's inescapable extension.

The inconsistency within the doctrine plays out over the question of character as qualification for ministry. Preachers want to play both sides of the Pervasive Depravity fence. They insist that man is incapable of choosing GOOD and therefore needs the hand of oversight and covering to enforce/validate his GOOD actions and in the next breath say that the qualification for ministry is longstanding, observable, measurable character. And here is the full rational disaster of the "logic." If depravity is our metaphysical assumption, then environment is **required** to enforce action. But if a man has character—and thereby qualified for ministry—he cannot be metaphysically depraved.

So, now back to the Larry issue. According to the "sound doctrine" of the Reformation kind, Larry fulfilled the only biblical standard of redemptive action: He confessed. For God to be **sound** to the doctrine being ascribed Him, He cannot ask Larry to give what Larry does not have.

That means that SGM leadership demanded something in addition to the confession, which means they

---

these two doctrines."

John Immel

overstepped the bounds of "sound doctrine." Somehow they are seeking to take credit for affecting GOOD action, by imposing their judgment as the measure of righteous standard. But this is a doctrinal absurdity. There is **no** human agency in God's plan of salvation. And that would include **their action.**

Do they think God is the author of sovereign grace or not? If it is sovereign, then what do **they** bring to the equation? How are they at any point relevant to sanctification?

The answer is, by their own doctrinal advocacy, they are not relevant to sanctification. And herein is the real function of the doctrine of Pervasive Depravity revealed to any who will actually look. Condemning Larry's assessment of himself is a full-on effort to steal volitional judgment out an individual's metaphysical existence. Booting Larry Tomczak had nothing to do with a higher moral standard, or the aspiration to the purest righteous standard. Larry is only relevant to the issue because he shared, on some level, the moral authority to shape the SGM worldview. But that worldview can suffer no rational challenge. It needs unconditional control of all definitions of TRUTH to sustain its autocratic existence. Using the Doctrine of Pervasive depravity to embezzle free will from man is the ultimate weapon **against** human existence. This weapon gives Mystic Despots the ability to wreck moral clarity and thereby destroy any foundation for critical enquiry.

Make no mistake; the goal is absolute control over the lives of men.

18.5
Why SGM Is Not a Cult

> Cults are easy to get into and hard to get out of. Covenant Life Church is hard to get into and easy to get out of.
>
> —Robin Boisvert

> Don't tell anyone, but on the pagan day of the sun god Ra, I kneel at the foot of an ancient instrument of torture and consume ritualistic symbols of blood and flesh. . . .And if any of you care to join me, come to the Harvard chapel on Sunday, kneel beneath the crucifix, and take Holy Communion.
>
> —Dan Brown

> It is a truism that almost any sect, cult, or religion will legislate its creed into law if it acquires the political power to do so.
>
> —Robert A. Heinlein

OK. With everything I've said to this point, this section should finally make sense. Robin Boisvert really did preempt the Cult/Covenant Life equation in one of our pastoral conversations. As I said in chapter 7, that was all him, which means the leadership of PDI/CLC/SGM is sensitive to the charge, which probably means they've heard it from many quarters. This is a wonderful irony. They like to point out that if many people observe the same "sinful" behavior, it must be true. But if they actually applied that standard to their conduct, they would have long since packed up shop.

John Immel

Anyway, enough of my love affair with irony and let me weigh in on this very issue.

Two temptations exist for readers of this book. Marginalize me, thereby reducing my comments as raving trivialities. Or marginalize PDI/CLC/SGM, thereby reducing them to a religious aberration and dismissing the problem as merely a bad apple in a very large barrel.

As to the first temptation, *shrug*. That is OK. I have a very long history of being proved right. I'm patient. People ignore me for a while and then come back and shake my hand: "You were right." To which, in my never to be Kantian disinterest, I universally reply: "Told you so."

>snicker<

As for the second temptation, this is augmented by being one of the leading blogosphere criticisms. With regularity, someone on the Ethernet insists that SGM is a cult.

This accusation immediately inspires this image: PDI/CLC/SGM leadership as a clan of patterned bald men, hiding tails and cloven hooves underneath black robes, chanting over Harry Potter books, and placing pencils under crystal pyramids.

You giggle at my absurdity, but this is what people envision when they hear detractors say cult. And this is exactly why the accusation gets zero traction.

PDI/CLC/SGM members have a noticeable reluctance to engage people outside the very strict realm of their church experience. The counterculture flavor of member social interaction is very hard to miss; it is almost in the DNA. Inevitably, outsiders find out that SGM has "approved" reading lists, and mandatory social functions, and a curiously homogenous collective expression. They find out because members talk endlessly of these differences: applauding the SGM way or frowning at something that is

Blight in the Vineyard

not SGM-approved. Then stories emerge where members claim to need pastoral approval for standard life decisions. Then a story of some potent dictatorial control surfaces and everyone starts chanting cult, cult, cult! All of these details, combined with some underlying manipulation of governmental force, and cult seem like a good descriptor.

But here is the problem.

The PDI/CLC/SGM men are upper middle class, sophisticated, and winsome. They overwhelm with how very normal, how very right, how very like everybody they really are. They are self-effacing, and self-deprecating, and have mastered the art of making everyone else in the room feel important by being associated with them. As I said in the beginning of the book, their presentation is a sweet mix: elitism so draped in the language of humility and character that the spice only lingers on the tongue for a moment before the rush of professional, winsome, culturally refined social acceptance slides down the throat and makes a ball of warmth in the soul. And then comes the aperitif of practical life instruction balanced with a lingering spiritual wonder.

And it isn't fake. It isn't some massive Svengali[1] act that beguiles people into dropping their guard. The bottom line is you would like them if you met them.

Their move to Reformed Theology was an overt effort to gain credibility by declaring themselves members of what they consider to be **the** historic Christian fraternity. They love to tell people they just believe what everybody has believed. They have a unique presentation of time-tested

---

1. From the George Du Maurier novel, *Trilby*, published in 1894, but in the modern mind better known by the movie starring Peter O'Toole and Jodie Foster. In modern parlance, the word has come to mean an evil hypnotist that beguiles people into doing his bidding.

John Immel

truths. The differences are nonessentials at best and at worst, mere eccentricities.

People come to see what the fuss is and walk into Mayberry RFD with a '60s rock concert energy and color. They see expressive Christianity combined with outwardly, culturally respectful children and preaching that keeps saying how to organize life into neat hospital folds and go, "OMG! How can I get this where I go to church?"

As a leadership, they have always trended towards the authoritarian model of Christianity, and PDI/CLC/SGM made a tactically brilliant move when they adopted Reformed Theology. That philosophy gave them the metaphysical progression that undergirds their governmental worldview and justifies their inclinations. They were in much greater danger of having the cult title wrapped around their neck from the time they were directly part of the Charismatic Renewal. When the marquee says Independent Church, the congregation's pathological determination to never utter unflattering words about the leadership—the homogenous bowing, smiling, and adulation for the pastorate—and heavy-handed authoritarianism look very different. As an independent church, what is the validation of authority? I'm an Apostle. I'm a Prophet.

Yeah? Says who?

But as a member of the historic Reformed Theology fraternity, no one really asks such a question. By preaching what "everyone" has always preached, they must be authentic. The PDI/CLC/SGM appeals to Reformed Theology as the foundational ideology gives them a get-out-of-cult status free card. Here is why.

The historic definition of cult—at least for the academic, doctrinal-minded—is related to confessions.

Blight in the Vineyard

"Cult," as a rule, is defined by a departure from orthodox catechism. But in this instance, the SGM leaders get a big dividend. The appeal to Orthodox is what saves SGM from real scrutiny. For the most part, the Apostle's Creed captures the elements of historic doctrinal accuracy: virgin birth, Trinity, Jesus made flesh, dead, buried, resurrected on the third day, et cetera.

The only way to unravel what happens within the walls of SGM is to fully grasp the cause and effect of the ideas to which they are committed. Those ideas are not the product of some universe-chanting, messiah complex Jim Jones wannabe. PDI/CLC/SGM has doctrinal statements aplenty. This has one function: to vet their authenticity and therefore affirm their authority.

So, here is what happens. Stories of their behavior come to the attention of the American Christianity celebrities and denominational big dogs. The big dogs hear cult and immediately sniff around for deviations from historic creeds and find a pathological adherence to those creeds. The big dogs go, "Woof!" which in Lassie speak means, "Nothing scandalous here." The denominational big dogs have long since decided that SGM is part of the big Reformation fraternity. The major players in the essentially reformed movement have long since decided that that they are all one big happy family and come out in defense of SGM. So the cult label dies, and the detractors look like raving lunatics.

Let me tell you straight out. SGM is not a cult, nor are they in the vernacular of the polite euphuism "displaying cultic behavior." Detractors need to stop giving them the greatest gift of all: irrational criticism. They are not a cult. SGM is merely acting out the logical extension of the doctrines under discussion. The leadership within SGM has been meticulous in execution of each "logical" step

John Immel

within the Puritan construct. And for all the reasons we have talked about, such "single-mindedness," and "humility," and self-proclaimed "selflessness" look really, really good to like-minded men in search of a justification for their own authority to dictate ideas. SGM receives no critical review because their "peers" are in foundational agreement. The only thing really being discussed at the denominational big dog level is over HOW MUCH autocratic control should they really wield.

There is plenty of rational criticism to offer, but it cannot be successfully leveled trying to straddle the ideological fence. SGM is deserving of intense and unrelenting critical review. There are serious problems with the content of their method and practice and the fruit is out there for anyone to see if they would only look past the marketing and packaging. But people are unwilling to take a hard look at the foundations because the realities call into question the core of dearly held beliefs. SGM is executing profound tyranny but not because they are preaching cultic doctrine. Their tyranny is derived from being consistent with historic Platonist/Augustinian philosophy under review. They are rigorous in their execution of their assumptions, presuppositions, and filters. Their zeal for doctrinal precision is the binding substance of SGM communal solidarity. Their use of authority enforces their group identity by removing any balancing power.

SGM is single-minded in their devotion and zeal to execute the inevitable conclusions of central Christian "Orthodox" doctrine. And in just a few more pages, you will be able to see why this is much, much worse than any cult.

19
Morality and the Sociopolitical Thingy

> A man's admiration for absolute government is proportionate to the contempt he feels for those around him.
>
> —Alexis de Tocqueville

> It was this very atheistic Declaration [of Independence] which had inspired the "higher law" doctrine of the radical antislavery men. If the mischievous abolitionists had only followed the Bible instead of the godless Declaration, they would have been bound to acknowledge that human bondage was divinely ordained. The mission of southerners was therefore clear; they must defend the word of God against abolitionist infidels.
>
> —Thomas Smyth, minister of 2nd Presbyterian Church of Charleston, S.C. 11/21/1861

> The State is the realization of the ethical idea.
>
> —G.W.F. Hegel

I'm going to pull back to the 5,000-foot view because I want to illustrate the broader picture.

In as much as I can be presumptuous and assign homework, here it is. Raise your eyes and ears to the social and political horizon. Start listening to the national and international discussion through the prism of moral advocacy. Of course, when I say morality, everyone assumes I'm talking about what people do with body parts as if sexual practice is the sum of moral conduct. While there are sexual moral standards, human sexuality is the leaf on the very end of the philosophical tree. The true force of morality starts long before we get to people baring skin at embarrassing moments.

Contrary to popular belief, Christianity is not the only group advocating morality in public discourse. To be sure, most of America's current political fight over social welfare and constitutional authority are rooted on moral arguments. To my great dismay, half the people talking don't realize it is a fight over morality. Those voices defending "freedom" are offering fiscal or mechanical or scientific justifications and getting their butt kicked in spite of the truth behind their urging. And this is because both sides have conceded the same moral premise: Man is incompetent, selfish, depraved, and a cog in a broader collective reality.

What form of social and political structure must one create when everyone assumes that man is **incompetent** and **collectively subordinate**? What choice does one have but to advance governmental structures that fetter man's existence?

Now flip this around. What social and political structure must one advocate when everyone expects that man is **competent** and **individually culpable**? What choice does one have but to craft a structure that follows this preamble?

> When, in the course of human events, it becomes necessary for one people to dissolve the political bands which have connected them with another, and to assume among the powers of the earth, the separate and equal station to which the laws of nature and of nature's God entitle them, a decent respect to the opinions of mankind requires that they should declare the causes which impel them to the separation.

Blight in the Vineyard

The above two questions turn on the morality at the root of both metaphysical assumptions. **Incompetent and collectively subordinate** Man is the core of European Christian thought, which is why European Collectivism has long been the source of tyranny in Western thought. The ideas persist because the source of the ideas has never suffered a prevailing challenge, because a challenge is seen as an assault on God. Thinking is often portrayed as divine treason so some people decide that God is the problem and rightly concludes that the only way to argue for freedom is to advocate atheism. But most people are unwilling to deny the existence of God. Though they may never be able to prove His existence to anyone else's satisfaction, they are hard-pressed to deny the glaring TRUTH blazing forth from creation and reject a Creator. They are caught in the trap of having to embrace ideas that demand slavery for fear of being insubordinate to God. They cannot sustain the irreconcilable worldviews of Freedom vs. Subordination. They cannot find any rational means to integrate how "secular," competent, individually culpable government can work when man is "Christian," incompetent, and collectively subordinate. Most people do not have the tools to enter the Arena of Ideas and do battle, so the philosophical system based on man's depravity wins by intellectual neglect in the face of Mystic Despotism.

So, it is no accident that we are seeing a resurgence of European Religion concurrent with a tidal wave of European Collectivism into American political life. The result is a catastrophic erosion of our national identity under a relentless moral assault.

The cruelest irony is that for all of America's grandeur and unmatched success—by almost every

John Immel

measure, spanning the whole of world history—she struggles with the value of her identity. So pervasive is her contemporary crisis of worth that the conversation fodder in the pubs—after exhausting three-hour Jägermeister stories—is the open concern that "the rest of the world does not like us." When Joe Sixpack cares one iota what the French say about American existence or whether Kim Jong-il looks down his nose at our lives, the message of depravity is destroying us at the root.

And Church social commentary is no better. It is not uncommon to hear the average benign preacher say with a straight face, "I don't want to be a typical American." To be followed by a cavalcade of "Amen. Preach it, brother." Spurred on by collective agreement, the mostly benign preacher will then, with perfect assurance, flip open his Bible and start thumping the pulpit about the great depravities of man to illustrate the cultural arrogance of American apostasy.

To which I want to respond, "You mean the typical American that shed his blood on the beaches of Omaha? Or in the Philippines? Or in North Korea? Or liberated Afghanistan?"

"Or the typical America that has been responsible for financing and participating in the greatest missionary outreach in world history in the last fifty years?"

"Or the typical American whose ingenuity and resourcefulness is responsible for 90 percent of all technological advancement in the world?"

"Or the typical American whose production success has fed the world for the bulk of the last two hundred years?"

Unfortunately, I rarely get to ask those questions as the mostly benign preacher filibusters his way through a Sunday sermon. Curiously enough, eventually, the mostly benign preacher will get around to applauding the virtues of the American Constitution and lay claim to its brilliance by insisting on Christian roots.

Remember what I said above? What doctrines do you preach if you believe man incompetent and collectively subordinate? The only logical conclusion is to destroy objective measure by disallowing those **with ability** to advance a higher standard. The more able a man is, the more disqualified he becomes to advocate his cause. This has seeped into every crevasse of our religious, social, and political life. What is true of individuals is also true of nations. By destroying the cause and effect between uniquely American ideas and her subsequent great action, this mostly benign preacher can engage in the moral denunciation above without ever taking into account the balancing virtues of American culture. He can pound the pulpit, railing against the individual errors of human action and make them equal to a prevailing apostasy.

Notice how often contemporary social arguments seek to make America (and her citizenry) the greatest social villains **because** of their success. Then notice how often these same critics demand that America (her citizenry) continue being successful so the world can eat at the public trough. The piglets scream, "Feed me, Seymour. . . ." and Seymour is impotent to say no to this little shop of horrors because the people with ability do not own themselves. They cannot morally object to what amounts to a little more than extortion by government force, because success is a gift, or an exploitation, or product of "winning life's lottery." Success can never be because of superior effort, or action, or ability, or ideas, so American culture is put down with all the zeal of Jonathan Edwards, sinners in the hands of an angry God.

John Immel

The inevitable conclusion of this moral equation makes the most degenerate **nations** the ethical standard.

Do you doubt me?

Really? Take a fast look at members of the United Nations.

How America's "human rights violations" can ever be on the same moral footing as the former Soviet Union or the current North Korean regime is beyond absurd.[1] But that moral equivalency is offered in public discourse regularly.

In the face of overwhelming proof that these ideas are at the very roots of tyranny and destruction, the average harmless preacher so mindlessly parroting the social argot of the day is falling in line with this very phenomena, making all of American vices equal to (or transcend) her virtues. And this presumes that he will allow American culture any virtue.

Considering Jesus' insistence on measuring bad trees by the nature of their fruit, I find it curious that Americans tolerate anything much that comes from the European Christian or political philosophy. If for no other reason, America has absolutely demonstrated how to do peace and freedom, and prosperity and generosity, and life better than anyone else . . . ever. And it is ridiculous that in the 21st century we are apologizing for the nature of our exceptionalism. We have freely and willingly exported the power of that exceptionalism anywhere in the world willing to have it.

But set the American track record aside for a moment and judge accurately the track record of Europe. For two millennia, religious strife and destruction has washed

---

1. For a full treatment of this very issue, see Natan Sharansky and Ron Dermer, *The Case for Democracy: The Power of Freedom to Overcome Tyranny and Terror* (New York: Public Affairs™, 2004).

Blight in the Vineyard

across the face of Europe fueled by the ideology that man does not own himself, man is a ward of the state, and the state owns TRUTH. History shows forth the tide of destruction **that** philosophical assumption creates in the hands of monarchists, oligarchs, papists, Calvinists, Puritans, Islamists, Marxists, collectivists, fascists, Fabians, and national socialists.

And this is no medieval aberration. Today, in the 21st century, the social democracies that dominate European polity are burning before our eyes merely because larger and larger segments of the culture demand that other "selfish" and "decadent" people refuse to give to everyone else. And these social movements are not limited to the atheistic Bolshevism of the old Soviet Union. The Catholic Center party movements and the Protestant Social Gospel ideologues are front and center, marching arm in arm with their atheistic AND Muslim social justice comrades. (Talk about curious bedfellows.)

This is the disaster of our chosen course. American Christianity is crawling into bed with overtly hostile ideologies. American Christianity is advocating the premise of those ideologies and therefore unable to reject their inevitable end. The end of these ideas is war. This is the same European religious despotic path, but we are patting ourselves on the back for being willing to speak of our great unending depravity, fully impressed with our moral narcissism. All the while, the rest of the world is desperately hoping the United States will snap out of it and come to their rescue once again.

But we cannot snap out of it because our leading thinkers are merely historical shills repackaging and resurrecting doctrinal justification for Protestant Papacy in modern American Piety. This is no easy feat because American intellectual heritage was founded on ideas that

John Immel

resisted European Mystic Despotism. And American Christianity had, at its root, the assumption of intellectual freedom and an utter distaste for collectivist doctrines. So to achieve the outcomes of old, they have dug back into history and revived the historic Platonist/Augustinian assumptions to justify doctrines of Dictated Good. These doctrines place one man, or a group of men, in seats of power to compel right action, which is to compel right ideas.

If there was ever a manifestation of the truth "you reap what you sow," the current social political age is it. Large segments of American Christianity have driven thinkers from their midst. The result is that no one is present within the local congregations to resist the ideological and theological disaster.

Take civic action? Take up the cause of persuading in the open square? How could someone suggest such unspiritual action?

We are insulted when people imply rebuking demons, and having yet one more prayer vigil will fail to change the political climate. Never once noticing that if praying was the only necessary thing, Jesus could have stayed on the Mount of Transfiguration blabbering away and all would have been well with the world. But whatever prayer achieved, Jesus deliberately took his ideas into public discourse for a free and open debate amongst the people. It was there that he impacted people because he impacted minds.

American Christianity has no interest in impacting minds because it is insulted that it should have to offer better ideas. So the only ideas it ever offers are the ones it steals from its European counterparts. This only serves to make us a bunch of intellectual schizophrenics advocating ideas that are mutually exclusive and

Blight in the Vineyard

wondering why the outcomes do not improve. We pound the pulpit proudly for our return to European Religion and in the next breath insist that God founded this country and Christians wrote the Constitution, never once realizing the two outcomes are diametrically opposed. The European Collectivism to which we are now laying claim is the very autocratic-oriented religion those Founding Fathers abandoned. The framers of our constitution were determined to created absolute barriers to the ascendancy of religious despotism in the United States.

The result is inevitable because you reap what you sow: We are planting the philosophical ideas of despotism deep into the hearts of the people. So just like our European religious forefathers, the American Church is aiding and abetting the rise of political tyrants. The American Church is doing what the European Religion has always done when History's Hitlers start beating the drums for hope and change. They become the leading force of pacifying the populace in the rise of every fascist, despotic state in the last 500 years. Christian leaders use doctrine to stifle inquiry because they cannot abide the barest critique from the pews, never once realizing that morally enforced intellectual passivity does not stay contained in the four walls of the church. People take that mindset to the streets. Once they learn the habitual dependence on authority's right to determine TRUTH, they are incapable of rendering effective individual judgment.

There is a reason that Marx called Religion the Opium of the Masses. There is a reason why Hitler courted the Catholics and the Lutherans—in the beginning. The easiest way to persuade the people that they shouldn't fight for liberty is to tell them: **"You are ineffective in**

John Immel

God's Kingdom if you don't play nice."

Passive people become empty people, primed for whoever will fill the void of their mind. The doctrines of Protestant Papacy are really doctrines designed to pacify the body politic. They are teachings designed to strip away the means and method of resistance by undermining your moral clarity to resist anything. Christians are heading for disaster because we have been primed to be compliant. We are being conditioned to believe that our spiritual function is conciliation, pacification, and appeasement. If we are a fountain of sweetness and light, somehow the world will get the point and be a better place to live.

But this never happens because a passive body politic has no power to resist tyranny. And a passive body politic was a core function of European Christianity in the medieval Three Estates. The social organization of Medieval Europe was enforced by the same Mystic Despotism. The same Mystic Despotism justified the Divine Right of Kings by insisting that all government was intended by God's hand, and therefore, all acts of despotism are just the way of a sinful world. And what can you really do?

Dear Jedi, we are at the crossroads of tyranny, and it is time we take a hard look at those who insist they are our covering

.

20
Covering

All hurricanes are acts of God because God controls the heavens. I believe that New Orleans had a level of sin that was offensive to God and they were recipients of the judgment of God for that.

—John Hagee

A society that will trade a little liberty for a little order will lose both, and deserve neither.

—Thomas Jefferson

When you see that trading is done, not by consent, but by compulsion, when you see that in order to produce, you need to obtain permission from men who produce nothing, when you see money flowing to those who deal, not in goods, but in favors, when you see that men get richer by graft and pull than by work, and your laws don't protect you against them, but protect them against you, when you see corruption being rewarded and honesty becoming a self-sacrifice, you may know that your society is doomed.

—Ayn Rand

Let us return one last time to the Larry Tomczak vs. SGM dealeo. We will be addressing the concept of covering that has gained so much traction in American Christian circles. The doctrine goes by different names and has a number of proponents who arrive at the same essential conclusions from different starting points. I won't rehash the names or the starting points, but the loose logic says that there is a spiritual authority structure (both good and evil) that manifests in a physical organization within the here and now. This otherworldly authority is conferred on Protestant Saints to combat the evil forces in the heavenly places and their counterparts on earth. The proclaimed function of this hierarchy is to **somehow** keep **something** from filtering down to those underneath the authoritarian umbrella. So, the process of sanctification and the daily outworking of life require a specific individual subordination to someone above. If you submit to someone in authority, you are covered. If one stays "under" the leaders, they will be shielded from life's bad stuff . . . kinda, sorta.

What does that mean practically? Well, addressing this issue is exactly why I am writing this chapter.

Let us pretend that SGM was Right

For the sake of this discussion, let us pretend that the Jedi Mind Trick is still in force. We know none of the available details of SGM's threat of extortion—Larry stays quiet in return for SGM leadership not spilling the beans on some problems with one of Larry's [then] minor children.

These are not the droids you seek.

Move along.

. . .

. . .

Larry and I talked at length about his part of the doctrinal refocus—his subsequent leaving/booting—starting in '96 and ending sometime in '97ish. From his account, he was made to sign a letter that he didn't write. He has his own take on what that meant. Whatever the truth of the events, here is the reality: He signed the letter endorsing the accusation. If he didn't think he was guilty of the charges, he should have refused to let SGM define the terms of the issue. If he really didn't think the letter or the consequence was warranted, then being compelled to sign it at pain of some other punitive measure represents dictatorial force to compel an unjust and immoral outcome. That is pretty close to the definition of tyranny. Which goes to the core of my comments—the specific nature of covering in context to what should be a slam-dunk opportunity for apostolic authority to blaze forth its relevance. Let us not lose sight of this glaring fact: PDI was Larry's co-brainchild. He called himself Apostle and demanded submission to his authority-ness. That demand would include the congregation and the sub-leaders, and sub sub-leaders of the egalitarian pyramid.

Not long after his ouster, Larry was stumping through the US claiming Apostolic authority and advocating that correct church government requires that pastors, and evangelists, and teacher, and prophets must come offer their gifts and callings to apostolic central planning. This is in exchange for the vaunted "covering." But this is the very doctrine to which he ultimately refused obedience.

Consider the scope of this event: He concludes that the doctrine is **accurate**, but the **application** by his PDI/CLC/SGM homeboys carried no moral **authority**.

Do you see the implicit conundrum?

Since the assumptions are the same, someone's "covering" is in error. If Larry's "covering" is disqualified, then SGM leadership were the only people acting consistently with the doctrine. They are the ones who brought force to bear to "cover" erroneous behavior. But if SGM's authority is in error, then where is Larry in all his

John Immel

apostolic covering glory? Where is the same zeal to bring force and correct the wrong? If his rejection of their moral authority is correct, there is a group of men who, by the terms of submission and authority and covering doctrine, are in desperate need of his apostolic glory to set things right. So, where is the proportional counteraction of nationally circulated denouncing letters and the open declaration of sinful behavioral patterns? Why the silence?

The reason I am seeking to enforce the Jedi Mind Trick is so that we can grant SGM some momentary credit for acting consistently with their doctrinal proclamations because it is essential that we see the fraud being brazenly perpetrated in the name of God.

If SGM acted correctly, there is no "offense" to be reconciled. There is no moral equivalency between Larry's and SGM's actions. In other words, Larry cannot say, "Guys, you wronged me. And therefore, you need to apologize." If SGM was correct to require Larry a redemptive sabbatical, the error is fully and entirely Larry's rejection of their right of action. There is no offense in the "you hurt my feelings" sense of the word.

By the terms of the covering doctrine in conjunction to the Calvinist construct, Larry was on the hook for subordinating his rational judgments to their edicts. He does not get to judge the SGM leadership actions in terms of Justice or Injustice. He doesn't get to judge. He does not get to hold out a separate doctrinal position. He doesn't get to disagree with the direction of the church doctrine. By definition, submission is a rational abandonment to someone else's rational conclusions.

This is important, so I am going to reiterate. Strip away all the rhetoric and the glossy veneer from the submission to authority doctrine and the teaching

Blight in the Vineyard

demands a self-imposed forfeit of rational faculties. "Covering" is what you are purchasing when you formally say, "I give you my brain and obedience to whatever you say." So, there is no Alakazam! Poof! "I disagree with your doctrinal refocus!" The moment Larry uttered the word "I," everything else that came out of his mouth is disqualified. He has abandoned the right to egoistic critical review. He possesses no right to object because he has no effective epistemological means to apply critical review.

This is why Pervasive Depravity is such a key element in the submission and authority doctrines. As I said before, depravity is the ultimate disqualifier, and a full justification why one man is—somehow—morally correct to stand in the stead of God and dictate "His" will to the spiritual barbarian masses. Larry cannot offer a counter-rational conclusion because the issue is authority and the power to compel cognitive compliance. Independent rationality is the stuff of cramped narrow perceptions and symptomatic of the church in captivity. Those in leadership are the sole owners of doctrinal conclusion: This is the essence of the submission and authority covering doctrines.

These doctrines are the very ideas that Larry proclaimed for years and demanded from those within his congregations. This teaching is what he has persisted in declaring since his leaving the SGM fold. This is the fealty he was proclaiming when he strapped the title Apostle around his neck. But more important, the very function of joining an "apostolic team" was the symbolic declaration of mutual subordination. He formally decided that the PDI hive mind was better at making rational conclusions than he was capable on his own. This forfeiture prevents Larry from objecting to PDI/SGM edicts. Whatever his disagreement, he is required to wait in the wings, out of ministry, until God changes the minds of those in authority. And this assumes that there is any change necessary. In the world of Sovereignty and Predestination, events are God's revealed will, so the "doctrinal refocus" is a manifestation of divine will. Being commanded to leave ministry is a function of God's dictate. So, sit down and shut up. The grownups are talking. When they want your opinion, they will give it to you.

Being consistent with the doctrinal predicate, Larry's actions—since his self-appointed split with the governing authorities—are a full-on lawless rejection of righteous church standard. By definition, Larry deserved his sabbatical. His lawlessness proves the truth behind the "patterns of sinful behavior" accusation. It stands to "reason" that the pattern was merely the precursor to his culminating action—a departure from the true faith. Being consistent with "sound doctrine," Larry's conduct is proof that God did not grant grace. Larry's departure is proof that he did not persevere, and his Christian confession is inauthentic. All ministry since his spiritual anarchy is in fact the function of deception, and the "fruit" of that ministry is false doctrine and false teaching. And the people that participated in his lawless rampage are false spiritual children.

SGM governing authority is acting appropriately, a benevolent judge who has the unenviable task of bringing a wayward son to heel, or winnowing out a budding heretic before he can do harm to the flock. Under this scenario, C. J. Mahaney is merely the lowly servant seeking to do the hard but necessary thing, refusing to let a man evade the true source of his deception: his sinful nature. To be sure, having flouted SGM judgments for the better part of fifteen years, the leadership would be fully within their

Blight in the Vineyard

rights to bring full-on heretical condemnation.

Larry was not free to play both sides of the doctrinal fence. Doctrine cannot be the highest charge **and** a minor disagreement at the same time. Pervasive Depravity **and** Ethical Egoism cannot live in the same metaphysical world. Submission to authority cannot be an absolute authentic Christian demand **and** a negotiable theory when it serves. Church leaders demanding rational subordination to their edicts are not free to eat at the smorgasbord of Christian ideas picking and choosing whatever satisfies their momentary appetites. Failure to live to the same standard, they compel the average pew-sitter to embrace what is called hypocrisy. So, this fiasco does not magically disappear because the parties say, "Oops, C.J. and Larry have kissed and made up. So, you just never mind."

In context, "reconciliation" has **one** definition: Larry steps away from all ministry, disbands all structures bearing his name, and proclaims everything he has touched, advocated, or taught as error. The only person who bears moral responsibility for proactive action is Larry Tomczak. He must reconcile himself to the original SGM plumb line. He must sit in SGM suspended animation until God sovereignly appoints whatever comes next.

Everything I just wrote presumes that all parties involved were fully consistent with the submission to authority and covering doctrines they are so quick to demand from those who sit in the pews. As we will soon see, this presumption has no basis in reality.

There is a cesspool of evasion and dodging swirling before our eyes. The public is being played for chumps by the primary players in this specific drama. For Larry and SGM to summarily declare the last decade and a half an "offense to be reconciled" is a raving trivialization. This linguistic manipulation lets the parties pretend they are pursuing some biblical high-mindedness while evading the true meaning of the specific conduct and treason to the very ideas they claim to hold so dear. The brazen contempt must be revealed for all its ugly disdain. I am going to hammer on this festering sore and repeat what I said above. If SGM acted **correctly**, then there is no "offense" to be reconciled. C.J. is admirable for being consistent with this own philosophical integrity, executing flawlessly the "righteous" practice the doctrines demand. There is no moral equivalency between Larry's and SGM's actions. Larry was not free to go do his own thing and start his own church. His authority was disqualified the moment he declared himself independent. And whatever wreckage that occurred within his family was merely the outworking of **his** sinful choices and the inevitable consequence of **his** unrighteous actions.

Did that finally get real enough for some of you? This is the review of the doctrine without all the cute proof text references. This is the ideological content without the marketing and packaging. This is the bare knuckles version of the one-two punch that this generation does not get much of. This is the gut level explanation without the fawning, bowing, witty self-deprecation that hides so many pastoral logical sleights of hand. They only get away with it because people turn their brain off.

Let us pretend that Larry was Right

OK, now I am undoing the Jedi Mind Trick. As aspiring Jedi masters with full and effective rational capabilities, I'm confident you saw through the ruse.

So, after a four-month "redemptive sabbatical," Larry

Blight in the Vineyard

decides to bolt the SGM covering authority because he doesn't agree with the trend towards Calvinism. Since this trend had been in steady ascendancy since 1991, it is a curious reality that he takes until late in 1996 to conclude that the doctrines are unpalatable. My, how convenient. Get charged with patterns of sinful behavior . . . Alakazam! Poof! It is the doctrine. It is the doctrine I say! Calvin bad. Me good! Me take ball and go home.

Anyway, I suspect that Larry Tomczak thought the "doctrinal refocus" could be merged with the existing charismatic worldview, thinking the additions of "sin" and "Cross-centered Christianity" necessary to combat the problems in American piety. It is in the Bible after all, and lots of people think that Calvin and Charismatic can live in the same world. And since Christians need the hive mind to be correct, then it must be true.

These "scriptural" ideas are just one big happy smorgasbord, and we can pick and choose whatever pleases our palate for the moment. No one is going to **make** me believe anything, so we can slurp down what we like and spit out the rest. If we are going to obsess on our faults for a few years, we can embrace the theory with gusto. What is the big deal? We can quibble over some vague theological exactness, but at the end of the day, there is no error. We are raising the bar. We are not like other churches. We are thinking big thoughts. We are reading thick books with big words. We are really cool—oops, we are wretched sinners.

It is always all fun and sins until somebody gets hurt. Suddenly the high-minded pretense and the groveling super spiritual, sin-sniffing, heresy-preoccupied preaching was transformed into the wicked political tool it was designed to be. Well, it was always that tool and had been used exactly like a political battering ram

John Immel

romping through people's lives for all those years. The only difference was it had finally gained enough moral authority within the SGM leadership structure to wreck Larry's life and as we shall see, wreck the lives of his family. Since he sowed rational neglect and the lack of doctrinal rebuttal due diligence for five years, it is no surprise that he reaped the whirlwind of his own apostolic complacency. Even if he would like to pretend that he was working "behind the scenes" to bring some balance, that explanation only illustrates incompetence. If he could not successfully counter doctrinal error that emerged over the course of five years within the very group he founded, how can he, at any point, be qualified to counter the big bad worldly wolf lurking outside the church? Complacency or incompetency, it doesn't matter. At the end of five years, the doctrines bit him in the submission and authority covering butt. He got caught in the SGM witch hunt vortex, and they presumed to romp through the deepest recesses of he, and his family's life.

When a man is guilty never to be proven innocent, the inquisitors found the evil they expected to find. Since guilty men are disqualified men, he was sent to the sidelines, wearing the scarlet letter "A," the price for being an Apostle, I guess. But Larry is not a sidelines guy. So, after four months of Reformed Theology navel-gazing, he decides that the sin and temptation gig is not for him. He engages his brain and concludes that he has a right to make up his own mind about leadership edicts and the SGM doctrinal refocus. "Oops . . . whatever I said before . . . never mind." Larry Tomczak emerges from his meditations a born again anti-Calvinist.

And SGM Central promptly said, "No, you are not."

That isn't an exact quote, but it is pretty close.

Just prior to the original release date for this book,

someone dumped about 600 pages of SGM internal documents onto the internet at http://www.scribd.com/sgmwikileaks. At first, I thought it would require a major rewrite of this specific chapter. But on further review, it became clear that my assessment remained exactly the same. To be sure, now that the details behind the event are available for review, the fraud of the covering doctrine is now a provable, brazen reality.

Larry Tomczak's silence in addressing SGM mistreatment has long since puzzled the broader PDI/SGM world. The disproportion between his treatment and the lack of his response has led to endless speculation on what could have so fully muzzled the wonder of his apostolic glory. As more and more stories of SGM abuse emerged, the conundrum grew ever more perplexing. As I said above, this seemed like a slam-dunk opportunity for him to blaze forth in covering wonder. Enquiring minds want to know: Why was the Apostle of Covering being vewwey, vewwey quwwieeet?

Well, now we know. Extortion.

As of the time of this writing, the person responsible for posting the internal documents for general consumption has not been revealed—well, at least their identity has not been revealed to me. Their identity is of little consequence, but the originator of the documents is rather important to this discussion. It turns out that Brent Detwiler former (or current depending on when you end up reading this) member of SGM leadership fame, kept meticulous notes on the sundry happenings within the SGM leadership. For various reasons, over the course of years, he was determined to confront C. J. Mahaney for a list of sins . . . to no avail. Hundreds of e-mail and letters and years later, C.J. remained intractable to

John Immel

Brent's efforts. The compilation of those documents was circulated amongst the SGM big dogs for roughly two years. Then in July of 2011, someone with access to these documents dumped them on the internet. It is my understanding that no one is challenging their authenticity. To be sure, SGM Central authority reacted to their content as if they were authentic, with their usual warnings to their congregation about reading things that were really none of their business. And Brent Detwiler has vouched for their sum, having joined the blogging world at www.brentdetwiler.com to weigh in on his efforts at reform within the SGM hallowed halls. Considering the detail presented (details that can be easily verified) and the players specifically named, it is highly unlikely that the documents are fraud.

I will not be detailing the sum of the documents. They are available online for consumption at www.scribd.com/sgmwikileaks and will remain available at my website www.blightinthevineyard.com/notes for the duration. However, I am going to direct your attention to part 3, subsection titled *C.J.'s Blackmailing of Larry Tomczak*. Starting in section 3 on page 131 (the document page number, not the PDF reader page designation), Brent chronicles the events with correspondence and commentary leading up to the moment that Larry steps down for his redemptive sabbatical. On page 135, the plot thickens. Brent notes a letter written on September 13, 1997 where Larry declares he is leaving for "a clear change in direction and doctrinal emphasis." That whole letter is not supplied, but C.J.'s response a mere five days later is supplied in total on page 135. The second paragraph says:

> Please know that if you do leave, (the thought is so grieving and all most inconceivable to me), it cannot be due to doctrinal differences. Your [September 13] letter is a serious (slanderous, actually, in its present form) misrepresentation of both the attitude and doctrinal position of the team. And there are those within PDI who hold a similar position as yours, and they see no reason to leave having only experience the support of the team in the midst of disagreement. No, trying to walk away due to supposed doctrinal disagreement is simply not legitimate. It appears to be fabricated to avoid the real issue.

And then further on, C.J. said this:

> And to attempt to describe your separation as due to doctrinal differences is simply not true. Larry, when you are ready to return to ministry cannot be your call. Given the sin revealed in your life and how imperceptive you have been, you are in no position to declare yourself mature and ready to return.

Anyone else ever notice that **every** uttered word that does not pass SGM muster is slanderous?

But anyway, like I said, Larry decided he was opposed to Calvinism, and C.J. said, "No, you're not."

And notice that most everything else I have been discussing is contained in C.J.'s words. C.J. is being utterly consistent with these doctrines . . . almost. He presumes Larry's rational incompetence. He presumes Larry's motive is flawed—he is using doctrine to cover for the real failing—moral turpitude. He presumes Larry's "immaturity," which is to say that he presumes to judge Larry's character. This means C.J. believes his character and judgment are by default superior. His "I'm the greatest sinner I know" is such pretentious rot.

John Immel

But in spite of C.J.'s doctrinal consistency, Larry was right. It was about the doctrine. No matter C.J.'s objection, it was always about the doctrine. Larry finally had a clear picture that his complacency had a price. He finally understood what so many others had long since encountered: the force of church government to compel people to commit to ideas and actions that were against their own judgment.[1] He finally grasped that the price of admission to the "sound doctrine" fraternity was the very sum of self. It sounds like a grand idea when **you** believe you are one of the Protestant Saints in charge of everyone else's life. But when it is **your** life being grazed over and picked through for the express purpose of destroying the sum of individual volitional judgment, it is no longer all fun and games. Larry was finally introduced to the fight of the ages: the ideological battle ground for man's existence.

You think this is me just exercising some literary hyperbole.

Yeah, huh?

Once it became clear that Larry was not going to go away quietly, the SGM leadership went into overdrive to do what they have always done when confronted with challenges to their authority: search and destroy. After a series of conversations where C.J. voiced some vague threats to tell the whole story behind Larry's "sins," there was a phone call on October 3, 1997 between C.J., Larry, and his wife, Doris. They had the foresight to secretly tape the conversation. On page 139, Brent details this exchange:[2]

---

[1]. Note on page 137, paragraph 2 of the SGM WikiLeaks documents, Larry Tomczak went on record refuting the judgments of the SGM leadership and rejecting their compulsory judgment from his earlier letters.

[2]. Transcript of phone conversation between C.J., Doris,

Blight in the Vineyard

C.J.: Doctrine is an unacceptable reason for leaving P.D.I.

Larry: C.J., I'm not in sync with any of the T.U.L.I.P. So, whether you agree or not, doctrine is one of the major reasons. I believe it is God's will to leave PDI and it does need to be included in any statement put forth.

C.J.: If you do that, then it will be necessary for us to give a more detailed explanation of your sins.

Larry: Justin's name has been floated out there when there's statements like revealing more details about my sin. What are you getting at?

C.J.: Justin's name isn't just floated out there, I'm stating it!

Larry: C.J., how can you do that after you encouraged Justin to confess everything, get it all out? Then when he did, you reassured him, "You have my word. It will never leave this room. Even our wives won't be told." I repeatedly reassured him: "C.J. is a man of his word. You needn't worry." Now you're talking of publically sharing the sins of my youth?!

C.J.: My statement was made in the context of that evening. If I knew then what you were going to do, I would have re-evaluated what I communicated.

Doris: C.J., are you aware that you are blackmailing Larry? You'll make no mention of Justin's sins, which he confessed and was forgiven of months ago, if Larry agrees with your statement. But you feel you have to warn the folks and go

---

and Larry Tomczak on October 3, 1997 [pp. 10-11]. Brent's note tells us there is much more to this conversation. This specific exchange occurs on page 10 and 11 of the transcript. It would be interesting to know what else is on that tape.

John Immel

> national with Justin's sins if Larry pushes the doctrinal button? C.J., you are blackmailing Larry to say what you want!

Justin is Larry's son. In 1997 he was a minor. Get the scope of what you just read. C.J.'s goal is to discredit Larry by exposing his son's sins. In a campaign to defend "Sound Doctrine," in an effort to silence an ideological opponent, C. J. Mahaney threatens to make the indiscretions of a minor child national public knowledge. Doris was right to call it blackmail, but that isn't really sufficient. Blackmail is merely the means. Beyond the illegality and the rank abandonment of any "Christ-like" pretense, what we just witnessed, what we just read, what lots of people who have heard this tape and read the transcript have failed to successfully name is the true core of C. J. Mahaney's actions. The moment he took aim on a minor child to shut down his father's doctrinal disagreement, he declared ideological war. If memory serves, there is another religion in the world that uses threats of harm to advance its ideological goals. So, are their methods biblical?

I told you from the beginning that this hinges on our affections and our fears. I told you in chapter 6 that Mystic Despots extort our compliance based on our highest values. And a man's family certainly tends to be at the top of his highest values list. And some of you, dear readers, still doubt my assessment that this is a Blight in the Vineyard? You doubt that the progression of these ideas executed to their logical end leads towards destruction? You doubt that orthodoxy is really the deep and abiding root of tyranny?

Evade my words at your own peril.

What no one seems willing to understand or name is this reality: SGM is in the Mystic Despotism business.

Blight in the Vineyard

They are utterly consistent with the doctrines in service to this specific end. No matter their big alligator tears and hand-wringing "grace, grace, grace" bromides, they are cold, and calculating, and fully intent on waging a planned war. So thorough was their actions against Larry they sought legal counsel. On page 160 and 161 of Brent's documents are two letters from lawyers detailing Georgia law and the subsequent legal ramifications for pursuing their course of action. The lawyers said it was a very bad idea to execute the strategy.

No matter how much C.J. would like to pretend it was all just one big misunderstanding, this was no idle threat spoken in the heat of the moment. The documents show this threat was repeated several times in the presence of many leaders and was held under considered deliberation. The fact that they abandoned the battle tactic does not mitigate anything. All it means is that they encountered a superior force that was not subject to their edicts. And having the wisdom of Sun Tzu, they chose not to fight. Well, maybe better said, they chose to go to war on a different battlefield. For almost two decades, for all intents and purposes, they refused to acknowledge Larry Tomczak's existence and let whatever rumor and speculation persist. The full-on implied message being that Larry was some form of habitual deceiver and evil public figure. And if that didn't work, they overtly condemned anyone who raised the subject with their perennial disqualifiers: gossip and slander. As Sun Tzu said, "All men can see these tactics whereby I conquer, but what none can see is the strategy out of which victory is evolved." If one cannot topple the World Trade Center from the bottom, try blowing it up from the top; a change of strategy does not change the ideological fight. Allahu Akbar!

John Immel

So, here is a question. What if Larry had not had the force of Georgia Law as his defender? What if the State had been subordinate to SGM edicts? What if state authority and SGM authority had been one and the same? Does that fill you with shivers and shakes? If it does, what does that tell you?

The answer to these questions is simple. Young Justin Tomczak would have been one more casualty in the endless tide of Puritan despots running over humanity in the name of God. One of the leading themes that the blogging world has revealed is the number of women and children caught in the vortex. Do a casual review of www.sgmsurvivors.com and www.sgmrefuge.com and notice how often women discuss the treatment of their children. Notice how often mothers comment on the longstanding distress the PDI/CLC/SGM experience had on their kids. Eventually, you will read stories that will make your stomach churn. And after about three of those stories, you will ask the obvious question: Where in the hell are the fathers? How could any self-respecting man let his wife and kids get chewed up and spit out like this?

The answer is simple. No man can be "self"-respecting under these doctrines. He cannot hold any value higher than what Church leadership demands. So when they say **sacrifice**, the automaton says, "Do you want me to hold the knife or will you?"

Man only sacrifices something of value if he has been told the destruction is in service to a higher morality. And the doctrine at hand overtly teaches that all human values are trivial to the pursuit of sound doctrine, and the definition of "sound" is commanded by authority. So, while some of you are vaguely shocked by extortion, it is important to grasp that C.J. is being utterly consistent when he threatens to put young Justin Tomczak in the national crosshairs. The reason he can represent the SGM leaderships as being "bound to integrity" to make these sins known is because the purity of the doctrine comes first, last, and always. **The purity of the authority must be defended at all cost**. And this is why (when it serves their purpose) the SGM leadership team has tended to treat Larry Tomczak like a bad memory. If they for a moment challenge C.J. in his conduct, they are ultimately challenging their very governing authority.

So, now let us turn our attention to the core issue, the ugly baby in the room that no one has the nerve to call ugly. How does this disastrous manifestation of moral, ethical, and doctrinal bankruptcy as perpetrated by the patriarchal thugs and pretentious Mystic Despots not qualify for apostolic intervention? If it doesn't rate the apostolic big dog bark, how about a mild pit yorkie whimper? How about some sign language of protest? At this rate, an emoticon eye roll would register some dissent.

Remember, Larry left because of doctrine. Doctrine was the motive power for his departure. Rational disagreement was used to leave SGM because of the break with Calvinist Doctrine. He affirmed over and over and over and over the problem was the doctrine. Larry correctly identified the injustice of his treatment centered in the body of Reformed Theology. He decided that the doctrine was error.

OK, so riddle me this: Is SGM still preaching Calvinism? How can there be reconciliation? Where is the ongoing effort to undo the practical error driven by the erroneous doctrine?

SGM has produced a tidal wave of Calvinist materials and delivered them to the masses. Where is Larry's

John Immel

proportional effort to undo the damage? He has written how many books in the last decade and a half? Only one effort at a "comprehensive" rebuttal to Calvinism was written titled *What do you Believe?* published in 1998 and that was pathetic. I've read papers written by college freshman coeds who wrote a more compelling review of Calvin's doctrine and they have never preached submission to their female apostolic glory. I fully expect that SGM Central got a copy, read it in forty-five minutes, and smiled at each other and said, "And what were we scared of?" That book told them all they ever needed to know: Larry, in all his apostolic covering glory, was no appreciable threat to their doctrinal domain. Larry who?

Larry has had fifteen years to get in the game and do what he insists covering is supposed to do: combat bad ideas. That was his self-written job description. By his own self-proclaimed social contract, he is on the hook for combating the tidal wave of Calvinist resources pouring out of SGM drop for drop. So, where is this covering? Is he covering quietly behind the scenes? How does that work? Did Paul think good thoughts and expect those corrections to proliferate into the Christian hive mind? Why then write one letter?

This question has lingered in the background of the blogosphere conversation: How come Larry has not been more vocal in his actions to address the SGM authoritarianism? I have taken him to task in four separate articles on my blog, SpiritualTyranny.com, over this very issue. For the longest time, I assumed that Larry was being driven by some misguided altruism. In many Christian minds, self-defense is disqualified because it is self-serving, and self-serving is being selfish. Since Christianity has conceded—without a

Blight in the Vineyard

fight—that Altruism is the foundation of human ethical standard, did Larry think championing the cause was a violation of ethics?

Well, that is what I get for assuming. There would be something almost noble if Altruism were the force of his ethical standard. Or maybe better said, I would understand why he thought it noble. But now I know there is zero altruism and zero nobility in the fraud called covering. As near as I can tell, from the available information, it appears that Larry really never quit championing his cause privately with SGM leadership. They ignored him for years, but he never quit contacting them. Brent Detwiler details a number of letters that were sent by Larry over the years, demanding, cajoling, pleading, wheedling, and summarily beseeching C.J. and the Apostolic Team to reconcile his offenses.

Brent was kind enough to compile a list of Larry's public statements about his treatment at the hands of SGM. If you notice footnote 317, Brent references that there are over a thousand pages of Larry Tomczak documentation, so they were busy little apostolic beavers behind the scenes. Maybe this is why Larry didn't write much else: He didn't have the time.

Anyway, after reviewing the compiled letters from Larry, here is what screams off the page. It is all about Larry, Larry, Larry, and Larry. His reputation, his family, his ill-treatment, and the litany of offenses **he** sustained. Larry's definition of the reconciliation was merely that SGM Central say they were sorry for being mean and give him the respect he feels due as a "co-laborer" in the gospel.

Fast forward to 2011 and read Larry's letter of reconciliation with C.J. and SGM for yourself. It was originally published on the Sovereign Grace Ministries

John Immel

website on July 11, 2011. Notice its focus: Larry, Larry, Larry, Larry, and C.J., and oh yeah, Doris, her parents, and his child.

Doctrine? Uh . . . .

What is that?

Doctrine? Errr . . . .

Other people? Who else is important? This is the C.J. and Larry show and everyone should be impressed that we, we, we, we have kissed and made up.

People's lives being destroyed in the name of God? Why . . . whatever are you gossiping about? That is slander. We are trying to reconcile. We are trying to practice the wisdom of Proverbs 14:9, "Fools mock at making amends for sin, but goodwill is found among the upright." So, all you fools out there trying to second-guess our actions and motives . . . you just never mind.

Here is what becomes glaringly apparent once the sum of action, the paucity of his proportional public statements, and the content of Larry's letters are tallied on the bottom line. Larry has never considered the SGM issue past his Apostolic covering navel. His self-absorption could not be more obvious. While he may empathize on some level with those who have suffered, he treats this whole dynamic as if it begins and ends with **his** spiritual good pleasure. He has demonstrated almost no responsibility to the broader issue.

The fact that Larry got kicked out (or walked out) is irrelevant. He started that group and called himself apostle over that group. People gave their submission in exchange for covering. How does the term of his departure mitigate his responsibility to his self-proclaimed social contract? He departed SGM leadership edicts over **doctrine**: doctrine he condemned as part of a broader pattern of mistreatment. By his own doctrinal mandates, he is on the hook for combating the **doctrine**. His covering doctrine requires that he address all mistreatment outcomes on behalf of the people who purchased his covering with their rational abandonment. Period!

This is exactly the kind of issue that Paul waded into with relish. When called to account for his many personal failings and logical conundrums, he charged in brandishing quill and insult to combat his foes. (So much for altruistic morality.) When Paul thought his adversaries carried no moral authority, he took no prisoners. When he thought the outworking of doctrines affected people, Paul waged ideological war by calling on Satan to beat the snot out of his intellectual adversaries. OK, well, maybe that isn't a good idea, but the very Pauline writings—stacked up like so many Legos for the submit, submit, submit part—are the same ones where Paul kicked some *gluteus maximus* when churches he had founded rejected him. It didn't matter that the churches didn't want Paul around or that he had been defamed in the minds of the local church. Paul refused to remain silent. Paul had the onions to stand against those with whom he disagreed. He was not shy. He took his argument public and would not back down. If Paul is your measure, then—**if**—apostolic covering is anything, it is a pair of danglies combined with the intellectual capacity to carry an argument.

So, where is the other side of this vaunted social contract? How does an apostle earn his keep? Covering? What bad things is he shielding people from? What does he safeguard? The prophecy mic? Keep demons from attacking?

And this is the crux of the issue. Leaders are demanding quantifiable action from those they cover, i.e.

John Immel

church attendance, serving the local church, tithing, and an intellectual subordination to whatever they say. But yet, there is no quantifiable measure of their protection. To be sure, Larry's 2011 reconciliation letter is almost defiant in its silence. Larry said:

> We have agreed that we don't need to go into specifics, but we can tell anybody and everybody that we came together, every major issue was put on the table, we endeavored to humbly repent, ask forgiveness, and honor God by forgiving.

This is their way of saying "This is none of your business."

So, if church leaders are empowered to "cover" in secret, how do we measure authority's covering effectiveness? Larry said that every issue was put on the table? The split was over doctrine. But if Larry is representing they have reconciled **every** issue, then what about the doctrinal divergence? Again, did SGM step away from their doctrine?

Notice that Larry is declaring an end to his responsibility. If every major issue was put on the table, then everyone else's mistreatment is not his concern. For Larry, this issue is closed. Larry bears no accountability beyond his cushy apostolic backside.

So, what is this covering that he is so hot to preach?

Does covering stop one earthquake or two? Does the earthquake in Haiti in 2010 mean the Christians were not sufficiently covered?[3] New Orleans would have been saved from Hurricane Katrina—in spite of being built

---

3. From the January 13 edition of Christian Broadcasting Network's The 700 Club: Pat Robertson said that the earthquake in 2010 was the product of the Haitian people's deal with the devil some thirty years prior. So, I'm wondering if covering would have stopped the geological shift of tectonic plates.

below sea level and forty years of levee neglect—if only they had been covered by a pastor? Does covering shield the flock from smallpox, or should you hedge your bets and get a vaccination just in case the preacher isn't as spiritual as he says? Does covering mean you will never sin again? Or does covering mean you will commit fewer sins? Or maybe it means you will quit doing the **big** sins if you are the worst sinner you know. Is a woman covered if she has a husband? Or does she need to add a pastor to fully cover her? Or is she covered, that is mentally subordinate, to every man in a congregation? Or does she need a hat on her head, a husband, a pastor, and an apostle to be fully fortified against her chromosome-driven tendency towards deception? If one is covered, does that mean his doctrine is perfect? Does covering mean man no longer has to think about anything important because the preacher behind the podium does the heavy lifting? Does covering stop one demon? Maybe it stops a thousand demons from nibbling on our butt. Is it a multiplicative authority? Two *El Primo* authorities put 10,000 to flight? How many demons are there? Does that mean Christians need one "authority" per X number of spiritual powers? Anyone out there in Christian land who is currently living a covered life suddenly have a problem-free existence?

You do get the joke, right?

Here is the dirty little secret of the doctrine of covering. It is a little more than spiritual protectionism. We would immediately know it was a con job if Tony Soprano was making the pitch. We would know that the extortion had one function: to extort us to give **them** stuff. Is it any wonder that C.J. responded with extortion? This is the foundation of this whole doctrinal cesspool.

John Immel

Now I want you to notice this: John Gotti Mystic Despots can only exist in an atmosphere of implied chaos and pending violence. In other words, they count on your fear and insecurity over forces that are never quantified to gain relevance. Vito Corleone pastors act like the Don on his daughter's wedding day, sitting behind their desks implying that the bad thing plaguing your life would not exist "if only you had submitted to me," which is really code for "Just believe what I tell you and give what I demand, because I'm making you an offer you can't refuse."

Maybe they fork over a few dollars from the church coffers in the name of charity, but they will only do that a couple of times before demanding you serve the local church full time. (Which means their benevolence wasn't free; it came with a vig.[4]) But when it comes down to actually doing anything, actually preempting bad things with the power of the vaunted covering, actually waging a **measurable** battle in behalf of the people they claim to cover, where are they?

And this is the fraud under the doctrine. Leaders can define covering any way they choose and defer all life failures to the great mysteries of God's intent, or the feebleness of faith, or the impropriety of self-interest (altruism) or . . . just fill in the blank with Christian excuse for bad things.

Once again, raise your eyes to the horizon. The Larry Tomczak vs. SGM anecdote is an example of a much graver ill, the symptoms of a horrific conclusion in American Christian thought. Get the scope of this one-two punch: enforced passivity to **any** authority's edicts

---

4. Vigorish, or simply the vig, also known as juice or the take, is the amount charged by a bookmaker, or bookie, for his services. In the United States, it also means the interest on a shark's loan.

Blight in the Vineyard

coupled with protectors that have no responsibility to **any** outcome. You can't seek your own self-appointed strength and fortification against bad spirits, or bad ideas, or bad actions, or bad authorities because to take independent action is to fail in subordination. Or said another way, self-reliant action is sin. Or as Dave Harvey said:

> For Christians ensnared in subjectivity, spiritual experience can carry an implicit authority that has the effect of overriding Scripture. Such expediencies are commonly used to validate an ungodly decision, justify disassociation from the local church, or claim the right to live a life unexamined by others. {. . .} Such is the fruit of a church in captivity.

So, you are stuck in an abyss of passivity while men insisting they are the protection over your life decide how to justify why bad things don't stop happening to you. They have a smorgasbord of tried and true options:

- Piffle. I don't feel called. Besides, who has time to understand "vain philosophies"? We already know people just have "religion," but we have a relationship with Jesus. Maybe Europe needs more missionaries.
- Who cares about Marky Mark or whatever his name is? I believe in social justice.
- What would Jesus do? Let us pray! Harder! Longer! Louder! Quieter!
- Judgment starts in the house of God. America needs to repent. Her chickens have come home to roost.
- We just need Character. We just need Faith! We just need Love! We just need ...
- Read the Prayer of Jabez 5,000 times so God will surely enlarge your coast.
- Rebuke devils! The authority of the believer!
- Name it and Claim it!

John Immel
- Preach Christ and Him Crucified, and all is hunky-dory.
- God is Sovereign! This is God's will.
- Even so come Lord Jesus! The Rapture! The Rapture! The Rapture!

These men have no responsibility to **any** outcome. So, it doesn't matter that there is ideological disaster taking this earth by storm. Church leaders can be as practically incompetent as they choose and as theologically narrow as they please. As I said, they are unquestionable authorities, so you dare not call them to account. And they are unquestioning authorities because reason is just "the old Adamic nature of pride," and besides, it's just too damn hard.

. . .
. . .
. . .

The result is a passive church ill-equipped to deal with the philosophical rigor within the Arena of Ideas. The winds of doctrine blow and swirl and everyone panics at the cultural postmodernist polyglot hell. All leaders can do is sniff derisively at the boogieman of bad ideas and demand that everyone bunker in the church against the bad, bad world.

The moment the church hears the magic words "I'm an authority," we are stuck with accepting whatever comes next, because the average pew-sitter has been indoctrinated with inaction in deference to a leadership that has no **moral responsibility** to any outcome. The leadership is impotent and left to bicker and squabble about which church is preaching the most wholesome authentic doctrine and pretend that theological purity will magically transform all bad-thinking people.

Blight in the Vineyard

Political tyrants couldn't care less about the ideological purity or pedigree, but History's Hitlers are quick to sounding like Jesus in the Garden of Gethsemane reminding everyone that **your** individual will is irrelevant, and woe to us when the political powers marry the force of government with the religious authorities. You are immoral, decadent, and require the strong hand of government to compel right action. Sunday preaching takes on a whole new meaning when TRUTH is the property of a state with the will to bring real violence to the flock.

It doesn't matter that these wondrous covering apostles don't know how to address the tides of destructive ideas. By their own submission and authority covering doctrine, they are supposed to know. This is exactly what the doctrine says: Select men are the ideological and theological watchdogs appointed the task of defending the stupid sheep from the ravenous wolves.

How can they get a pass on executing a job description they wrote for themselves?

It doesn't matter how sincere they are; they don't get credit for sincerity when History's Hitlers come to pillage and plunder at will. And if the Parable of the Talents illustrates anything, it is this: Mere good intentions are penalized harshly; results are rewarded absolutely.

If one is going to claim apostolic authority as a precursor to covering and guarding the prophecy mic is the sum of task, shut the flipping thing off and get a job that makes something useful. If any stray word will upset the delicate sensibilities of those sitting in the pews after six months of instruction, if the people in the pews can't immediately discriminate between truth and falsehood, if they cannot sustain their own minds within the Arena of Ideas, then the problem is **not** the mic.

John Immel

The problem is incompetence.

Demanding absolute control over the spiritual peasantry must mean more than collecting tithes and offerings for the cushy job of telling everyone to give everything to central planning. Covering must mean more than the power to commanding the flock to purchase permission to live and work in their own behalf. If this were a secular job, this would be called graft.

Far too many nationally known church leaders have treated authoritarian method and practice and their counterparts like a polite secret, like the inner wrangling of wayward children against a strict father. They are far too eager to close an already blind eye to tyranny. And the reason is simple. They are *persona non grata* because they do not have anything to say.

Make no mistake. National leaders have been fully aware of the dynamic within SGM, if for no other reason than the blogosphere has been doing just about everything but standing on its head to draw attention to their conduct. But thanks to good ol' Brent Detwiler we now have on record (page 156 and 157) seven players in American Christianity who heard the tape declaring the blackmail of Larry Tomczak since 2002: Stephen Strang, Rick Joyner, Michael L. Brown, Che Ahn, Mike Bickle, Lou Engle, and Ken Roberts. Oh, they weighed in with some letters that contained sundry claims to nausea and some general complaints about injustice, but the sum of covering is an apostolic and prophetic sick stomach and a letter from a word processor?

Really?

How many of you have ever heard a peep of effective criticism out of these national ministries about the SGM phenomena? Some of these men have a full national stage with the communication power to connect with millions.

Blight in the Vineyard

If I hadn't named them, would they have immediately leaped to mind as defenders against the SGM juggernaut? Or when you think of defending against SGM mistreatment, do you think of some lowly bloggers called Kris, Guy, and Jim?

Considering many of these men preach a very similar brand of submission and authority covering doctrine, the silence is deafening.

And here is the ugly baby that I am going to finally call ugly. The wonders of apostolic covering glory are hiding because they cannot bring any real authority to bear, because authority is nothing more than force. They can chant covering all they like, but at the end of the day, it takes the force of **ideas** or the force of **violence** to bring despots to account. And there isn't anyone in American Protestant piety that has either (ideas or force) in sufficient potency to bring another ministry to heel.

If they had the ideas, they would be doing what I am doing. Or better yet, they would have long since beat me to the one-two punch and set out to dismantle the philosophical power under the tyranny. They would never have conceded the SGM right to wage ideological war by using women and children as pawns in a theological battle field. They would never speak of such terrorism in terms of "offense" or "reconciliation" or "co-laborers" in the gospel. They would not grant SGM the dignity of being named in the same sentence with themselves any more than they would give the 911 hijackers that dignity for using the same methods of extortion: Believe what we believe or else! They would not pretend that men who will destroy the innocent in the name of God are creatures of reason. If the "worst sinner they know" were a pedophile, genocidal, degenerate on par with Caligula, the cries of denunciation and doctrinal rebuttals would fill the airways by the pound as the Apostles of covering scrambled to get out in front of the heretic. They would not grant such a man the right to be called a brother.

The fact that national Christian leaders continue to embrace the grand theory of SGM method and practice and refuse to openly challenge the ideas powering their doctrines is not a demonstration of their Christian love. It is really a manifestation of their philosophical impotence, the full-on wreckage of their moral clarity. So, even on their best day, exercising the greatest spiritual authority, raising the dead, casting out demons, and sliding down the Mount of Transfiguration, what are they gonna do? Quote another scripture like everyone should care and whine about the evils of postmodernism when no one does?

Who is kidding who? They only thump the pulpit to intimidate those who give a rip about their submission to authority posturing. The rest of the time, all they can do is sit very quietly and hope above hope that no one ever notices that the only subjects to their authority are the very ones whom they claim to cover

21
Felt Needs

> Although we may not know it, we have, in our day, witnessed the birth of the Therapeutic State. This is perhaps the major implication of psychiatry as an institution of social control.
>
> —**Thomas S. Szasz**

> A fanatic is a person who can't change his mind and won't change the subject.
>
> —**Sir Winston Churchill**

> People say I make strange choices, but they're not strange for me. My sickness is that I'm fascinated by human behavior, by what's underneath the surface, by the worlds inside people.
>
> —**Johnny Depp**

All renewal movements get their start when the disenfranchised are stimulated by a message of revitalization, empowerment, and hope. From the days of Ezra to the days of John the Baptist, the renewal themes dominating preachers' mouths are a return of economic, social, governmental, or spiritual power back to the hands of the common people. The trend of authority-based institutions is to consolidate power into the hands of the few at the expense of most anyone else. That power feeds on increasing its despotic control in service to sustaining its own existence: Its existence serves its authority and its authority serves its existence. The people at the helm of such institutions use taxation and enforced service (a.k.a. slavery) as fuel for their organization's actions. They use tradition and philosophy (a.k.a. orthodoxy) to shape the moral justification for their organizational survival.

As John the Immerser stood in the riverbanks pronouncing his submersion in water for the remission of sins, the smoke from sacrifice raised thick into the air for sins appeasement. Centuries of tradition and scriptural interpretation focused Israelite culture to venerate all facets of temple practice even though the people groaned under the demands. The orthodoxy was unquestionable, the practice unarguable, the leadership unassailable because it was exactly what God had appointed from times immemorial. Yet there stood John, hip-deep in a river, insisting that the water was sufficient to the task of cleaning the soul in spite of the blood of bulls and goats dripping off the temple mercy seat. The message rang clear and true, as people across class lines flocked to the Jordan's banks listening to his words of kingdom immediacy and commit their lives to the "fruits worthy of repentance." Our modern ears having been so indoctrinated into traditional interpretations that we utterly miss the overt message of political and social and religious rebellion: the condemnation of the old order and the return of personal individual relevance and power back to the hands of the common man.[1] Of course, the established denominational powers of 1st century Judea criticized the populist renewal for being inauthentic, its leadership unrecognized by approved authority, and driven by

---

1. For a treatment of the sociopolitical environment of first century Judea and John the Baptist's contribution, see Richard A. Horsley and John S. Hanson, *Bandits, Prophets, & Messiahs: Popular Movements in the Time of Jesus* (Harrisburg: Trinity Press International, 1999), chap. 4.

Blight in the Vineyard

erroneous theology. But the people did not care. They wanted the power to encounter God, in their own way; they wanted their own relationship with the Lover of Their Soul.

Fast forward to the modern day, the Charismatic Renewal was no different. People wanted their own relationship with the Lover of Their Soul. Men emerged, standing by their own metaphorical riverbank, preaching doctrines that laid the ax at the root of traditional Catholic and Protestant church practice, claiming they did not need existing authority's approval to fulfill the purpose of God. People left denominational churches in droves, drawn to the immediate, heartfelt, personal, subjective interaction with God. The word traveled that some men worked miracles and advocated that a new day had dawned. Faith became something more than a vague assent to the unproved and was transformed into the stuff that moved mountains and raised people from the dead. God was close, His kingdom was within. He was in the process transforming the world for His immediate return. Hope poured forth from pulpits exhorting people to ever higher levels of divine expectation: The power of the Spirit, the "full gospel," was present to transform the sum of man's existence.

The critics emerged making the claim that the populist renewal was not authentic, lead by unrecognized authority, and driven by erroneous theology. The proof of the heretical nature was this "observable" truth: People don't act any different than unbelievers. After all the praying, and preaching, and faith, and power, and freedom, and life-filled churches, and contemporary music, and expressive worship, Man still sinned. In spite of the touted outpouring of God's Spirit and the spiritual-gift-driven meetings that sprung up, human beings still did bad stuff.[2] With all of this reported divine power, how was it that Christians failed to act any better? Some suggested that the persisting sins disqualified the manifestations. Others said that the manifestations were merely a small taste of something greater to come, if only man could quit sinning.

By the time 1990s rolled around, the Charismatic part of American Christianity felt the need to answer why the behavioral mysteries about human existence still persisted. The sources and solutions had many subtle variations but they all tended to revolve around three primary schools of thought.

The first explanation said that overarching spiritual powers, i.e., spirits, demons, or otherworldly powers somehow have the ability to influence human behavior. The solution was an understanding of the vast hidden world of demons that tempted and moved people to sin. These evil spirits were subject to Christian spiritual authority based on the New Covenant, the name of Jesus, and his shed blood. All Christians needed to do was master the power bestowed on them and that would keep the gremlins besetting humanity from causing bad actions. Church's teaching this explanation often ended services with altar calls for rebuking spirits and other importunate prayers of freedom.

The second explanation came from behavioral sciences teaching a "Christian" version of psychology. For some people, spiritual calling meant obtaining counseling degrees and hanging out a shingle. They blended the "secular" behavioral science conclusions of Freud, Jung, and reflective listening techniques with favorite Bible passages and prayer. And others suggested that the

---

2. Referring to the reported renewals centered in Toronto, Canada; Brownsville, Florida; and Kansas City, Kansas.

therapy in the average pastor's office was little more than peer counseling and insufficient to treat true illness recommending psychiatric care with a Christian emphasis. The behavioral science solution for Christian sin problems was known by some as the Therapeutic Movement.[3]

The third explanation was a resurgent move back to the doctrines of old, back to the teachings of the mainline churches but with a fresh twist: peppy songs, clapping and shouting. True to their counterculture genetic predisposition, PDI/CLC/SGM waded in as the voice of dissent. They staked the claim to the best of both worlds—the best of the Charismatic and the best of the Orthodox—eager to get out in front of the ideological bandwagon.

Devils were not the source of human failure but an excuse for failed personal responsibility. Spiritual gifts were wonderful, but they were just that: **gifts** distributed by forces beyond human keen and therefore not something to be pursued. They made this comparison: We don't want to be gift-rich like the Corinthian Church but doctrinally deficient.

The PDI/CLC/SGM counterculture answer to the question befuddling Christian minds was the drumbeat of C. J. Mahaney's sermons denouncing the Therapeutic Movement: Man is a wretched old sinner in need of sound doctrine. He dedicated endless Sundays addressing the evils of "felt needs," needs that are derived from the wellspring of experiential drive and justified merely

---

3. Brent Detwiler's comments briefly stated in the third chapter were a critique of the Christian cultural environment briefly summarized above. People were watching all sorts of vision, and dreams, and doctrinal fads and pop physiological trends, but they were not watching their lives or their doctrine.

because of urge. The book of James chapter 1 verses 14 to 15 and James 4:1–3 says:

> 14 but each person is tempted when they are dragged away by their own evil desire and enticed. 15 Then, after desire has conceived, it gives birth to sin; and sin, when it is full-grown, gives birth to death.
>
> 1 What causes fights and quarrels among you? Don't they come from your desires that battle within you? 2 You desire but do not have, so you kill. You covet but you cannot get what you want, so you quarrel and fight. You do not have because you do not ask God. 3 When you ask, you do not receive, because you ask with wrong motives, that you may spend what you get on your pleasures.[4]

A specific reading of these two passages together seeks to locate the source of sin as the fight for gratification, an unloving war with other people to satisfy sinful needs. Felt needs are the pathway to sin. Or said another way, man's "sinful cravings" are at the source of his sin. The key to change is man's self-subordination to authorities that hold him accountable in the face of his internal desire towards sinful wants. Pastoral counseling is superior to the counterfeit based on worldly thinkers; and besides, the local church version is free.

Change is not the product of having his esteem affirmed by endorsing Man's every action deeming it OK. Indeed, his actions are shot through with sin, disqualifying desires, and feelings. The solution to sinful action is recognition of the source of human depravity. This leads to an understanding of the trivial nature of human felt needs and places human existence in correct proportion to the measure of eternity.

Blight in the Vineyard

Because the "light of eternity" dwarfs any human preoccupation, the wants, desires, and felt needs of man's life are microscopic in the grand scheme. There is no pleasure that man can deem good in its own right; therefore, his motives and actions have no moral justification. This indoctrinated triviality is manifest by the abrupt acceptance of his indwelling sin, which manifests in the fear of God. The fear of God then transforms into despair as man recognizes that he is a valid recipient of divine wrath. Then—if God grants Grace—Love. For he who is forgiven much will love much. Much love—in light of the cross—manifests in being "visibly moved."

The doctrinal outcome means that the only **moral** feelings in human existence are fear, despair, and love. But this love is exclusive, directed supremely and entirely at one source. Any other manifestation of love for any other person, place, or thing is ultimately the roots of idolatry. Because man has deep, deep roots of sinful pride and idolatrous love, the action of walking out his sanctification ". . . with fear and trembling. . ." means he needs a strong hand of leadership pressing him towards righteous action. The only place to obtain this guidance is in context to the local church. Like an onion, man "changes" by constant scrutiny of a community as he is made aware of the endless layers of his innate depravity. Man must renovate his spiritual affections by committing to absolute truth, i.e., sound doctrine. Once the mastery of pure doctrine is achieved, his only appropriate response will emerge—by God's Grace—in holy action. And when man inevitably fails to manifest righteousness, the church's specific function is to evaluate, confront, and administer discipline. Church

---

4. New International Version

discipline is the privilege of the truly authentic Christian.

Now, take a deep breath and ponder that summation: the proposed reasons for human failing and the subsequent proposed answers. You need to wrap your mind around the particulars to grasp what is ultimately being demanded.

Mastering the cause and effect of our actions is an important human function. If we understand the levers of our existence, then we can become masters of our existence. These are questions we need to answer. Therefore, let us briefly review the three proposed location of man's problem.

- Man is at the mercy of demonic spiritual forces tempting his weak soul.
- Man is at the mercy of environmental forces abusing his delicate psyche.
- Man is at the mercy of his own consuming devilish depravity.

Now, let us evaluate the proposed solutions.

I suspect that there are people who would insist that they prayed against evil spirits and their sins stopped. Maybe it is true. Or maybe there is another factor that impacted the behavior. The weakness of the "man moved by spirits" explanation means that the power of human action to unseen and unknown demons reduces man to a puppet on a string, moved by malevolent forces beyond his control. This reduces man to an automaton utterly detached from the cause and effect of the world in which he lives. At the end of the day, every behavior is summed up by that master of theology, Flip Wilson: "The Devil made me do it."

Other people equally committed to solving the riddles of human action would swear by the techniques embedded in many therapeutic methods. The power of environment to shape the human psyche is observable; sometimes mommy and daddy really don't love us and that lack has a profound effect on our self-value and personal development.[5] And just because we feel does not specifically mean that need is trivial, irrelevant, or immoral. But the weakness of the therapeutic approach is its amorality. Or maybe better said, the weakness is its a-philosophy, its unconcern with the integration of the scope of human existence that defines a moral standard.

But in a small defense of Behavioral Science, it never sought (to my knowledge never claimed to provide) a comprehensive metaphysical system that developed a code of human conduct, Christian or otherwise. Some people may have tried to offer such an explanation, using the science, but science as a discipline is limited by the character of its inquiry and does not address the metaphysical and by its very nature accepts a specific epistemological standard. The goal of behavioral science was merely to discover a toolset that unlocked another facet of man's mechanical existence similar to biology that had unlocked medical practice. The failure was not the mental ratchet set but rather a cultural determination to treat all of life as if it must be lived as an open, reflective listening, a-judgmental Sigmund Freud therapeutic session.

Think back to the 1990s. Transactional Analysis from Dr. Thomas Harris's book, *I'm OK, You're OK*, was still reverberating through the American psyche. Self-esteem was making a bid for the top of Maslow's pyramid.[6] The

---

5. Kingsley Davis, "Final Note on a Case of Extreme Isolation," *American Journal of Sociology* 52 (March 1947).
6. Referring to Maslow's hierarchy of needs from bottom to top: physiological, safety, love/belonging, self-esteem, and actualization.

John Immel

Jerry Springer show was considered entertainment (for some). Divorce rates continued to climb from decades when everything seemed much more stable. Relational chaos seemed to reign as neurotic autonomy was the sacrosanct domain of mommy or daddy's instilled hang-ups. Diversity was the buzzword that sanctified any and every deviancy. And tolerance meant people could not be told that their actions were bad, or harmful, or destructive.

Man's actions were unassailable because pop culture treated everyone as if they were on the metaphorical couch, helpless in the face of forces pounding our delicate souls, abusing everyone into neurosis. This mindset was blended with Postmodernism's intentional ideological chaos and placed in service of removing moral judgment from man. Man's house is made of glass, so put down the rocks. Or said another way: "He, who is without sin, can get off the couch and play nice with mommy." But since no one is really without sin, they forfeit all moral authority; so just lay back.

The PDI/CLC/SGM solution wanted to combat the "Devil made me do it" theology **and** the therapeutic ratchet set for its implicit a-judgment. Blaming spirits for personal actions is irresponsible. Saying that Man has spiritual authority to combat demons seems like stealing what should be divine authority. The therapeutic solution requires professional level qualification to do little more than offer a counterfeit to shaping felt needs. Man is not blameless because his actions were the product of some insurmountable environment-driven neurosis. Man is fully and entirely responsible for the sum of his emotions, actions, and choices, and the solution is not **his** spiritual authority but God's sovereign authority. No matter how much man tries he can never escape his implicit, devilish depravity unless a God chooses to sever the internal puppet strings and replace them with his own imputed grace strings.

And here is the richest irony, the greatest manifestation of philosophical/theological farce: The PDI/CLC/SGM solution to man's behavioral problems concedes the very elements it seeks to condemn.

1. Pervasive Depravity/Indwelling Sin reduces man to a reprobate automaton without any power to correct his own conduct.
2. Divine Sovereignty/Predestination renders human existence a static determined reality, a pawn in a mystery wrapped in an enigma at the mercy of forces beyond his control.
3. Man is at the same time utterly guilty for the evils of the world, but powerless to change the fated order of the universe.
4. The theological structure merely offers a different mental ratchet set and insists—like its secular counterpart—that it must be used by professionals: "First Among Equals" that stand in the stead of God.
5. It robs human existence of moral authority: "We're all just sinners," so just lay back down on the pastoral counseling couch so they can hold you accountable to what you can never achieve. (You get what you pay for.)
6. Spiritual Authority is still used to compel actions but in this instance the target is Man. Notice the irony. Compel devils = usurp God's authority but Compel Man = Righteous? Really?)
7. And last, it gains its power from "felt needs": emotions shaped by the force of spiritual authority.

John Immel

Give me a minute. I need to laugh . . . a lot.

. . .

. . .

. . .

OK, for those of you who haven't gotten the humor just yet, let me violate the first rule of comedy and explain. Of course, when I do that, it won't be amusing anymore, but then it really isn't funny. The Blight in the Vineyard is a tragedy.

The Shaping of Spiritual Affections

Fear, despair, and love are all feelings. It is strange that this needs to be pointed out, but these human emotions are the power behind the doctrines under discussion. The very emotional subjectivity that C.J.'s sermons sought to combat in the therapeutic movement is at the core of this doctrinal execution. No matter how cerebral, academic, or theological the conversation, the doctrinal **practice** turns on feeling. This will scandalize many of you pointy-headed academic types, but emotionalism is at the very depths of Luther's Law and Gospel.

Let us mentally reflect by summarizing. The Law is preached. Awareness of sin manifests. **Fear** emerges as the response to God's justified wrath. The inescapable vortex of law and sin produces hopelessness as man realizes he can never escape the consequence of his sin nature; the result is **despair**. Assuming that God chooses to grant Grace, **love** emerges from absolution; the greater the sin, the greater the debt, the greater the forgiveness, the greater the love, the greater the emotive manifestation. These are the presumptions of Protestant Orthodoxy. This means that the steps to salvific

Blight in the Vineyard

experience are rooted in "felt needs." You **feel** fear. You **feel** despair. You **need** grace to **feel** love.

Since this whole sanctification dynamic starts subjective, it **might** be harmless if it remained subjective. Individuals could define for themselves how the fear, despair, and subsequent love manifest, but this is not where it stops. By using the intellectual sleights of hand detailed in previous pages, men insert themselves into the process and demand the right to measure the emotional authenticity. It doesn't matter if it is John Owen, or Jonathan Edwards discussing religious affections or one of the Puritan groupies currently residing in pulpits, the result is select men create doctrines that secure authority to shape individual emotional expression. That shape might be the utter lack of emotional expression, with a stiff upper lip and the Queen's decorum, or that shape might be the utter abandon of emotional restraint with lots of alligator tears and chest-thumping sackcloth and ashes—pinstriped Puritan or tie-dyed turmoil or anything in between. But the source can be directly traced to the expressive tastes of one man. That man is the First Among Equals who hired everyone else on his staff—oops, the divinely appointed egalitarian team—and they would not get on the team unless they subordinated their tastes to his.

The second chapter opened with a discussion on the power of our emotions, our affections, and our fears, our drive to live up to the standards of the Lover Of Our Soul. I told you then, this dynamic turns on **our** fears, and **our** affections. This is the lever of the tyranny.

Notice how much power the doctrines discussed gives leaders. Your fear, your terror, is the key to the sum of you. If a Pastor can **demand** your expression of fear, he does not even need a collar around your neck to drag you where he wills. You will willingly go wherever for the small assurance that the sum of your fears are put off till another day. So, no matter how often you hear grace, grace, grace, grace, grace, no matter how many sermons on God's great mercy, at the end of the day, if a church leader tells you that God's disfavor is heaped upon your head because of some failure to adhere to pastoral judgments, the yoke of terror yanks you back to obedience. You hope above hope that your actions are a sufficient sacrifice against the great penalty of divine wrath. And you dare not risk your own self-appointment because any failure is a manifestation of God's judgment.

No matter how much the leader slaps you on the back and tells you it's all a great egalitarian party, no matter how often he insists he is just a "First Among Equals" and hugs you in expansive *bonhomie*, this is the foundation to every leadership conversation: He owns your fear. This hinge of fear is what ultimately shapes the lever of your love. You have no choice but to generate affection for whatever leadership demands. Failure to emulate the appropriate affection is ultimately a failure to love God. When you are not "visibly moved by the wondrous work of the Cross," there is serious doubt to the proof of your salvation.[7] How can you be so hardhearted to not weep, wail, and moan at such great suffering? How can you be so callous not to grieve your great sinfulness at every appearance of the Cross? Maybe God is not filling your mouth with imputed shouts of praise? Maybe that means your Christianity is suspect?

---

7. "Visibly Moved" is C. J. Mahaney's euphemism for crying big alligator tears in service to this exact dynamic. He presumes to quantify the authenticity of salvation on the willingness and ability to cry. Just go listen to him preach about half a dozen times. You will see to what I am referring.

So, you just better get to crying, so God can tell that his Limited Atonement was effective.

You doubt my assessment? Are you tempted to say, "Good leaders don't do such things. They don't extort our affections like that"?

Yeah, huh?

How many of you immediately remembered the Joshua Harris article? Read the whole section again and on this read-through notice his overt emotional manipulation.

> Ultimately, we have no excuse for not pursuing deeper knowledge of God. We can't allow our culture's apathy towards truth, or our own laziness, or wrongheaded ideas to keep us from the study of biblical doctrine and theology. Without it, we cannot love God with all that we are.

Mr. Harris presumes that men are full of error, cultural apathy, personal laziness, and wrongheaded ideas, and seeks to trump those presumed failings by a blatant emotional appeal. He wants you to love a specific theology like he does. To achieve his outcome, Joshua plays on the pinnacle of man's felt needs: his fear of failing to possess **authentic affection**.

Under the current dynamic, you don't get your doctrine and then your affections. Your affections are the force that confirms your doctrine. Your felt need drives you to an inescapable emotional vortex. Man is doomed to remain in despair until he takes up residence where it is warm and smoky . . . unless God intervenes. So, emotions come first, the doctrine come some place down the line in service to explaining an "authentic" Christian salvation "experience." Unless you are "visibly moved by the cross," there is serious question about the nature of your sanctification. If only you were diligent with sound doctrine to shape your spiritual affections you could be assured of your eternal location. Alakazam! Poof!

John Immel

Protestant Saints enter the equation to validate or condemn Christian authenticity.

Some of the resident Reformed Theology aficionados just choked because I just told them their ideas are the product of their feelings. But how can it be any other way? In as much as other men shape your emotions in service to shaping your affections, they own the lever to your ideas.

22
Sound Doctrine Subjectivity Beast

> Philosophy is questions that may never be answered. Religion is answers that may never be questioned.
>
> —**Unknown**

> Evil is not to be traced back to the individual but to the collective behavior of humanity.
>
> —**Reinhold Niebuhr**

> Luther, we grant, overcame bondage out of devotion by replacing it by bondage out of conviction. He shattered faith in authority because he restored the authority of faith. He turned priests into laymen because he turned laymen into priests. He freed man from outer religiosity because he made religiosity the inner man. He freed the body from chains because he enchained the heart.
>
> —**Karl Marx**

It turns out that sociologists study the dynamic between group participation, relational emotional attachment, and ideological commitment. In other words, they study Felt Needs as they shape theological orthodoxy.

In the early 1960s two sociologists, John Lofland and Rodney Stark, went to the streets to study the specific process of religious conversion. They published their initial findings in 1965, and other studies conducted by other people soon followed, augmenting the conclusions and expanding the evaluations across denominational and

John Immel

religious movements.[1] The findings bore out what is called the Control Theory of Deviant Behavior. The fact that the group was organized around religious themes did not change the basic functions of social dynamics.

Sociologists seek to grasp the central utility of social interaction. The leading discipline revolves around conformity and deviancy. In 1901 E.A. Ross published Social Control, arguing that the primary forces behind social stability were family and community. In 1957 Jackson Toby[2] introduced the idea of "stakes in conformity," as the foundation of social integration.[3] In 1969 Travis Hirschi published *Causes of Delinquency*, a study of the underlying forces of social deviancy.[4]

This aspect of social science seeks to answer this fundamental question: "Why does **anyone ever** conform?" The Theory of Deviant Behavior is one answer to that question. Rodney Stark, in his book, *The Rise of Christianity*, makes this comment: "People conform when they believe they have more to lose by being detected in deviance than they stand to gain from the deviant act. Some people deviate while others conform because people differ in their stakes in conformity. That is, some people

---

1. John Lofland and Rodney Stark. "Becoming a World-Saver: A Theory of Conversion to a Deviant Perspective," *American Sociological Review* 30:6 (December 1965): 862-875. See also Rodney Stark and William Sims Bainbridge, *A Theory of Religion* (Bern: Lang, 1987).
2. Jackson Toby, "Social Disorganization and Stakes Conformity: Complementary Factors in the Predatory Behavior of Hoodlums." *Journal of Criminal Law, Criminology, and Police Science* 48:1 (May - June 1957): 12-17.
3. For a full treatment of Toby's concepts, see *Contemporary Society: Social Process and Social Structure in Urban Industrial Societies* (New York: John Wiley & Sons, 1964), chap. 9.
4. Travis Hirschi, *Causes of Delinquency* (Berkeley: University of California Press, 1969). See also Travis Hirschi & Michael R. Gottfredson, eds., *The Generality of Deviance* (New Brunswick: Transaction Publishers, 1994).

simply have far less to lose than others."[5]

Don't trip too hard over the word *deviancy*. It is merely used to describe a departure from a cultural norm. For example, deviancy could be choosing strawberry in a world of grape jam lovers but utterly normal in a strawberry kingdom, or deviancy would be doctrinal celibacy in a world of heterosexuals. The point of the sentence is the value placed on conformity is measured by social cost. The highest cost for most people is the security of their relationships.

Stark's study noted that the driving force of conversion was relationships within the group. He said: ". . . the first thing we discovered was that all of the current members were united by close ties of friendship predating their contact with [the group leadership]."[6] So let me summarize what he is saying. Conversion is not about seeking or embracing an ideology; it is about bringing one's religious behavior into alignment with that of one's friends and family members.

Stark goes on to evaluate the fundamental elements that drive joining and commitment to the religious group. I have summarized the core of his chapter presentation with these three points:

- Membership is driven by interpersonal attachments.
- The group growth is proportional to multilayered social networks.
- Social conformity fuels ideological conformity.

The first two elements are the driving force behind the

---

5. Rodney Stark, *The Rise of Christianity: How the Obscure, Marginal Jesus Movement Became the Dominant Religious Force in the Western World in a Few Centuries* (Princeton: Princeton University Press, 1996), 17.
6. Ibid., 16

third element: Stakes Conformity. Stakes Conformity is the constant inter-relational calculus we all do in pursuit of social interaction. It is the ongoing differential equation that we do to answer the question: "What price will I pay to maintain interaction with the people around me?"

For example, on the right side of the ledger sheet is Mom and Dad in the real world; on the left side is fighting Captain Hook in Neverland. What is the cost for authentic social interaction with Lost Boys? Mom and Dad are mean, so crowing like a rooster and Tinker Bell orthodoxy (happy thoughts) is a cheap price for flying. And besides, Wendy is a real cutie pie.

Anyway, the greater the cost for being removed from the group, the higher the theological zealotry. Stark noted that "because . . . people retrospectively describe their conversions, they tend to put the stress on theology . . .."[7] But because he and his partner had been observing the group from the beginning, they knew the initial stages; they had already noted a lack of doctrinal interest from the early period of involvement. However, once part of the group, the price of admission to group resources was directly related to group authenticity, which is expressed by greater and greater adherence to theological orthodoxy.

It doesn't really matter what church is under discussion. People go to church because of felt needs. They attend because that is where their friends are, and then they make adjustments because the music makes them feel good, or they want a sterile environment to raise their kids, or they want to feel like they belong. The doctrines are secondary and will change in emphasis depending on the political wind within the organization.

The PDI/CLC/SGM leadership fully understands the

---

7. Ibid., 19

Blight in the Vineyard

power of interpersonal commitment to shape church involvement. The Protestant Saints within leadership have gone to great lengths to elevate interpersonal affairs to the highest Christian responsibility. I could also write that sentence this way: They have gone to great lengths to elevate relational "felt needs" to the highest Christian responsibility. They describe their organization as **Impassioned** Orthodoxy. That one-two punch marries the emotive power of relational commitment to the doctrinal authority of their leadership practice.

They demand an emotional reaction to qualify commitment which makes it very consuming to participate in church. Sundays are a rush of expressiveness from a broad array of personalities. In fairness, this is no mere emotionalism (they would never tolerate such a thing), but rather an ongoing encouragement to encounter Christian practice with an outward abandon. The loose logic offered from the pulpit says that if you can cheer for an NFL team with abandon, how much more should you cheer for the wondrous work of the Cross? This is blended into a relentless evaluation of motive, doctrinal consumptions, and cultural participation. The passion and the preaching are combined with an identity akin to the military—precise, ordered, authoritative.

This makes it very hard to remain on the fringes of church. If one does not gravitate to the prescriptions, they almost immediately stand out. And members are not shy about asking why one is hesitant. Remember Dave Harvey's comment?

> Such expediencies are commonly used to validate an ungodly decision, justify disassociation from the local church, or claim the right to live a life unexamined by others.

The leaders instill into the congregation a demand for

relational transparency. Participants are expected to dig into the middle of everyone else's life. They may accept some timid distance in the first few meetings, but if the months pass and your face is common, eventually, someone will ask you to reveal your soul. They will expect an overt commitment to the collective: "Are you 'plugged in' to a Care Group? Are you going to serve here at the church?" If one shows the slightest interest in using the church resources, a leader will raise the subject: "Are you planning on being a member?"

Relationships and absolute commitment to relationship are the leading force of PDI/CLC/SGM participation. Whatever PDI/CLC/SGM leadership would like to pretend, for most of their congregation, doctrine is secondary (at best). Inevitably, a few noisy people dominate the public conversation fully enamored with all things Puritan theology, and everyone nods and smiles because they have been told this is specifically valuable. But for most people, doctrinal details are irrelevant. If the ideas happen to confirm to their take on the world, that is a bonus. But they attend for other reasons. This means that most people do not evaluate preaching in terms of a philosophical whole. They hear in piecemeal snippets of devotional moments: how what they heard made them feel, how it addressed a current pressing need, how the sermon should have been preached for someone else's benefit.

This is not limited to someone's itching ears who just want to have their pleasure centers tickled. If men have been told that their highest moral and spiritual expression is to weep, wail, and moan through church and that standard confirms a deep-seated self-contempt, they will relish the indoctrinated despair with all the gusto of Al Capone consuming caviar and champagne during Prohibition. They will emote themselves empty with

Blight in the Vineyard

metaphoric sackcloth and ashes and say, "Sir! Yes, sir, and three bags full!"

By the power of stakes conformity, the average pew-sitter will pick up the stock doctrinal summary. But beyond the script, they will have no thoughts. Peg them down on the Joshua Harris pursuit of theology and they are appalled, or worse . . . just bored. Stakes conformity drives the collective dynamic: The greater the felt need payoff, the greater the stakes in social deviancy.

So, the cycle is:

> Social interaction → relational interdependence → "felt needs" → leadership approval/rejection → doctrinal refinement = collective authenticity → stakes conformity → social interaction. And so forth.

So, if the stakes for participation is keeping one's mouth shut, so be it. No one talks about what they really think, and they cash in on the sterile environment to raise their kids, or keep their friends or, maintain their business contacts, or pay their bills from the church coffers, or . . . the felt need *du jour*. Stakes conformity scales to the desired interpersonal payoff. A greater measure of participation, i.e., entrance into the inner leadership circles, and people raise their zealotry to politically correct levels accordingly. If the coin of the realm is becoming a Puritan groupie . . . shrug . . . we are not like other churches. Put the checks in the right boxes. Read the right books. Say the right things. Alakazam! Poof! Stakes Conformity.

The Highest Stakes

". . . God opposes the proud but gives Grace to the humble. . . ."

Paul said, "If God be for us, who can be against us?"

John Immel

But that is not nearly so compelling a thought as, "If God opposes you, you're screwed." To memory, that specific quote is not in the Bible, but it is in the Gospel according to John Immel chapter 5 verse 21.

There are no higher stakes than divine sanction. So being able to define pride (conversely Humility) is the power to define divine sanction; this is the highest moral high ground. This is why the PDI/CLC/SGM community works so hard to seize it as fast as possible in every interaction.

One of my first encounters with Robin Boisvert went like this: "Hello, John. My name is Robin. You are prideful."

OK . . . that isn't quite right. I'm exaggerating a little bit.

He didn't say hello.

Ehem . . .

The blow-by-blow of the hour or so conversation is actually irrelevant because his conclusion was assumed. I mean, I'm sinless most days, but on the occasion, I do squander the grace of God; I'm not guilty of that error.

>snicker<

OK . . . so seriously, pride (and its evil twin arrogance) is context-dependent. But Robin's assumptions made pride a state of existence.

What was he specifically referring to with the accusation? He leveled the opinion when evaluating the content of my life. He presumed pride was the underlying force that had shaped the whole of my choices and outcomes. As cause and effect explanations go, I thought this was weak. My response was: "Robin, you don't know me. How can you possibly make that assessment?"

His response was to accuse me of arrogance. That judgment didn't make sense either. And since I didn't

Blight in the Vineyard

realize it was **not** a big egalitarian party (even though that is what I had heard from the pulpit), I asked him to define arrogance. He just steepled his fingers below his chin and looked at me. He thought I was debating semantics.

SGM has a particular method of dealing with what they call conflict. Most people call it a fight. They have an elaborate social structure and a full-blown doctrinal statement to pursue what they refer to as reconciliation. They overtly and repeatedly demand this social interaction. So, I did what was preached: I reached out to others to mediate the presumptuous and erroneous judgments about me as a person.[8]

C. J. Mahaney called me to "communicate" about my frustrations with Robin because "We take these kinds of accusations very seriously." Not too far into the conversation, he made the same charge: "You are a proud man." And I said, "C.J., you've talked to me for less than thirty minutes on the phone. How could you possibly know what kind of man I am?" Within a few sentences, he trotted out the "You're arrogant" line. When I asked him to define that, he said, "This conversation isn't fruitful."

Those years ago, I didn't do any better than anybody else at getting away from the vortex. I wanted someone to tell me I belonged. I was up against some hard places in life. Some hardship was my own bad stuff; some of the hardship had nothing to do with me. (Not Pol Pot and Joseph Stalin bad stuff, but not the sneaking of a pack of gum either.) I went to find someone who could help me fix the bad stuff. Like most of you, I had a longstanding desire to be a part of God's church. I wanted to bring my skills, talents, and passions to the party. Or said another

---

8. SGM uses Ken Sande's book, *The Peacemaker: A Biblical Guide to Resolving Personal Conflict*, 3rd ed. (Grand Rapids:

way, I had sufficient stakes conformity. The coin of the realm, the price of admission for all of these things, was being willing to say I was proud and arrogant regardless of definition. So, I accepted the judgment. I willingly, even happily, subordinated myself to their assessment.

But notice that my two questions "What is pride?" and "What is arrogance?" are not rhetorical, and they are most certainly not semantics. By refusing to define the specific actions that constitute the charge, the leaders have laid a very specific foundation for all subsequent interaction.

Very few people have the nerve to reject the theoretical premise of their own pride and arrogance. Such a self-defense would require a highly defined moral clarity and an effective, clear, measurable, ethical standard. So, by making any self-assertion a manifestation of Pride and any self-defense the product of its evil twin, Arrogance, leaders destroy moral clarity and obscure ethical standards. This is the wreckage of moral clarity brought down to the interpersonal level.

Notice how this shapes all conversations. If authority can persuade you that self-expression is indefensible because it is pride and God opposes people like that, leaders control your actions. The stakes of your conformity are absolute because God is in the business of screwing up your life in **their** behalf. Finding a foundation of rebuttal to their considered judgments is like standing on quicksand. Confidence is pride, so a man can have no assurance about what he knows without being guilty of the ultimate disqualifier. Arrogance is a denigration of any superiority, which takes genuine ability and expertise and makes them the doorway to the highest spiritual failing. So, you never have firm footing

---

Baker Books, 2004) as a full theology on this subject.

to reject anything Mystic Despots assert.

And this is the goal. By defining any personal security, any personal motivation, any personal confidence as Pride, and any ability or expertise from which to reject Pastoral judgment as Arrogance, they remove the possibility of peerage and set the stage for your absolute dependence.

Notes

23
Addicted to Elitism

> I never will, by any word or act, bow to the shrine of intolerance or admit a right of inquiry into the religious opinions of others.
>
> —Thomas Jefferson

> Great ambition, the desire of real superiority, of leading and directing, seems to be altogether peculiar to man, and speech is the great instrument of ambition.
>
> —Adam Smith

> Every form of addiction is bad, no matter whether the narcotic be alcohol or morphine or idealism.
>
> —Carl Jung

With the previous chapter in mind, you can now grasp the upheaval during the time period of the PDI to SGM "Doctrinal Refocus" had on its members. The leaders spent years shaping its congregation's religious affections presumably towards a "biblical" set of ideas. Then they decided that they wanted everyone to shift their allegiance ostensibly to another "biblical" body of ideas. People listened to the content of the "Doctrinal Refocus" and were aware that the doctrine ran diametrically opposed to the teaching from previous decades. When people challenged the ideas, the fraud was revealed. PDI didn't want allegiance to "biblical" doctrine; they wanted **personal** allegiance for one purpose: to demand ideological conformity.

If doctrine and practice really turned on ideas, a PDI/CLC/SGM pastor would never—could never—ask this question: "Don't you trust us?" Yet when challenged on a doctrinal issue—when asked to explain their mental reflections—they offer a mental deflection. They make a demand to relational loyalty, which means they really use personal allegiance to shape people's minds.

Appealing to trust is not a rational argument. Actually, this is no argument.

During the years of ministry, somebody realized that this was a good response for deflecting Pastoral scrutiny because the question put a person in an awkward place.

If one says, "Yes, I trust you," they respond, "Then why do you question me, God's duly appointed authority?"

If one says, "No, I don't trust your intellectual conclusion," then they respond, "Why are you here under our authority?" This succeeds in positioning contrary mental reflections as a betrayal of God's authority.

This is a masterful piece of relational manipulation.

This is an exquisite piece of "Felt Needs" extortion.

Let us mentally reflect.

If we all are wormy deficient creatures subject to the deceptions embedded within our Pervasive Depravity, if "we can't allow our culture's apathy towards truth, our own laziness or wrongheaded ideas," to keep us from loving God with all that we are, shouldn't they be pleased for people to say, "No, of course, I don't trust you. Your motives are mixed, your intentions flawed, and your actions are shot through with sin. Now justify yourself against my criticism!"?

I do so love irony.

Anyway . . .

Blight in the Vineyard

This relational manipulation is most readily revealed in the following PDI/CLC/SGM assertion. From the mouth of my favorite pastoral autocrat Robin Boisvert: "So many other Churches are not about Sound Doctrine. What good is being healed if you don't have character? We, PDI/CLC/SGM, would rather not be like the gift-rich, doctrinally-deficient Corinthian Church."[1] Whatever the biblical teaching on health and healing might be, I want you to see what is really buried deep inside this "biblical aspiration."

You, dear aspiring Jedi, now have the tools to evaluate this comment. You know the assumptions, presuppositions, and filters undergirding the claim. Let us start unraveling the manipulation together. The endless determination to compare their existence to the failure of other churches knows no bounds. Robin is overtly claiming superiority to even the Church in Corinth, with a subtle critique of churches in general tacked on for good measure. This functional elitism is the spice to the heady SGM tonic and a blatant emotional appeal. Who doesn't want to be elite and have the most righteous, most doctrinally superior church? Who doesn't want to be part of the best and wear that status proud?

However, the superiority presumes that the Corinthian Church would have pursued character if only they had teaching about character and personal accountability. And since doctrinal sufficiency is of the Reformed Theology pedigree, it means personal accountability can only be found in the doctrine of

---

1. I don't remember where I was when I first heard this comment. To be sure, the refrain during the early parts of the "doctrinal refocus" was said in many instances by various leaders. I just happen to remember this specific comment during one of my sessions at Robin's office away from his office: Hunan Best in Gaithersburg, Maryland. They have great Chinese food, by the way.

John Immel

Indwelling Sin/Pervasive Depravity. This is a rational curiosity considering the doctrine does not find formal shape until circa 450 AD (at minimum) and more precisely, as taught in the 16th century. That is a strange standard by which to judge the poor Corinthian Church, since all churches have their problems, but even more bold is a general critique of other churches:

- This assertion presumes that PDI/CLC/SGM has an inarguable standard of Character.
- This assertion presumes that the SGM yardstick applies to all people at all times in all instances.
- This assertion presumes that character is specifically the product of "Sound Doctrine."
- This assertion presumes that they know the mass conduct of church participants who do not hear what they teach.

How many churches do you have to visit so you can consider yourself an expert on people's character? And how many Sundays has *El Primo Doctrinal Mover and Shaker* been absent for the express purpose of doing this statistical study?

Just for fun, let us apply the logic in reverse. Are there examples of failures within their congregations that could be used to extrapolate doctrinal failures in their movement?

Hmmm . . . let me ponder. . . .

OK, here is one. Rumor has it that people—family members deeply involved in PDI/CLC/SGM and its teaching—have committed suicide. So, people under Reformed Theology commit suicide. What good is having sound doctrine? And sadly, people who have sound doctrine kill themselves. Isn't it better to be doctrinally deficient and be alive? Or if you think that is an absurd reason to indict a body of teaching, then what about what seems like an epidemic of adolescent boys from within SGM congregations that molest little girls? That should be a big blaring warning bell to avoid their doctrine at all costs.

How is that for a pejorative judgment about the sufficiency of their doctrine?

Did that last comment seem indelicate of me? Did that seem like gross speculation? Did it seem presumptuous without having all the details?

Yeah, huh?

"But, John, they are just trying to raise the bar. They are just trying to do the best they can. They are just taking their jobs very seriously. Besides, all churches have their problems."

Well, misplaced bargaining aside, this defense gets trotted out with surprising consistency in behalf of PDI/CLC/SGM conduct and practice. It is a beautiful subterfuge designed to get people to concede a vague truism for one purpose: absolve SGM leadership of despotic outcomes. Considering their relentless determination to differentiate the wonder of SGM from even the Corinthian Church, it is glorious that they justify failures by pointing to "other" churches when called to account.

"We at SGM are the best of the Orthodox, the best of the Charismatic! Stand and applaud our great leadership! We have character! We have sound doctrine—and sadly, other churches do not!"

"We are set apart. We are uniquely qualified to shepherd your souls! We offer you the privilege of Church discipline! We are not like other churches."

"Viva la SGM!"

"What?"

John Immel

"Problems?"

"Uh? Err . . . Hmmm . . ."

"Well, you know, we are like all other churches that have problems."

All hail the moral equivalency.

This is knee-slap funny. Can you imagine if a pastor called a mere mortal to account for his actions and the response was: "Well, Pastor, all people have their problems." Parents, here is a question for you: If your teenager trotted out this moral equivalency, "But Charlie did it!" what would be your response?

But beyond the silliness, this whole intellectual dynamic is really an insidious, false choice. Character versus health or health versus "sound doctrine" is a false choice. Whatever Corinth's doctrinal problems, there is no tradeoff between ideas and character and physical health. At the very least, good ideas about nutrition combined with character tends to lead to good health. Duh?!

How many of you refuse to take your kid to the doctor because they misbehave? Do any of you?

I thought not. And don't trip over the idea that health of the spiritual gift kind makes this equation somehow different. How can the source of health matter when the outcome is being denigrated—be healthy vs. be without character vs. possessing specific doctrine? If the overriding concern is character in service to elitist ideas, then the source of health is irrelevant: God or a Doctor.

Of course, this is absurd. No sane person pretends that the pursuit of being healthy is an inferior activity to learning better ideas. No sane person places physical health behind a manifestation of character because no rational person believes they are specifically connected.

Yes, true, you can play in the street and get hit by a

car, have sex with prostitutes and get syphilis, and smoke fifty packs of cigarettes a day and get emphysema. And maybe these are all illness brought on by a lack of character. But is anyone going to honestly say that a person should refuse to pursue health care in service to ideological purity?

Really?

It is to our shame that I need even make this point. It takes almost no interpretive skill to identify Jesus' attitude about this very issue: doctrinal precision vs. health. Any number of fights end with Jesus flat defying theological exactness (Great words, Bob, but really, really, misapplied) to get health and wholeness to men and women. Never once do you see Jesus vetting the qualification for the gift of health against a broader character. And you never see him demanding health recipients qualify their worthiness by their grasp of Calvin's "sound doctrine." Jesus held doctrinal precision in contempt and health, life, and freedom in the highest esteem. I will say it again: It is to our shame that I even need to say this.

But the most important part is the insidious subtext. The false choice is really designed to place a **moral** authority on "Sound Doctrine." If sound doctrine is more valuable than health, then shouldn't you be about sound doctrine? Which is really code for, shouldn't you be more concerned with what the Pastors teach than anything else?

This is what I want you to see. SGM's goal with this ideological rotgut has nothing to do with advocating better conduct or elevate a higher intellectual standard. This elitist sales pitch is just the window-dressing. This is the bait dangled before your ego so you cannot see the values switch, the rope-a-dope before launching the intended assault. This is really one more salvo in the ongoing campaign of intellectual and spiritual violence. The goal is to embattle you to lay down one more value that benefits you.

Your health benefits you. Seeking health is effectively seeking LIFE. And preachers cannot preside over advocating death if seeking life trumps their sponsorship. So, by creating a false choice that implies temporal, fleshly concerns are a product of spiritual inferiority, they can demand you embrace any doctrine. This Neo-Gnosticism is a blatant effort to get you to despise your "flesh" concerns up against an elitist illumination called Sound Doctrine.[2] How can you consider your health more important than God's very gospel? How selfish must you be to elevate a temporal need above the greatness that is the Cross? Your real standard of physical indifference should be measured by Jesus on the Cross. Your healing means nothing by comparison.

Jedi, this is by design. This false choice is calculated intellectual violence to undermine your life no matter the choice. You are damned if you do and damned if you don't. Health is a gift that God may or may not bestow. To spend God's precious time seeking an uncertainty in light of Jesus' suffering example is to further reveal your flesh-mindedness. Your carnal-mindedness is a doctrinal deficiency; like the Corinthian church, you don't have your mind right. This makes the only righteous action an absolute abandonment of all flesh concerns. Subordinate health enough and you will physically die. (So, maybe those people who committed suicide were the ones really listening? Hmm . . .)

This redefinition of LIFE values is in service of

---

2. If this isn't Gnosticism, what is?

elevating DEATH's value. This is a deliberate attempt to obscure the dynamic tension between righteous values to create moral ambiguity. The goal is to shape your spiritual affections so they can stand unopposed in advocating a religion of utter dependence.

Spiritual Crack

"We doubt you. Why don't you doubt yourself?" This gem of saint-equipping counsel was said by my favorite spiritual tyrant, Robin Boisvert. On the surface, it looks like he is trying to convey the general opinion of the SGM hive minds about *moi*. I don't remember the specific conversation, but I do remember this was a response to my confidence about something that he didn't think I should be confident about. But notice this: His words are really an implicit doctrinal statement. His words sum up the leading ministerial assumption: the quest for Indoctrinated Self-Doubt.

Notice that Robin's pithy statement is the logical conclusion of the Platonist/Augustinian Pervasive Depravity. By Orthodox standard, humanity's great transgression is self-will. Self-will is the sum of our corrupt appetites, desires, and aspirations that get lumped into the general category, lusts. Corrupt human nature requires a sanctification that is little more than confining that nature, binding it, placing man in ever more sterile circumstance to incarcerate his action. If he is not near bad things, he will not be tempted by bad things. Holiness becomes the absence of temptation enforced by a community of busybodies holding each other accountable to the social tastes of Protestant Saints. The only place of blissful emotional security is the absolute abandon of self to those who are appointed caretaker of the souls.

John Immel

So much of what is being advocated by Puritan groupies today is a little more than the moaning echo of haunted people subordinated to the same ideas from the annals of human history. William James captured these thoughts in *The Varieties of Religious Experience*, in lecture XIII. He recorded the inevitable conclusion of indoctrinated self-doubt from a voice almost 200 years ago.

> One of the great consolations of the monastic life, says a Jesuit authority, is the assurance we have that in obeying we can commit no fault. The Superior may commit a fault in commanding you to do this thing or that, but you are certain that you commit no fault so long as you obey, because God will only ask you if you have duly performed what orders you received, and if you can furnish a clear account in that respect, you are absolved entirely. Whether the things you did were opportune, or whether there were not something better that might have been done, these are questions not asked of you, but rather of your Superior. The moment what you did was done obediently, God wipes it out of your account, and charges it to the Superior. So that Saint Jerome well exclaimed, in celebrating the advantages of obedience, "Oh, sovereign liberty! Oh, holy and blessed security by which one becomes almost impeccable!"

As this Jesuit rightly identified, indoctrinated self-doubt ultimately means that man is absolved of sin if he is obedient. He carries no moral responsibility to any action as long as he can say he obeyed. The motivation for this full abandonment is harmony within his embattled soul, because the only place a man can find peace, assurance, and moral security is to utterly defer the sum of self.

From the pastoral perspective, the Platonist/Augustinian worldview makes crushing out any ability or self-inclination a good thing. Said another way, my favorite spiritual tyrant thought he was doing me a favor. Crushing my confidence was the goal of his counsel, because my confidence, in his mind, was evidence of a lack of sanctification. I wasn't dead enough. Under Platonist/Augustinian assumptions, the fivefold ministry is really nothing more than a bureaucratic spiritual death panel ever advocating that man's lot in life is inability, insufficiency, and inequity. This makes fivefold ministry an endless appeal to individual self-destruction measured by increased levels of subordination. Since we don't advocate the bullet in the head brand of suicide, the Christian definition of death means "equipping the saints" to ever increasing surrender.

To whom?

The current Church marketing and packaging says it is surrender to God, but since He isn't holding office hours and since you are incapable of getting to Him on your own, that leaves those He charged with governance in His stead. Men who stand in the very Stead of God are the manifestation of God's Grace for your civil and spiritual life.

Man must subordinate his action to the guiding assertions of authority. This seems sort of right; what better yardstick of human action than governmental authority that God appoints? But this yardstick makes the definition of right and truth the sensibilities of men who feel it is their God-given duty to squash any dissent from those they lead. And never forget: Government is force. So, put this together, and you have defined Christian sanctification as death by bureaucrat: unelected and unaccountable authorities who can, by force, crush those they administrate. In any other

John Immel

context, this would be called despotism.

But in the Platonist/Augustinian worldview, this Mystic Despotism is the logical progression of ideas. The progression gets called biblical and everyone who is anyone knows that if it is in the Bible, man is supposed to believe it. To defy the idea is to defy God, and no one wants to do that. So, man caves to his spiritual insecurities and accepts the premise unchallenged. This is the definition of Mystic Despotism: the use of man's spiritual insecurities combined with governmental force to control those ruled.

A fivefold ministry of Mystic Despots is nothing more than bureaucrats of destruction responsible to drive people into the cult of death that has become the cross. They beat people down the path of self-abandonment until there is nothing left to abandon. Individual destruction suppresses every desire, every want, every inclination, holding up as an ideal a man so stunted in restriction that he is unrecognizable as man. The individual—if it could even be called that—becomes a squat, square, rigid, sexless curmudgeon suspicious of any unapproved concept or pleasure, rabidly evangelistic against elements of human individuality.

The product is inevitable: a meek social conformity to all "authority." And as John Stuart Mill correctly commented about the cultural effect of this doctrine perpetrated by Calvinists: "I don't mean that they choose what is customary in preference to what suits their own inclinations. It does not occur to them to have any inclination except what is customary."[3] Karl Marx referred to this narcotic-induced state of human

---

3. John Stuart Mill, *On Liberty and Other Writings*, ed. Stefan Collini (Cambridge: Cambridge University Press, 1989).

existence as "the opiate of the masses."[4]

I call this Spiritual Crack.

Crack is cheap. The doctrine of self-doubt is cheap. It takes nothing to undermine a human soul by manipulating their spiritual insecurities. It takes no pastoral skill to rip out a person's confidence. Supply the brute force of authority to crush ambition, and turning a man into an empty husk of inert of self-destruction is a matter of course.

Crack is highly addictive. The outcome of Mystic Despotism is highly addictive. "We love you, so we care for you. You belong, so make our work a joy. If you don't, God opposes the proud. Your self-assurance is a measure of pride." This is the beginning of the addiction as people go to bed feeling the warm, heady rush of inclusion. The words "you belong" inject ecstasy into their souls. The price of hearing those words over and over and over is just a tiny bit of self-doubt. Just a bit more surrender. And self-doubt is really humility, right? And surrender is spiritual, right?

Like the crack addict revisiting the street corner, people go back to the church building to get their fix of pastoral "care" deferring one small choice and another little assurance chipping away at **self**, trading it for pastoral validation. At first, the need for injected affirmation is infrequent. But as the **self** is eroded, the junkie jones grows until one day there is nothing left to exchange; the addiction complete. Leadership opinions are the only opinions. Leadership passions are the only passions. And leadership's mannerisms are the only mannerisms. Having lost track of their identity, they adopt the group personality and then the collective; the

---

4. Introduction to *A Contribution to the Critique of Hegel's Philosophy of Right*.

hive mind is complete.

Man cannot live without an identity defined by a coherent worldview because his worldview is the source of his interior energy. Man is moved by the interior energy of his values. And when nothing is within, he looks for something to fill the emptiness. He cannot help this drive any more than he can help needing to breathe. Left without power to originate anything, he turns to whoever will fill the void. The result is an endless cycle of dependence driven by an indoctrinated addiction. Any preacher teaching spiritual dependence is as much a drug dealer as any South American cocaine lord.

His drug is Spiritual Crack.

And the effects are equally horrific. People are robbed of everything that is dignity.

The disaster is harder to see because people appear "respectable" in their Sunday best, and live in neat and tidy houses, and retreat to the very sterile safe haven of steeple-topped buildings. They hide behind crosses like Bram Stoker's vampire hunter and spice their conversation with Bible verses like garlic. But underneath the good church boy and girl façade is a destitution and spiritual squalor that makes a crack whore look noble. Indeed, we have all met these putrid souls, automatons of sanctimony, poster children for Paul's "filthy menstrual rags" righteousness. For all of their insistence that by virtue of their submission to authority they have mastered life, terror rolls off them like a stench at the thought of venturing beyond a very narrow-controlled environment.

Hardship sends them to their knees in penance for the smallest perceived sins. They cower and quake at the capricious god of the universe who piteously drubs them about the head and shoulders for his great mysterious

Blight in the Vineyard

purpose. Every hardship is some divine effort to teach dependence and inability, a WWF smack down with God doing flying elbow drops from the turnbuckle, eye gouging, and biting until man taps out.

Sinners in the hands of an angry god more loathsome and vile than any serpent might be in man's eye. This truth from the pulpit makes people detest their reflection and sends women into campaigns of intentional drabness, ruining their beauty with all the energy of a flail-ripping flesh. Heaven forefend that they make their pathetic, weak, incompetent, hopeless, useless brother stumble with the skin of a shoulder or the flesh of an ankle.

This self-detesting, self-loathing doctrine so castrates men from their drive to prevail that the smallest choice sends them to the pastor's office to facilitate a decision. Should I nap or is that sloth? Should I watch G-rated movies or dare I see PG? Is it sinful to use a spoon or should I only use a fork? This produces men so absent that their ethical power is atrophied and cannot stand against **any** moral seduction. Their world is a bewildering endless dark tide of destructive hostile gremlins of bad that they are incapable of mastering.

Is it any wonder the overriding emotion of this life is fear? Is it any wonder that they look at the sky in terror expecting it to fall?

A life addicted to spiritual crack inevitably produces this outcome. The addiction is the affirmations and sensibilities of other men. Indeed, addicted souls were force-fed a substance more consuming than drugs. Drugs bind the body. Spiritual crack binds the spirit and mind to a putrid state of anonymity that needs any confident and able person pretending authority. Without this crucial substance, the world tilts, and the boogieman of bad stalks in the shadows of insecurities.

John Immel

How dare you miss church? Without a man measuring right thoughts, how will you know what to think? Without a man defining right actions, how will you know how to act? Oh wretched man, who can save you from this world of death?

The answer: only those appointed by God to shepherd your stupid and ignorant and degenerate soul through this life of justified woe and pain and suffering.

Is there a way to rehab? Don't be absurd. In the Platonist/Augustinian worldview, to even ask this question shows the measure of your deception. Your choice maker has been so atrophied, so shriveled, so bent and corrupt that such an action is impossible.

Or is it?

Dear Spiritual Crack Addict, here is your first choice.

24
Interpersonal Train Wreck

> 1) All people act logically from their assumptions. 2) It does not matter how inconsistent the ideas or insane the rationale, they will act until the logic is fulfilled. 3) Therefore, when you see masses of people taking the same actions, find the assumptions and you will find the cause.
>
> —**The Gospel according to John Immel 3:1-3**

Jesus crosses the Sea of Galilee and his favorite denominational critics meet him on shore. We remember the story, right? The Pharisees demanded that Jesus defend the source and substance of his actions. By what authority do you do these things? Justify your actions to us! Implicit to their demand is the assumption that they were uniquely qualified to measure Jesus' authentic existence. Of course, Jesus had no interest in their affirmations, so he defiantly refused and left that little fishing village and moved to another place. Interestingly enough, he was overtly asserting his right to live a life unexamined by the appointed authorities.

As he and the disciples traveled, Jesus gave this warning: "Beware of the Leaven of the Pharisees." Unfortunately, the warning sailed right over the disciples' heads. The disciples were focused on food or the lack thereof: a curious preoccupation in light of their most recent experience of feeding the 5,000. So, they never really thought to get explicit clarification, and Jesus got wrapped up in their bread preoccupation. Of course, this meant they fell ill with the very leaven of

John Immel

Jesus' warning. The Pharisees' fixation with authority tended to dominate the disciples' worldview till the very end.

The subsequent generations of Christians have not done much better in understanding or heeding Jesus' warning. In the modern age, people hear Pharisee and immediately think legalistic, sanctimonious condemnation. Our historic doctrines shape our preaching filters, so we miss Jesus' exhortation with equal catastrophic measure. So, the warning to beware of leaven is read as a warning against being a Pharisee, which is a condemnation against legalism. And depending on the audience, this can be an appeal to license or the proclamation of liberty. And who defines the truth? The answer is: those with the authority.

Exegeting the length and breadth of Jesus' exhortation needs its own treatment—another work for another day. But this needs to be said now. The Leaven of the Pharisees was the measuring of authentic spirituality through the lens of doctrinal precision empowered by force. The Pharisees' obsession was rooted in an endless quest for authority. Their arguments to condemn Jesus revolved around their moral claim to authority's exclusive right: Whether it was the authority of Torah (scripture), the authority of pedigree (Abraham), or the authority of orthodoxy (Moses); every fight with Jesus is rooted in this preoccupation. In spite of Jesus' warning, many of the disciples' internal squabbles revolved around who had what authority to take what action and compel an outcome.

The case can be made that the preoccupation with authority dominates the whole of Paul's writing and eventually found formal foundation in Constantine's use of Christianity in the Roman Empire and Augustine's

Platonist syncretism that dominated the rest of Western history.

"It all comes down to an issue of authority." Dave Harvey could not have been more right. Once authority becomes the standard of judgment, **everything** does come down to authority: the acquisition and qualification and use. This statement is an ominous foreshadowing of the underlying reality of every relationship, friendship, and intimacy. So, it should be no surprise that this leaven has infused every corner of human interaction, from the least to the greatest. The result is a bunch of elitists seduced by spiritual roofies into spiritual crack addiction that produces an endless interpersonal train wreck.

Spiritual Roofie

> "We are strongest when we are connected to others. Why do we run from this reality? Could it be that in our pride we don't like the idea of exposing our weaknesses to others?"

This is a spiritual roofie.

> "Well, you know that iron sharpens iron. You need to have more friends that will hold you accountable. You need to come be a part of our group."

This is a spiritual roofie.

> ". . . But encourage one another daily, as long as it is called today, so that none of you may be hardened by sin's deceitfulness. We need each other every day. We need unbelief-splitting encouragement that God loves us through the cross and only at the cross. If God loves you, my desire is to love you the same. We need to get together."

This is a spiritual roofie.

John Immel

The unstated theme of these exhortations is the not so subtle effort to make people morally responsible to provide a level of intimacy that has not been earned.

Flunitrazepam is the drug's trade name for roofie. Its medical uses include anti-convulsant, anti-anxiety, and a sleep aid. When used correctly, people benefit from the relief of suffering and an improved quality of life. Twisted, distorted, and abused, the drug is used to disarm women (or men) so they can be exploited by removing their will to resist anything. The drug steals their power to enforce personal boundaries. Said another way, the roofie is used to gain unearned intimacy. Well, that assumes disarmed exploitation can be called intimacy.

The above Bible references—the quasi-spiritual exhortations—are used the exact same way. And like the drug, the passages and sentiments have their own truths to be revealed and benefitted from. Strength can be increased by numbers. Sometimes it helps to be with another person in the face of a challenge. But true partnership is not a function of weakness, but rather the mutual exchange of strengths. Enforced collective participation is not proof against hardship, or temptation, or failure. Being connected sounds like a rich, warm, and fuzzy state of being, but "connectedness" is too ambiguous to be a yardstick of intimacy. Fellowship is not the default outcome of being part of a crowd. Friends may sharpen friends, but not everyone is destined to become friends. And even if someone does become friendly, it doesn't mean they have anything to sharpen. So, just because a person hangs out in a community doesn't by default qualify them for any interpersonal involvement.

The endless advocacy to a collective utopia where all

Blight in the Vineyard

would be right with the world if everyone would just embrace communal harmony, sing Kum-by-yah and fellowship—Oh the Liberty! Oh the Unity! Oh the Fraternity!—is based in a mystical crack pipe dream. There is no such emotional or relational utopian existence where everyone links arms in brotherly love, sings hymns to Heaven while encountering a cosmic group-ness. It doesn't matter that we are all "Christians" or "Brothers in Christ" or "Children of God;" the moniker is not a broad brush to account for individual tastes, needs, and desires.

There is no such thing as community. Community is merely the aggregate actions of many people: individuals acting consistent with their cultural assumptions. Those cultural assumptions may or may not be good, effective, just, or righteous. A group might provide an identity. It might give a collective direction. It might afford a location to galvanize action. But a group cannot give intimacy. Closeness is not a magic function of location or imputed by participation. Intimacy is earned. Anything earned is the result of work, and investment, and commitment, and perseverance. But when people are compelled to enter the "community" as an expression of authentic Christianity, they are being required to give what no one has worked to obtain. Spiritual roofies manipulate familiarity that has not been earned and grants access to the mind, spirit, and talents of another human being. They disarm men and women to be used for whatever spiritual gratification that can be justified. It steals the individual's right to enforce personal boundaries and sets the stage for full-on spiritual crack addiction.

The only people who must use manipulation to gain relationships are the social beggars who need group interactions to fill the void of their own vacancy. These are the church version of the college frat boys who can't get a woman, can't get **any** form of intimacy without some outside force destroying the will to resist. These are the people who frame their appeal to "deeper fellowship" as a rejection of God and the Church. Only the worst sort of humans need to manipulate personal insecurity and spiritual commitment to command intimacy, control transparency, demand familiarity.

The next time you are standing round the church frat house, drinking your grape juice and a sorority sister or fraternity brother start quoting scripture as leverage to demand unearned intimacy, implying you are not an authentic Christian if you are unwilling to bare the deepest part of your soul, check your drink. They are slipping you a spiritual roofie.

However, even checking your drink has its limits when authority can demand you reveal the sum of self. At a frat party, the predators are relying on their victims being unaware; they can't compel anyone to do anything, so they have to dose the drug on the sly. But when authority condemns people for "claiming the right to live a life unexamined by others," they are morally obligating everyone to reveal whatever they demand.

In an environment where the individual has no moral right to personal boundaries, people have no relational responsibility. Authorities are entitled to your transparency, and you are obligated to their judgments. They don't have to make **any** investment to gain **every** intimacy. Add the functional suspicion of Pervasive Depravity and this creates an atmosphere where no one can be at rest because everything is forcibly laid bare, and sin is determined by the observer. (What you think your motive or purpose is irrelevant; you are guilty, and

Blight in the Vineyard

how dare you defend yourself.) The result is a culture of busybodies nitpicking every action, word, motive—perceived, actual, or fictional.

People come to conversations, sifting, logging, evaluating, looking for the opportunity to offer "correction" or "exhortation" or "encouragement' or "offense." The paranoia lingers deep and undergirds every phrase as an endless string of caveats and qualifiers poured fourth in a desperate attempt to avoid any appearance of political incorrectness. There is no such thing as a candid conversation or a truthful exchange for fear that a single word will reveal a sewer of selfish sinfulness, and someone will criticize, or condemn, or expose to the church KGB. "Fellowship" persists as an endless posturing for scriptural justification or spiritual sanction. Everything and everyone is measured for authenticity by the presiding authorities.

Who are the authorities? It is not hard to tell. Listen for about thirty minutes and someone will start declaring the pecking order. If a few minutes don't make things clear, presume to offer a public independent thought or plan or interest and then step back and listen. Pay close attention to the people in charge of chair-stacking "ministry," or church bulletin "ministry," or greeters "outreach" (any menial task so labeled). These people will be the greatest zealots because they are showing themselves "faithful in little" so they can be deemed worthy of much authority. They will be the most tuned into the authority structures because they have deliberately put themselves on the path of authority acquisition.

Sometimes it is subtle and sometimes it is blunt, but it won't take long for the collective identity to illustrate who carries what power. When the coin of the realm is authority, people use their "fellowship" to jockey for an authoritarian fiefdom. I mean this in the purest feudal sense. The payment for loyalty is lordship over something called ministry which is the highest validation of collective identity. Of course, Christians can never admit to such a thing, and we pretend that no one wants to rule his brother or sister. We have created endless justifications to sanctify the very authoritarian preoccupation that Jesus sought to short-circuit when James and John's mother came looking for a political appointment to governmental power.

It doesn't matter how small the group; someone is considered the authority. Someone emerges as the alpha male to organize the pack around his edicts. Between husbands and wives, the husband is the authority. Between "friends," the authority is the one who represents formal approval. In Home Groups, it is the Home Group leader. Where two or more are gathered in the midst of them is a microcosm of authority acquisition playing out its authenticating role.

In every church function, the pack leader moves about keeping tabs on the sundry attendees—measuring, evaluating, guarding. The alpha males are determined to enforce their territory directly proportional to a perceived threat. If an interloper is deemed weak, they are treated as potential recruit to the collective. If one is considered a potential risk, they are treated with doctrinally justified suspicion, and the forces of stakes conformity are employed to determine loyal commitment. If a person demonstrates the force of personality, drive, and capacity to advance any individuality, the pack survival instinct growls to the forefront. Those deleterious souls are driven out by any means—isolated or devoured by the justified moral absolution of authority.

People who achieve the status of authority have enormous relational power. They can pick and choose which intimacy fits their purpose and define for themselves the boundaries on their own self-revelations.[1] In one second they can be pals patiently listening to a friend pour out their soul, and in the next second deny them participation in social interaction for a failure of attitude, expression, or action—perceived, actual, or fictional. In one breath they are declaring themselves eternally trustworthy confidants and in the next breath blab those secrets in a leadership meeting. Authorities are free to stand at a distance and lob character pot shots while never taking any ownership of the interaction. They are appointed to the task of character affirmation, but their actions are really the work of character assassination. Resist authority's sanctifying judgment and suffer the accusation of the aforementioned *uber* sins of Pride and Arrogance. These two judgments also go by the names Unfruitful and Un-teachable.

---

1. Notice that the church leaders teaching submission and authority lead intensely private lives. Notice that they shield their own lives from mass consumption by the force of their doctrines, and yet demand utter transparency from those who grace the sanctuary of their pastors' offices. Their friendships are few and revolve around family. Their social exposure is always expressed in the confines of church where they are uniquely in charge of the dynamic. They will pay lip service to their submission to authority, claiming to have peers who have veto power over their lives and ministry. But if pressed about WHO exactly those peers are, they almost always live someplace else far, far away. If you point out that distant friends cannot hope to use the veto power of true submission, they will have a list of caveats and hedges against summary judgment the leader presumes to wield over their congregation. Press this conversation far enough and it will be clear that these submission and authority leaders do not come close to living the very standard they proclaim.

John Immel

Unfruitful?

Un-teachable?

What do these criticisms mean exactly?

In context, character assassins are offering a specific counter judgment when they are expected to account for the accuracy (read authority) of **their** declaration. This means that **your** attitudes and actions are the only thing open to scrutiny. So, "unfruitful" means you are too proud to understand the value of their precious time. Because they are an authority, their time is more valuable than yours; their relational objectives are the only objectives. So, you just pay attention and say, "Yes, sir. You are exactly right." Because the moment you resist their observations, they remind you that they are taking time out of their Saturday night sermon prep and you are displaying and un-teachable spirit.[2]

Since an authority is spending their precious time to impart wisdom to mere *Untermenschen*, un-teachable can only mean **you** were too arrogant, too personally superior to see the profound wisdom of their words. Since they are the authority, of course, their counsel is better. Their ideas have been vetted by greater minds, and they agree with those greater minds. Their minds are better because

---

2. I have said repeatedly that this dynamic is not limited to SGM. A pastor who was **part of another denomination** in Montgomery County, Maryland said this very thing. He presumed that his time was valuable, and I was the relational problem because I would not give him whatever satisfaction he believed he deserved. I pointed out to him that the only reason we had any social interaction was because I invested MY time to be where he was. So, for him to suggest that I was wasting his time was the height of hypocrisy. And this is true of most every "authority." The only reason they ever know the name of the average pew-sitter is because the pew-sitter spends enormous energy and expense getting to the church. If we are going to measure importance based on time sacrifice, then it is a profound conceit to overlook the relational energy spent by those who attend the church as valid sacrificial qualification.

Blight in the Vineyard

they have thought big thoughts, so how dare you discount the wisdom of the ages? You must be proud and arrogant, which means you can't be taught the TRUTH.

The character assassins conveniently overlook this glairing reality. Maybe their canned speech wasn't as profound as they thought. Maybe their righteous judgments didn't rank on the so-what meter. Maybe the truth is they inserted themselves into a conversation that was none of their business. Maybe their authority-appointed busybody-ness isn't worth the bowing and fawning they bully people into giving. Maybe they are incompetent and they use authority to hide from effective evaluation. Maybe they didn't have the authority to compel anything because it is not man's job to compel another man to rational subordination.

Oh, the memories.

Good times. Good times.

Is this relational freight train ringing any bells, dear Jedi? How many of you are thinking back through church relationships gone bad and seeing the train barreling down the track of unearned intimacy and authority? How many of you see the damsel tied to the track desperate to avoid the inevitable like some campy Hollywood silent movie? The only difference is that the character assassins don't look like Snidely Whiplash twirling a mustache. They don't look like villains. They are sincere, zealous, committed, average people, but they keep you tied to the train track just as surely because they remind you, you are disqualified to save yourself.

Do you remember their reaction when you dared tell them—blunt, emphatic, without apology—they were wrong? Do you remember these quaint phrases in response to your enforcement of personal boundaries and an expectation of relational responsibility? Did you hear these curious rejoinders: "Be released," or maybe "I just appreciate you!" or even, "I'll pray for you," or "I'm old enough to be your father, but I don't feel the least bit patronized"? These are the character assassins' escape hatch. When it is apparent that the engine is jumping the tracks, they flee to the caboose, transforming themselves into victims. They are saddened. They repent of anger. They concede that **we** are all just sinners as justification for being wrong. Laying on the sanctimony deep and thick, they say: "Be released."

From what exactly?

Hahaha . . .

The best guess is they are releasing you from hurting their feelings.

They were just trying to help. They were just trying to follow the leading of the Spirit. They were just trying to be iron sharpening iron.

They were just . . .

They were just . . .

And you are a big meaner 'cause you didn't see the wonder that was their nosiness for the great spiritual effort it was intended.

The last man that offered up the "be released" manipulation, I said, "I don't need your absolution. And you are the one who started this conversation."

And to the man who said "I just appreciate you," I said, "You should, because I am one of a kind."

And to the woman who said "I'll pray for you!" I said, "Specifically, what will you pray? We can do it now." She was mad. She left. I guess she really didn't want to pray for me.

And you already know what I said about the Geriatric Enlightenment Club.

For most people, the academic, theological, and

philosophical minutiae behind their spiritual life doesn't register much up against the responsibilities of getting their kids ready for church and the immediate needs of their social interaction. So, they might not be able to diagram the ideas undergirding their church pains and frustrations. But the Interpersonal Train Wreck is what they live out in painful clarity. To be sure, this train wreck is what Christianity is really known for. Step out of the church walls and listen to people comment on their experience, and this complaint will emerge in seconds. We are the poster children of dysfunctional relationships and a byword of interpersonal meddling. People are flat terrified that we will gain sufficient government force to dictate the content of their lives. And here is the sick joke. They are justified in that fear because they hear our words and watch our actions and know with certainty we would require access to their bedrooms and sexual positions and demand **more**.

By doctrinal tradition, Christianity is so infused with the preoccupations of authority that it has soaked into every crease and crevasse of our interactions. This is the thread that undergirds most everyone's church experience. It becomes fully habitual, so we take it into every social contact sniffing and snorting disapproval at whatever is not church-approved. We prowl through video game stores, bookstores, and movie houses like we have stepped into an outhouse that somebody else **must** clean. We criticize and condemn any and all spiritual pursuits as revelations of demonic counterfeits declaring our "revelation" superior, never once realizing we just made Christianity one revelation in a list of subjective revelations. When asked to explain our superiority, we are insulted that we should have to offer a better argument, a better idea, a better cultural choice, or a

John Immel

better quality of life. We vault into the wonderful irrationality of "I just believe," defiant that such words are sufficient for everyone to bow down at the force of our faith. And then in a fit of hypocrisy, we approach perfect strangers and demand they give account for their spiritual health and eternal wellbeing and call it persecution when they don't give us the satisfaction of our righteous authority to win the world for God.

And people wonder why Christian is a curse word?

In the introduction, I wrote the following:

> That set me to thinking. How was it possible that from state to state, even country to country, people could recount similar life events with stunningly consistent conversations, outcomes, and backlash? What ideas could constantly produce such underlying fear, and anxiety, and spiritual frustration? What ironclad logic could cause masses of people to act out similar conduct that produces such invasive outcomes? What thoughts could lurk under the titles of authority that would lead average men to believe they wield unchecked control over people's lives? How could a denomination produce such unswerving reproducibility? Companies spend billions of dollars to produce a brand in the minds of people and they fear it being undone in a blink by the smallest bad press. As far as I know, a church denomination managed to do it without a single TV spot.

I opened this chapter with a quote from *The Gospel according to John Immel* that diagrams the driving force behind mass action. Man is a rational creature of foundational thoughts, turned integrated ideas, turned to habitual action, turned inevitable to outcome. This is why from congregation to congregation, from city to city, state to state, even country to country, masses of unrelated people, even unrelated original cultures, can emulate the same interpersonal priorities, recreate the

Blight in the Vineyard

same leadership conversations and advocate the identical social control outcomes by the power of stakes conformity. In every instance, they are operating from the identical assumptions. The undercurrent flows underneath every interaction. Those who do have authority must guard it with tireless energy for fear that some usurper will violate the order of things and everything will descend into Postmodern Polyglot Hell. Those who don't have authority are constantly seeking to obtain it because they can't express a **self** without. They can't speak about their passions, or play their guitar for group consumption, or talk on the prophecy mic, or bring any skill or talent to public use, or have any peace of mind about personal expression until they are expressly authorized. Unless an authority deems them authentic, they are a nonperson fit only to go with the collective flow; they are a faceless cog addicted to the spiritual crack used to fuel the collective machine.

No one can really suffer this kind of anonymity, so people are forced to find co-conspirators in nonconformity. People dabble at the fringes, out of the sight line of collective eyes with things they know are not leadership-approved, winking and nodding at their bold self-appointment as they sneak some improper pleasure into the relational speakeasy. Depending on where the improper pleasure falls on the unofficial sin hierarchy scale, the co-conspirators are thick as thieves with blackmail material. They are brave champions of individuality living life with gusto, that is until someone whispers the word "Pastor," and then they scatter like bootleggers during prohibition, tucking their vices into hidey holes until the Big Daddy law dog leaves the scene. But Big Daddy preacher never really leaves the scene. The moment an authority starts preaching against

John Immel

"secret" sins, the guilt and anxiety carried around with every self-expression comes roaring to the forefront. Since no one can live with the sum of themselves utterly transparent for all to see, everyone has a "secret," so the condemnation always strikes a chord inside a shame-ridden psyche. This sends everyone to their knees in a fit of moral navel-gazing: a desperate effort to rededicate their lives to the pursuit of accepted self-expression. And the cycle of authority-approved existence starts afresh.

It doesn't matter how each congregation defines the acquisition of authority, because everyone is in a mad dash to emulate that unique expression. If the guy behind the podium is bald, wrings his hands, tells self-deprecating jokes, gives a slight bow of deference with every encouraging word, the Mini Me's bleed out of the woodwork with shaved heads, jokes, and genuflecting. If the guy behind the podium struts around in Armani suits and bullet proof hair and blows on people in the healing lines, the revenge of the clones buy a JC Penny's rip off, a case of hair spray, then huff and puff until someone falls down.

Walk into **any** church where the doctrines of submission and authority dominate and look for the guy who presumes to shape the group then note how he acts, how he measures his acquisition of authority. Next, look around the congregation and you will see the cookie cutter pattern displayed in neon lights.

As I said:

> Leadership opinions are the only opinions. Leadership passions are the only passions. And leadership's mannerisms are the only mannerisms. Having lost track of their identity, they adopt the group personality and then the collective; the hive mind is complete.

For those of you who lost longstanding friends after a

fight with church leadership, this is the reason. The mechanisms of the interpersonal train wreck are deeply embedded in the doctrines and designed to speed people down the path of abandoning every part of themselves in service to obtaining authority's validation.

The relational collateral damage is the inevitable outcome of people pitted against one another for the purpose of measuring authentic behavior. They were not your friends. Or maybe better said, they were only friends in as much as it served their pursuit of a spiritual fiefdom. Loyalty to you was always subordinate to the loyalty to the feudal lord. The leading value was the relationship cache represented in the broader church context. Maybe they liked you but they will close the door on their hospitality the moment the individual interaction threatens their standing. Their affection was always subordinate to the stakes conformity of collective identity. This is also known as a clique.

Here is the dirty disgusting secret of this whole dynamic. For all of the Christian insistence at selfless, moral superiority, intimate fellowship, brotherly accountability, and the righteousness of Church attendance, this dynamic is a cesspool of relational fraud.

Everyone is using everyone else against their will to buy their Christian authenticity from dictatorial church leaders. The coin of the realm is your soul grazed over like a buffet, picked at like a chicken bone in service to fulfilling someone else's spiritual project: evangelization, or service, or discipleship, or doctrinal purity, or leadership.

The sundry Care Group leaders dotting the Christian landscape open their houses in an expansive display of brotherly love and Christian fellowship, but that door closes the moment someone represents a challenge to congregational orthodoxy. Their doors were open because of a bid for a broader "ministry," i.e., they want to preach, or sing, or play their guitar under the klieg lights. Care Group was really a Pastoral minor leagues project.

The Jewish husband, married to the believing wife, is invited to church and home groups in an effort to "win" him for the kingdom. That is, until it becomes clear that he is not at all subject to the same local church values and resists stakes conformity. Then the motivation for the friendship becomes transparent: the Jew was a social engineering project.

The dinners supplied for the hardworking single mother is "service" until it becomes clear that she is not going to send her child to the approved church school (or quit her job and home school), but rather subject her child to the evil influences of secular school. Suddenly, the care group refuses to support the woman with any service because that might be seen as condoning a sinful life choice. She was a Care Group self-sacrifice project.

Basketball is not a game to be played by people who want to enjoy themselves but a pressure-packed metaphysical event revealing the deepest manifestations of sin and unrighteousness. Leaders stand around the court looking to pounce on some ungodly attitude so they can demonstrate righteous qualification to the Protestant Saint in charge of Zenball Ministry. Basketball is a leadership disqualification project.

A casual conversation about the movie *du jour*, or the book *du jour*, or the newscast *du jour*, or anything not church-approved *du jour* is an opportunity to correct a failing of doctrinal purity; the pastors might not approve after all. Conversation is an idea-policing project.

Men who sacrifice their wives to lofty pastoral affirmations because they can "biblically" demand full sexual and mental submissiveness and never once take an action worth following, develop idea worth listening to, or create a value worth desiring, are using their wives as a masculinity validation project. (Actually, any man who needs authority as an aphrodisiac is no man. You are despicable and loathsome and don't warrant bedding any living creature.)

Everyone is everybody else's church project in endless pursuit of authentic validation. "God's" confirmation comes by seizing authority by citing chapter and verse on every action, word, or deed. A quoted Bible passage transforms their intentions and actions into a God-approved mandate. People use Bible passages like a hammer as they proof-text every word, action, or motive, to establish their superiority in the collective pecking order. The zealots bludgeon everyone around them with scripture in mad pursuit of the ultimate affirmation: The day a church leader says "Yea, verily, I now pronounce you biblical!" From this moment on, fealty is owed to the lord.

In a blink, carefully cultivated longstanding friendships are destroyed when leadership casts a jaundiced eye. The "fellowship" so freely given—the giving lavishly bestowed—is suddenly retracted for fear that association with bad influences will harm **their** reputation. The *tsu casa me casa* fraternity is abruptly replaced with *anathema tsu nombre*.[3] The local church amicability is replaced with a thinly veiled suspicion. You quickly find out that friends were not faithful sounding boards but informants with a moral

---

3. Just a little Spanish and Greek lingo for you. Translated in order: "My house is your house," and "Cursed is your name."

responsibility to rat out your greatest peccadilloes in service to authority's right of judgment. Their co-conspiratorial bootlegging has more value as ransom for their authority-driven soul.

Now pause and digest the system dynamic I just laid out in detail, and then take inventory of the cause and effect of your emotional upheaval. This is why you feel so utterly betrayed and so deeply wounded. This is why you ache with despair that will not go away. You offered the sum of self and people presumed the moral right to accept or reject the deepest parts of you and call their actions spiritual. They spent your relationship like dollar bills in the pastoral G-string on a private authority lap dance. No one can sustain this kind of utterly personal rejection. No one can sustain others using unearned intimacy to fill out their Christian authenticity balance sheet. So, when you rightly complained about the mistreatment, they are brazen in defense: "Forgive me **if** I sinned against you but . . . since I'm the authority in this interaction, I can say that this conflict really exists because **you** are the problem."

Toot! Toooot! Chugga Chugga Chugga Chugga Boom!

25
Getting Healthy

A dictator is not a self-confident person. He preys on weakness, uncertainty, and fear. He has no chance among men of self-esteem. But in an age of self-doubt, he raises to the top: men who do not know their own course or value have no means to resist his promises or demands.

—Leonard Peikoff

The highest manifestation of life consists in this: that a being governs its own actions. A thing which is always subject to the direction of another is somewhat of a dead thing.

—Saint Thomas Aquinas

The most effectual means of preventing the perversion of power into tyranny are to illuminate, ... It is an insult to our citizens to question whether they are rational beings or not, and blasphemy against religion to suppose it cannot stand the test of truth and reason. Light and liberty go together. I look to the diffusion of light and education as the resource most to be relied on for ameliorating the condition, promoting the virtue, and advancing the happiness of man. Enlighten the people generally, and tyranny and oppressions of body and mind will vanish like evil spirits at the dawn of day. If a nation expects to be ignorant and free, in a state of civilization, it expects what never was and never will be. No nation is permitted to live in ignorance with impunity.

—Thomas Jefferson

Do I need to make the case that there is something wrong in American Culture?

If the answer is yes, we will have to take up that

conversation another time. If the answer is no, then that begs the question what is wrong. When people seek to answer this question, they observe the interactions of people and evaluate that conduct up against a standard of values. Since people arrive at their values from different starting points, the conclusions vary. The Marxists value collective revolt against the greedy capitalists. The Catholics value man's collective inducting into the "true" Church. The Nationalists value man's collective loyalty into a specific geopolitical genetic identity. The social liberals value the collective freedom to act on any physical pleasure. The social conservatives value standing in the way of individuals doing whatever they do with body parts. And so it goes through the list of constituencies: Their values drive their actions and political objectives.

People hear the word politics and tend to think of some slickster glad-handing his way through the crowds in an effort to win the government version of American Idol. That is not what is under discussion here. Politics is the next step on the philosophical progression and represents underlying values in the outworking of our social actions. Man first identifies the overarching nature of his existence, then he determines the scope and limitations of his knowledge, and then he identifies his moral standards. How he interacts with other people is the culmination of all those values. In the Arena of Ideas this is called politics. How man interacts with his neighbors is the branch on the end of the limb, growing out of the trunk of his philosophy.

From the first pages, *Blight in the Vineyard* has been focused on illustrating the impact of the specific metaphysical worldview of Platonist/Augustinianism as it unfolds to the next logical step in knowledge, then moral

Blight in the Vineyard

standard, and then interpersonal outcome. For the highest impact, this progression was shown in context to a specific group of American church leaders so that people can see this is no vague abstraction.

Like so many that have come before (and many of their contemporaries), PDI/CLC/SGM walked straight into the trap of these ideas offering them as "absolutes," inarguable conclusions that cannot be challenged or evaluated. So, in spite of their genetic predisposition to counterculture superiority, they ended up being parakeets singing the despotic song of the ages.

For the better part of two millennia, Christian leaders have pounded the pulpit insisting that "The Bible says it, you better believe it, and get your butt into our church" is the fix to man's problems. They have prophesied portents and disasters. Natural calamity is God's visitation on man's sinful ways. Christians have sounded like Marxists in the denigrations of evil materialism and the pursuit of mammon. If men would only give away their substance, all would be well with the world. We have acted as if our mere good intentions are sufficient to dismiss the work necessary to supply all the goods and services that elevate the standards of human life. We've made ourselves feel good by holding people's hands, washing their cars, raking their leaves, and passing out bibles. We've sung hymns and prayed prayers and conducted vigils and cried tears and wailed for deliverance. We have insisted that Faith is superior to every Reason. We've condemned the world to the four corners for its implicit sinfulness and then tried to woo the world by singing it lullabies: "God really loves you. God really loves you. God really loves you." And then when the wretched slobs get a glimmer of hope, and come to hear what we have to offer, we swat them upside the head with some variation of:

> He might love you, but he doesn't like you very much. You are a worm, detestable and loathsome and worthy of His wrath. Your ideas are deception. Your interests are trivial. Your desires are immoral. Your life is fit for nothing more than whatever predestined outcome God has appointed.

With almost no variation, this has been our explanation and remedy, but somehow the problems persist. Actually, better said, the more the message of man's mass incompetent, nature-driven depravity spreads, the worse the problem gets. The way of all self-fulfilling prophecies is to descend into the vicious cycle of declaration and "inevitable" outcome. The universal outcome concludes the message and the universal message concludes the outcome. We are very pleased with our ability to portend our own doom, tut-tut-tutting the feeble efforts of men to resist forces of divine power. But for the grace of God, we would all be on the streets slaughtering, and thieving, and rutting our way to utter reprobation. We like to say that the miracle is not that man does evil, but that God restrains us at all.

Here is a radical thought: What if it is not true?

Here is an even more far-reaching thought: What if the historic synthesis is the problem?

What if the "inevitable" outcome of human existence is not unavoidable at all?

What if the thing driving Man down the same path over and over and over and over is the force of the integrated ideas?

I suspect that for some, reading this book has been like trying to drink out of a fire hose: Before you even get to swallow, the next mouthful is pressing down your throat. The questions above brush up against the unthinkable and give voice to what seems like utter chaos. That is a very uncomfortable space to live. Here is my suggestion. Jedi, put this book down and mentally reflect on these questions for a day or two, or three. Maybe if you let the ideas simmer before continuing, the horizon line of possibilities will expand to as far as the eye can see.

. . .

. . .

. . .

Now that some time has passed and you, dear readers, have had some time to digest, I will offer my diagnosis. Then I will offer a glimpse at the leading idea that must take the place of the "inevitable" message.

Here is my take on the health and wellbeing of contemporary culture based on people's conduct. As I listen to our national conversation, the underlying theme is the drumbeat of inability, mass principled failing, and the threat of ethical sanction. These moral arguments are focused on a singular outcome: man's utter subordination to the collective will. People hear the themes and act logically from their assumptions: alternately painting themselves as passive victims of human ill will or demanding freedom to consume their neighbors at the public trough. The result is escalating agitation and unrest, a culture of busybodies lobbing potshots into everyone else's life, and lobbying political powers seeking to acquire the force to compel an outcome.

People come to conversations, sifting, logging, evaluating, looking for the opportunity to get offended while taking no responsibility for the rigor of their own lives. The paranoia lingers deep and undergirds every phrase, as an endless string of caveats and qualifiers pour fourth in a desperate attempt to avoid any appearance of political incorrectness.

John Immel

This is the logical extension of the moral arguments at the root of our cultural assumptions. I submit that the wellbeing of American culture is being undermined by the message of Man's depravity-driven incompetence because the purpose of the ideas is to compel men to fear, cower to any authority, and wait to be saved from what can never be fixed.

This leaves people only two social options:
1. Subordinate all choices to the affirmations of any man asserting authority.
2. Take lone action under the ongoing threat of ethical judgment that finds sanction in government force.

The result is displayed in stark contrast: men utterly passive slouching towards indolence **or** men defiant of any moral judgment. As generalities go, this is a fair assessment of America's cultural disposition.

For some people, their self-loathing conforms to a message of depraved incompetence. They love to grieve their great moral wickedness because it suits their self-image. They love their moral narcissism which gives them the determination to evangelize everyone else to the same groveling. And if they can't persuade you to join them in the state of moral narcissism, they will create a State where Man is compelled to weep, wail, and moan on penitent knee. Heart attitude be damned.

But no Man can survive his every action condemned by moral judgment. If he can find no peace between his ethics and his action, he will die or—in an act of self-preservation—he will abandon moral judgment altogether. Men who realize they can never live up to the moral judgment decide the only way to survive at harmony with their soul is to deny moral judgments as such. This defiant rejection of moral judgment is the lifeblood animating everyone's postmodernist boogieman.

These responses are the logical actions of people dominated by Augustine's worldview and the Altruistic self-sacrificial ethics. Or maybe I should say these are the answers of a free people in the face of no other philosophical choice. If we had a State compelling Augustinian subordination, there would be no alternative choice. It would be hard to imagine what a world without secular choice would look like. Oh, wait. We don't need to imagine; **that** world has already existed. And in some quarters of the globe, that world **still** exits. The picture of life in that world blazes forth and shows us that men are damned if they live and damned if they don't.

Man cannot live without moral judgment; neither can Man live passive, empty, and fearful. Man's life requires action. Man gets his action from his moral energy: The more important the action, the more essential his moral clarity. He cannot live with a moral clarity that demands his passivity.

This needs to be repeated because it is important.

Man **cannot** live with a moral standard that demands his passivity. This places man in endless internal conflict that can only achieve one outcome: death. Since Man cannot exist in this condition to live, he will bootleg all manner of self-appointment into his philosophy but will suffer endless fear for being vulnerable to a moral condemnation he cannot repel. Man's psyche breaks down under this driving pressure, so he self-medicates against the pain and self-loathing, blasting his mind into unreality, turning to any distraction to subordinate the pain. If Man is forbidden to find relief on his own, he will look for someone else to take action on his behalf, fill the void of his ideas, and find defense against the terrors of his existence.

John Immel

Nations made up with these two types of men are the seedbed of tyranny. They are defenseless against **any** assertion of authority, **any** offer of moral affirmation, **any** cohesive worldview, and **any** demonstration of strength. Like the crack addict drawn to the pipe, they have no power to resist and no ability to assess the leader's value. If history is any measure, such people are not able to tell the difference between strength of character and Will to Power.[1] The people will not distinguish between cultural stability and rank nationalism. The people will be ill-equipped to discern between peaceful co-existence and authoritarian obedience. Historically, the result is an inescapable disaster.

America has problems, but I submit that it is not what Christians have been told. The malaise has nothing to do with men having sex with men, or the movies in our theaters, or the conspicuous consumption of materialism, or the destruction of life from the womb, or the gremlins of chaos at the roots of Postmodernism, or which political party occupies the White House, or the pervasive rejection of Church in American life.

Followers of Jesus are to be salt and light. This is a metaphor to illustrate that they are to blaze forth the light of truth and season interpersonal interaction. I affirm the premise that we are to impact the world in which we live. For an age we have acted as if compassion and morality are ends in themselves: actions taken for their own sake with no regard for the outcome. And then

---

1. Friedrich Nietzsche developed this concept to describe man's driving motivation: the ultimate expression of ambition to any given individual end. Will to Power successfully sums up the autocratic actions of despots and tyrants. As an example, George Washington was a man driven by strength of character who used power to achieve liberty. Joseph Stalin had a will to power, an ultimate driving ambition to obtain the force to compel people to his Marxist ends.

Blight in the Vineyard

we have added an anti-rationally anti-reason predicate to Christian life. We have driven thinkers from our midst, equating their efforts to false ideas and spiritual sedition. The result is a bunch of neo-mystical cultural revolutionaries who cannot carry an argument into the public square any better than some carry a tune in a bucket. The weapons in their belt are limited to the intellectual conventions of the day: the pop culture wisdom and underling arguments.

Intellectual naiveté is bad enough but when a bunch of defiant anti-intellectuals march into the Arena of Ideas spouting standard social argot, presuming their self appointed non-thinker-ness is defined by resisting "The Intellectual Man," they are merely imitating the stock anti-institutional rhetoric and are clueless about the underlying philosophical assumptions. These marauders of Christian anti-reason have no choice but to become parakeets singing whatever Top 40 philosophy that has been playing on the radio. Because they are by definition vacant, when faced with intellectual pressure, they default to what they have heard over and over.

Thinking and ideas are intensely demanding work done by individuals utterly committed to their own judgment. A failure of commitment, or individuality, and the only choice available is someone else's ideas and someone else's judgment. Their self-enforced ignorance means they advocate ideas that are in service to tyranny. And since they are intentionally ignorant of **ideas** and are overtly hostile to **thinkers** who might know something they don't, they are bewildered that "somehow" all the bad stuff continues to manifest over and over and over. Defying the postmodern establishment in the name of God and Church is not intellectual courage any more than social activism for the sake "doing something" is political strategy. The disaster is monkey-see-monkey-do Orthodoxy. The definition of insanity is preaching the same Man-denouncing doctrines everyone else is preaching and expecting that Man will somehow find moral substance.

Here is what we have (almost) never done. We have (almost) never been the defenders of Man, which means we have almost never defended his greatest tool for integrating his existence: reason. We have roundly condemned every facet of his being, but we have never defended his right to live. We have preached of man's moral obligation to die, to sacrifice, and too self-destruct. But at (almost) no point have we defended his moral right to be fruitful and multiply, rule and subdue the earth. We have preached giving, the condemnation of poverty, and the moral obligation to bear burdens. But we have (almost) never demanded that Man be free to prosper, to be in health, and live a life consecrated of blessing. We have condemned the forces that impoverish man, but in a fit of madness condemn the counterforce that lifts man from the beggarly elements of the world. We have bewailed the plight of the downtrodden and then condemned the ones who find freedom to escape their bondage. We love men who wallow in the filth of their destitution, but condemn those who successfully clean themselves. We want credit for our tears and intentions for those who suffer but are insulted and antagonizing when a man gets healed. This is utter, mystifying insanity. A flat bewildering reality, since the very function of Jesus' death was to give man an abundant **life**.

Since the progression of all integrated ideas is founded on a metaphysical premise, here is my starting place: That man was created a rational creature, with logic as his greatest tool in service to his work/creative power. He was placed in an unruly world for the express purpose of finding his identity through the challenge of ordering the chaos by the force of his creative ability and the work of his hands. Just like his Creator, Man's greatest satisfaction comes from creating, ordering, categorizing, and then wanton sharing. But sharing is predicated on ownership, and ownership is founded on sovereign individuality; only free individuals can exchange value.

I submit that the problem was not in eating the fruit on the Tree of Knowledge but the violation of private property. The motive made it treason. The partner in crime made it cosmic rebellion. The aphorism that fences make good neighbors is in service to the implicit human understanding of personal boundaries. You can walk in the cool of the morning for a millennium sharing the deepest truths, but unless there is recognition of where one life stops and another starts, every interaction descends into presumption. The result is exploitation and if unchecked, descends into war.

Notice that this is the subsequent story of human existence; one anecdote upon another of men waging war against their brother to take his life, or his wife, or his stuff, and then the counter war of vengeance and conquest. Man cannot help his drive to rule and subdue because the mandate is built into his very DNA, so the world is a reflection of the directive twisted into an aberration of despotism and tyranny. Man's natural inclination to dominate is viewable in the twisted actions of secular powers and Mystic Despots seeking a moral justification to create man in their own image.

Since God created Man in His image, I contend that God is the first and original humanist and measures the sum of existence by man's existence. I contend that His efforts over the millennia have been to liberate man from the power of death and end Man's treasonous hostility to

John Immel

TRUTH. There are many facets to this event, but the overarching direction is to teach the philosophical foundations of LIFE. I submit that the story unfolding before our eyes is man's progressive liberation from the edicts of other men: men in solidarity with death. The end game is each man returned to his own LIFE consecrated to sovereign individuality. We may be bought with a price, but that sum is not a down payment to communal subjugation. Divine ransom does not necessitate collective slavery. A parent who pays ransom for his child does not obligate them to sibling servitude. The ransom is paid with the full intention of giving the child back the liberty **stolen by his captor**.

Sovereign Individuality has been proposed before, but what is being advocated here is no Nietzschean superman's Will to Power. Rather, I am advocating a human existence harmonized in ethical knowledge and moral action, free to categorize, create, and order his world to his own satisfaction. Then share the sum of self with those who value that sum in mutual agreement; all parties protected by the force of government in service to man's sovereign interests.

Defending what I just described is no small task.

The energy brought to bear to condemn man makes up the vast majority of academic, theological, and philosophical tradition; the intellectual heavy-lifting has already been done for each new generation of orthodox shills. The fortifications that protect the Mystic Depots are formidable. To dismantle the walls requires undoing the rationalizations that protect millennia of tradition in service to government force. The size of the achievement should give you a measure of the problem's scope. But failure, in my mind, is not really an option. America was the first nation created that presumed the universal competence of man and fashioned the monopoly of government force as his individual protector. For the first time in world history, Man was not property of the State. The State was the limited protector of Man. However, by ever increasing strides, we are abandoning that central galvanizing truth, and the American Church is growing in advocacy to the very historic doctrines of our European counterparts, laying the foundation for a depraved, universally incompetent, utterly obedient, helpless mass. This message has been at the forefront of most every nation's descent into despotism.

Our Founding Fathers were defenders of Man against all interlopers: the democratic masses, the State, and Statist Religion. The nature of their Christianity was fully tempered by the expectation of Man's sovereign rational existence, individual responsibility, and autonomous liberty. Whatever their reliance on divine providence amounted to, they fully expected that man was responsible to engage a world of his own making.

If we fail to reassert their philosophical certainty, galvanized by man's rational, individual culpability, our children, or maybe our grandchildren, will be thrust into the persisting dark age of unreason, barbarity, and Mystic Despotism that the rest of the world has really never left. Ronal Reagan was correct: If Liberty falls here, there is nowhere else to go. The essence of liberty is sovereign individuality.

To successfully take up this task requires a reevaluation of what we have been told is true. I would enjoy others joining the party, but be forewarned this is not for the faint of heart or mind. The upside is that the flaming stake is currently frowned upon.

For many people, the Theology stuff is largely irrelevant: marginally interesting but it kinda makes the

John Immel

brain hurt. I know that people don't live their lives out of their head, but notice this: The biggest reason people can be tyrannized is because they are so ill-informed. Uninformed people suffer from a relentless abuse of their naiveté. Many have paid a steep price for absolving themselves of learning (at the very least) the rudiments of Church history and the history of Church thought. So they persist in the state of deliberate ignorance at their own risk.

For those inclined to take up the cause, dig into Jewish history and theology. Most people don't think about Judaism at all. The few that do, at best, they think of the rather faceless religion of pre-Christianity. At worst, they parrot the historic judgment: a legalized religion preoccupied with externals, doctrinal minutiae, blind and cast out from God's grace because of their hardhearted obstinacy.

Christianity has a profound ignorance of living Judaism. The result is willful blindness to its essential, life-giving worldview that developed over the course of millennia. Historic bigotry has profoundly stunted and altered Christian doctrine and led us to advocate treating a race of people like a theological abstraction and ignore Judaism's resilient, vital foundation for Christian existence. The outcome is a disaster and directly related to this conversation about the *Blight in the Vineyard*.

Next, turn your attention to Church history and theology. With an understanding of Judaism fully in place, you will then see the evolution of Church history and thought in glaring, dare I say, disturbing light. You will have the foundation to see some very important departures that reshaped Jesus' words to mean things he could never have intended. Indeed, in Western Christianity you will see Jesus' warnings about the

Blight in the Vineyard

Leaven of the Pharisees come to full light. Do your homework well and you will be introduced to the Eastern Church who was conducting successful missionary campaigns into India, China, and made some in roads to Japan. This was happening at the same time Charlemagne was whacking the heads off 4,000 Saxons in the name of God and Church. You will learn of the massive propaganda campaign that has painted the Eastern Church as a minor irrelevancy at best or a divisive, un-submissive, heretical interloper on God's righteous plan centered in Rome at worst.[2] But if you have the smallest amount of intellectual courage, you will be introduced to spiritual and intellectual traditions that will shift your Christian worldview like Copernicus's proof that the earth revolved around the sun.

This is an exciting time to be alive because in the last thirty years, the scholastic advances in biblical studies, Judaic studies, and Church history have traveled light-years from the available knowledge in the 15th century. The archeological finds of Nag Hammadi and Qumran have had a few decades to reveal their truths, and the scholarship is rich and potent. A number of Greco-Roman archaeological finds have increased our knowledge of the Judean world to which Jesus preached, and some have increased our understanding of the spread and diversity of Christian expansion.

And last, dig into the evolution of thought from Plato to the present day. By the time you become fully acquainted with the gospel according to Platonist/Kantianism that has hijacked Jesus' teaching, you'll be about ready to address the ideological war being waged by the groupies of that historic syncretism. And

---

2. Very similar to the massive propaganda campaign that says Protestant Christian theology centers in Geneva.

make no mistake this is no gentleman's game. No matter how much advocates of the historic doctrines would like to pretend they represent love and grace, wring their hands and talk about the family of God, strip away the pretense and they will insist you are the enemy. History is replete with examples where those extolling the ideas of Platonist Kantian thought—men who hijack Bible ideas with impunity—if given free rein to government power, these doctrines have ended in bloodshed and despotism. Every arrow, every sword, every bomb, every bullet used in the history of warfare has its motivating power in the fight over the moral justification to subordinate man. The only lasting peace this planet has ever seen is directly proportional to man's liberty. To our great misfortune, the full philosophical case for man's sovereign individuality has yet to be published abroad to the minds of men, and the men who oppose those who seek to do so are open promoters of death. They make it sound righteous and spiritual. But at the end of the day, they are advocating man's death, and some are not particular about the means to get him there.

Even though the stakes are that consuming, don't be daunted by the gambit to triviality. Having done all of this research, prepare to be dismissed with a wave of the "I just preach Christ and him Crucified" wand "And you are just a big, unloving meaner who is hiding behind a veil of theological exactness." (Great words, Bob, but so very, very misapplied.) That is the nature of the conflict: aggressive denunciation or self-righteous, passive-minded pseudo thinkers. Be prepared to encounter all of the above.

Now let us briefly talk strategy:

1. Refuse to let Mystic Despots set the tone and standard of the conflict. Have the courage of Simon

Blight in the Vineyard

Episcopius and refuse to let pretend arbiters demand answers on their terms.

2. Quit scripture-stacking debates; they are tedious and useless. The real issue of Western theology has always been sourced in the Platonist/Augustinian worldview married to the power of the state. When the State can compel an interpretive methodology, there is no friendly debate over scriptural meaning. There is only war over their right to rule intellectual compliance. A theological ruling class has dominated this conversation by the power of academic orthodoxy, a manipulation of man's spiritual fears and the open use of violence to achieve intellectual conformity. Challenge their right to dictate revelation, and they scream heretic. Refuse to cower under that denigration, and some "predestined" leader will start looking for biblical reason to burn you (or your books) at the stake. And don't pretend that such things cannot happen in America. Church people burned black men and women in the name religious/doctrinal purity barely sixty years ago. And our current political, social, and religious environment is ripe for a repeat performance. But that is very defiantly another book.

3. Be conscious of your audience. Reformed/Calvinistic zealots are not the best choice. Their life purpose is to evangelize the world to Calvin's synthesis and scope out "heresy" in all forms; they are aggressive and relentless and will rat out the slightest deviation from their strict definition of Orthodoxy. Don't mistake academic familiarity with intellectual motivation. These people are typically lay systematic theologians that have read a dozen

John Immel

    books by leading contemporary Calvinistic writers who have been bitten by the academic/scholastic bug. And once the concrete sets, all conversations require a hammer and chisel. They are admirable on some level for their focus and determination, but their intellectual stubbornness makes them mostly insufferable and any probing conversation impossible. For all of their biblical posturing, their theological horizon is measured in minutes and seconds with a fundamental resentment of a counterargument headwind. They have chosen a narrow field of systematic theological study and tend to assume it is the **only** field of biblical study. If you choose to try this conversation on for fun, note that it will inevitably degenerate into their assertion to an expected authority. This gambit is easy to spot, because they will presume that whatever Bible passage referenced can only be understood as they demand.

4. And last, don't worry about being called a heretic. Without the bonfires to intimidate, many of the historic arguments are very easy to overcome or even better, just dismiss. No man has a moral, spiritual, or intellectual responsibility to dead men's ideas. History shows forth the disaster of these ideas for all who will actually look. For those who do look, you have a moral responsibility to judge the ideas and their outcomes correctly.

How often are everyone else's bad ideas, bad doctrine, and bad theology made directly responsible for bad actions? Why are these ideas exempt from critical review? How come Pervasive Depravity and Altruism get a pass on their outcomes?

The answer is they don't. The ideas (and their advocates) do not stand apart eternal and affirmed by the universal depravities of man. Orthodoxy's failures are painted large across history. Proponents do not get authority, power, and absolution all in one magic word. It is incumbent on men who pursue TRUTH to judge the cause and effect of ideas correctly. The title heretic pales in the face of that rational responsibility. And we do have a rational responsibility. For all our appeal to humility, the one thing that historic Christianity has shown itself utterly incapable of doing is judging the ideas behind its actions. The single leading criticism of the Catholic Church is directed at its steadfast refusal to judge Papal decree error long after they have been shown laughably, horrifically wrong. Protestants don't fare much better. We are utterly condescending when offered new evidence, new understanding, and new knowledge.

Never lose sight of this fact. Man is judged for bearing false witness. It does not matter how noble the cause or how much "confusion" people will suffer by telling the TRUTH; once we know it, we have a moral obligation to adjust our witness. Martin Luther was wrong; there is no good strong lie for the sake of the Church. Modern men do not have a moral responsibility to cover for the rational errors of their ideological forefathers. We cannot claim affection for TRUTH when we treat new and better knowledge with contempt. We cannot win the world for TRUTH by perpetuating what is observably false.

So, quit worrying about being called a heretic. The name carries no power because at the moment, they can't burn you at the stake. They may try to wreck your reputation, accuse you of teaching doctrines of devils or raise the Boogieman of Postmodernist thinking, but vindication will come one way or the other. If Man's defenders succeed, liberty and freedom, and prosperity and life will prevail in America and eventually around the world. The power of the message will improve human existence, just like it has done in the few instances where the proclamation of man's right and empowerment to live has prevailed.

If we fail . . . shrug.

As our elected officials in the name of Altruism confiscate the productive lives of American citizens . . .

As our representatives borrow "prosperity" in the name of good intentions, condemning our children, grandchildren, and great grandchildren to serfdom . . .

As politicians chain us to the government plow with ever more oppressive laws in the name of "community" and "service" and "brotherly love" . . .

As judgment is destroyed and reality is abandoned so that no one may challenge the angelic utopian socialist collectivism and its violent twin brother Marxism . . .

As Mystic Despotism is merged into the power of an American theocratic state and the war on drugs expands to a war on bedroom practice . . .

As people scramble for the last shreds of prosperity, and abundance, and life before the class war devours everything like locusts . . .

As everyone decries the depravities of American culture, "It wouldn't be this way if only man were better!!!" . . .

As tyrants rise to compel "Righteous Actions" and "Racial Pride" and "Civic Duty" and "Social Order". . .

As yet another "Christian" nation wrings its hands wailing and moaning their great misfortune . . .

As the proud will to be an American vanishes under an onslaught of moral denunciation . . .

As the world scrambles to find a galvanizing reason to oppose the Religion of Peace's endless effort to command *Sharia* law . . .

As preachers thump a pulpit condemning the great sinfulness of man pretending that one more sermon will make a difference . . .

As church leaders start making deals with tyrants and privately patting themselves on the back for saving some . . .

As academics and educators woe and tumult: "How come no one can **think**?????!!!!" . . .

As America watches her own demise, wondering why the people are asleep, why do they act like sheep, where is the action to turn back the evil, why won't somebody "**Do Something!!!!!!**" . . .

As all this is happening, we can say, "I told you so."

. . .

. . .

. . .

But before we get to the very lofty goal of resisting tyrants and saving the world, many of you need to get healthy.

Notes

26
Group Homoousios and Individual Homoousios

I like a man who grins when he fights.

—Sir Winston Churchill

I cracked wise about group and individual nature some pages ago. Since that tickled me, I thought I'd resurrect the joke. Since our doctrine of Trinity is based on the assumption that what is true of the whole is true of its constituent parts, I figure that our collective health must also be a reflection of our individual nature. If individuals are healthy, then the whole will be too.

When I left PDI/CLC/SGM, I had enough individual confidence to dare disagreement with the doctrines, so I was motivated rethink the implications. Plus, I had a decade of spiritual life that predated SGM, so my Christian identity was not a product of their affirmation. I was mostly secure in my authenticity even if they didn't hug me into the grand fraternity of believers. And in the times when I was not so secure, my little internal drummer supplied a marching rhythm.

But most importantly, I had the historic and Bible science tools I've overviewed in the preceding pages and that helped me wade through the interpretive methodology and identify effective departures. Combined together, I was able to get out from underneath some of the most oppressive ideas perpetrated on man. What you have read to this point are the high points of that intellectual path I've walked out over the course of years.

John Immel

However, in retrospect, I was far from healthy. This, of course, assumes that I am spiritually healthy now.

>snicker<

We'll talk about how I define that lofty notion in a minute.

I can't unravel all of the intellectual and spiritual issues bound up inside you with the limited space of the book, so I'm not going to try. The limits of my goals were stated from the beginning. I set out to discuss:

- The motivating power of our love
- The motivating power of our fears
- The assumptions of authority
- The means of manipulation
- The intellectual sleights of hand used to demagogue the sheep in the pews
- The power demanded over people's lives
- The specific doctrinal function spread abroad in Christianity

I have given you a snapshot of historic of Christian thinking. I have introduced you to some intellectual tools that will help find some confidence in your own ability to grasp the ideological world in which you live. This confidence will give you the courage to evaluate the doctrines to which you have been demanded to subordinate your mind.

Thanks to Dave Harvey's exhortation for mental reflection we've seen the truth. The select ability to ignore large parts of Higher Critical Methodology and subsequently use a presumptive authority to dismiss historical realities, men are able to declare a narrow strand of 16th century theology the only game in town. This demagoguery is fantastically limited in scope. No denomination with an existence measured in decades and a doctrinal tradition that has undergone dozens and dozens of revisions can make a rational claim to possess the **only absolute truth.** Two thousand years of Church history makes this underlying claim ridiculous on its face. Furthermore, church organizations are not free to create doctrinal machines that so terrifies intellectual and spiritual disagreement that people fear for their very spiritual lives. No single man or a group of men can claim exemption from intellectual critique on pain of divine reprisal; to do so is a profound conceit and the height of rational, logical, and intellectual fraud.

Anyway, we have talked about all of that. The part that hasn't been discussed is the aftermath of exposure.

Let me see if I can guess where some of you are.

It all started like a dream. In the beginning, there was church on Sunday. You participated in the "Local Church" because it was mandatory, but people don't complain. Leaders insist they are uniquely qualified to vet your gifts and place you in the service of their choosing. This is how **real** Christianity is done. You were told to abandon yourself to the church because it was the safest place a person could share their lives. You poured yourself into your friends and your service and the hope of your calling. And then somewhere between the New Members' class and walking out the door (or being tossed out), something **bad** happened. Suddenly, the church was anything but safe. A life event took you before leadership, and the result was disaster. Somehow the world according to them and the world of your life no longer matched . . . and you dared to say so.

You were told that Christians should not fight, and if they did, they were obligated to make it right. You thought you objected correctly. You did what you had been taught. You confessed your sin. You laid yourself bare. You granted leadership total accesses. And under the same presumption, they told you they would supply the same relational standard.

Suddenly, the transparency you offered freely in what you thought was secure friendship became their greatest lever of criticism. Somehow, all the service you had given, all the marks on the "committed" column, were irrelevant up against some charge of overarching pride, or arrogance, or manufactured spiritual sedition. To your growing dismay, leadership judgment was unhinged from any sense of proportion. Their actions were trivial relational failures. Your actions and attitudes placed you on par with murderers, and false prophets, and other biblical ne'er-do-wells. You tried to set the record straight, but that only seemed to dig the pit deeper. The recriminations of spiritual failing mounted with every counseling session.

You thought, surely, if you were diligent to the Matthew 18 reconciliation ethic, there would be some vindication, and then forgiveness, and then peace.[1] But to your growing dismay, leadership was unable or unwilling to hear your dispute. With shameless consistency, leaders and sub-leaders and sub sub-leaders worked to divide and conquer your marriage, pitting the masculinity and leadership of husbands against the delicate theological female sensibilities of wives. They had kibitzed and affirmed their mutual conclusions. Their reaction was monolithic: You are indeed proud and arrogant and in sin; ergo, your objections are irrelevant. And then it became clear that reconciliation had one definition: You were wrong, they were right. You were

---

1. A reference to the process of engaging offended parties, then bringing others into the interaction to mediate, then further involving people to establish the scope of the issue, unless and until the offending party is found irreconcilable.

given two options: to get onboard or withdraw . . . quietly. Everyone has objections about their church experience after all. This is no different. Whatever happens, do not talk about the pastors, but on the other hand, your character was assassinated at every turn.

As you take inventory, you realize your Christian experience has been a bizarre mix of trying to live up to "what should be" and the disastrous confusing reality of "what is." No matter how you seek to reconcile the two, you remain mystified in the pursuit of a solution: The hurt does not subside and you are terrified that the judgments pronounced against your very existence are true. The fear lingers on the horizon like a mist: unnamed, without full shape. The lack of definition paralyzes your soul. The thought of taking any action in behalf of your own life fills you with a tiredness that seeps into the bones. And then, after some time has passed, the only abiding conclusion is really no conclusion: resignation. You resign yourself to accept the judgments for failing to live the standards that Christians barrage you with at every meeting. And under all of this is a brooding anger that has no outlet, target, or expression.

Here you are: hurt, paralyzed, spiritually drained, fearful, resigned, and angry.

Fear, Bitterness, and Anger

That last emotion in the list is a big deal. You're not supposed to be angry.

Anger is a sin, and you shouldn't sin because . . . well, . . . you shouldn't, even though you can't help yourself because you are indwelt with sin, which compounds the despair because you sin but can't help it, which seems to validate what your preacher told you. And if that is true, then maybe the other stuff they said was true . . . and . . . and . . . and . . . you can't find anyplace else like that church, but that fills you with more pain, which drives your frustration higher because there is no one to talk to, because that would be gossip, and Matthew 18 says that you should go to your brother privately, but that didn't work, and the loneliness is excruciating and . . .

You walked out from underneath the "covering" and now you are looking around at the events of your life playing an elaborate game of divine charades. You're not sure that God's leading takes on specific words, but you have impressions that told you to RUN and your steps toward extracting yourself (and your family) is agony . . .

The questions come hot and heavy: "What if I'm in sin?"

"What if they really are right and it's just some massive deception on my part?"

"What if bad things happen?"

"Is that God telling me I'm wrong?"

Stop.

Let's **think**.

Notice that your internal conflict revolves around exactly what I told you it was designed to do. The force of your fears is wrecking your confidence; it is destroying your self-appointment moral clarity. The result is terror and passivity. Do you see it? This is the evil underneath the ideas we have been talking about: indoctrinated terror.

Before we talk about your proactivity, we need to engage our minds and wade through the misinformation. So, let's talk about bad things and God's revealed will for a minute. Let me flip this around. Let's say that you go into your pastor because something bad happened: losing a job, or a miscarriage, or a car accident, or whatever.

Blight in the Vineyard

You are under their "covering" but the bad thing still happened.

What will be their counsel?

Will they ever say to you, "Well, since you are here under our protection, this bad thing shouldn't have happened? We'll pray and tell God this bad thing is a great injustice in light of having honored His will. Since you are submitted to us, He will put it back the way it was."

Come on, laugh with me. That is really funny. You know they will offer this bromide: "God is Sovereign." So the bottom line is it sucks to be you. And depending on what they think of you, they will say something like "Is this revealing a secret sin in your life?" or "Pressure just reveals what is really on the inside of you," or "This is designed to show you an increasing measure of God's Grace. You need to trust God."

And your reaction after some contrite tears would be to nod and smile thinking: "My . . . what wisdom. What a privilege to have their insightful counsel."

What did the "covering" get you exactly? Did oversight get you a dispensation on that BAD thing?

I don't know which is worse, a pastor playing both sides of this intellectual fence or people **letting** them play both sides of this intellectual fence. If they are going to obligate **you** to doctrine, then **they** should be obligated to an **outcome** if you are obedient.

But anyway, bad things happen. By doctrinal standard, all bad things are good things anyway . . . so chasing your tail over the **meaning** of events will just make you want to sit in the corner and blither your lips and drool down your chin. Go outside and look up . . . the sky did not fall. Nor will it fall tomorrow, nor the next day.

John Immel

I submit you will figure out how to deal with bad things better and faster if you start with the premise that **you should** fix the bad things. When you accept that circumstance is some vague, hazy portent of divine wrath, some mysterious event of God's ironclad will, what action can you take?

God has infinitely better communication skills than we give him credit, and circumstance as intended "Divine Will" is a superstitious doctrine handed down from the age when man lined cathedrals with gargoyles.

It is time that adult Christians to start acting like rational beings and observing the cause and effect of our world. Looking for some overarching, Meta, Dao, Zen, the Universe is teaching portent rarely produces something good. The **meaning** of most life events is merely the outworking of choices—sometimes many people's choices—mixed with the laws of physics, economics, and ideas. By accepting those events on face value, people are, as a rule, way ahead of the understanding game.

But more importantly, it is time for Christians to start expecting that God is perfectly capable of talking to them like adults, explaining His will as simply as they speak to their own kids. You don't piteously drub your kids around the head and shoulders in response to a failed, bewildering game of charades. Why we think that God treats Man any different is flat bizarre.

So . . . choose peace and let Him explain himself.

He will.

The Soul-Sucking Need

"But John, they did help me . . ."

They did, huh? I assume you mean that **they** (whoever they are) somehow are responsible for an advance of your sanctification? Somehow men were a means of grace to your better action or conduct?

Jedi, how is that possible? How is it possible for mere mortals to take credit (or give credit) to what is undisputedly God's sovereign action? Man plays no part in his own salvific experience. If men are going to preach the doctrines we have talked about, they can never get any such accolades. At best, they are automatons in God's mysterious machine, acting out their predestined course, vessels of destruction with no right to pleasure or affirmation. Their reward is to avoid Hell and maybe, if God so chooses, access to His rest. No more, no less. All men preaching these doctrines are zeros, nothing, a nonentity, and a non-value worthy of no consideration.

Did that seem vicious? Of course it did. But it is not my comment that is the problem. That is the logical extensions of the doctrines.

Did I get your attention?

So, how can you be giving credit to men for your sanctification? For any help? All Good comes from God, right? No Man is Good, so how can you ascribe good to any mortal? What is this damnable display of spiritual treason lifting up men to Usurpers of the Irresistible Grace throne?

Is your mind reeling from the accusations as you desperately try to reconcile what you have been led to believe? Well, you are going to have to decide your faithfulness to the doctrines discussed. If you are going to remain committed to those doctrines, then you are stuck with the implication. Or you are guilty of the very Convenient Calvinism that lets people make the Bible say pretty much whatever they want it to say (all the while screaming about orthodoxy).

If you are going to muster the courage to reevaluate

the doctrines and find effective departures, then we need to address those vague foreboding fears that drive your soul-sucking need for **their** affirmation. Mixed into your terror is this lingering suspicion that if you don't act **flawlessly** after having left your church, a failure of conduct or attitude will validate the pastoral judgments. Let me remind you, this is what the doctrines are designed to do: compel you to seek men for authenticity and affirm your identity.

You are extracting yourself from a group that has for years been the source of your affirmation. Your identity has been mixed deep into the corporate image. Actually, it is more potent than that. You have been told and told and told and told that the corporate identity should **be** your identity. Most people have longstanding relationships—personal friends, children's friends, private school commitments—that are sourced in that collective personality. You **lost** your identity long ago. By walking away, you are cutting off a part of your very self. Whack off a finger and notice the pain. This is no different.

The challenge now is to rethink or even reinvent an identity. This is no easy task. You have some deeply embedded assumptions that dramatically affect your ability to find a strong, healthy, independent identity. I am going to make some suggestions a little later in the chapter. It does get better though, as your identity rounds out. Eventually, the soul-sucking need for affirmation will begin to pass because you will be all right with who you see in the mirror.

Be Perfect or Else . . .

You've read the first part of this chapter but

insecurity dominates your soul. You find yourself longing to have your pastor, and the local leadership team, and your friends think well of you—inexplicably needing their affirmation. You want to show everyone: "See, I'm not apostate. I'm not going crazy." So, you agonize over every word you say. You flip back and forth between being confident and being utterly weak. If you offer any objection to their treatment, you feel a powerful need stipulate and wheedle. You are terrified that if you fail to act exactly like they expect, you are the failure. This need, this fear, boils inside of you. You try to tell yourself this is "the fear of man" and its source is pride. You should repent of the pride. But that only seems to feed the idea that your pastors were right all along.

I understand. I've been exactly where you are.

But **think** of the stunning conceit the pastor to pew-sitter relationship represents. Preachers like to pretend that if people are not perfect in their criticisms and actions, then the person is in error, which means the criticisms are invalid. And mystery of mysteries, people fall for it. Indwelling Sin and the Doctrine of Pervasive Depravity mean that people live in abject moral, social, and spiritual wickedness. This should include pastors but no one dismisses their Sunday morning rants for the same reasons. Expecting the bearer of correction or rebuke to be perfect is absurd.

Don't fall for the myth. Don't let yourself be bullied into scrubbing your heart for every perceived, potential, or fictional failing when church leaders don't begin to hold themselves to the same standard. You are not disqualified because you **might** make a mistake. Your choices are not diminished because you **might** experience failure. Your New Birth is authentic even when you do fail. If all sin is the same horrific spiritual sedition, and if they applied the same standard to their actions, they would be compelled to shut the doors of the church a day after opening.

On its face, this should boil the blood in your body. But that isn't where it stopped, is it? The intention is to make you dependent. It is spiritual crack. Now, you are going through withdrawals. There is nothing neat and tidy about what comes next. The process of detox is an ugly, nasty event.

You will do yourself a huge favor if you don't feel the need to walk this out perfectly. Being mindful of your heart is admirable and desirable, but give yourself the permission to just be. Over time, you will be able to repent till your heart is content, but give yourself time to heal and get your bearings.

Even if you are angry . . . it is OK. I know . . . that is a hard one to swallow. You've heard endless sermons about sinful anger which preachers tend to define as any unapproved emotional reaction to their injustice. I think you will find that many things you are angry about you should be angry about. You have been exploited.

Theoretical Guilt

It is time to get out from underneath theoretical guilt. Men preach these doctrines in direct proportion to their contempt for you: your ability, and your life. Never forget the function of the doctrine is to seduce you to embrace a theoretical failing so you feel incompetent to uphold any standard so they can make any assertion. The purpose is to get you to abandon critical review.

Here is the reality. The preachers of theoretical guilt do not believe their own doctrines. Or maybe I should say, whatever the dearly held theory, they smuggle into

Blight in the Vineyard

their theology a host of caveats and addendums that lets them off the consistency hook. Most of what you see pouring fourth from Christian pulpits is theater. When you see a man wailing and moaning his great depravities, you are watching a morality play, a not so polite fiction designed to yank on your heart strings. The tears and the anguish and the soulful consternation come forth in a fit of moral narcissism. But eight minutes after he walks off that stage, he is dry-eyed and smiling and receiving the accolades for his great homily. Oh, he will pepper the acceptance with all manner of Altruistic rot, and self-deprecation, but this pales in light of Total Depravity Eternity. The very enemy of God should be looking for a mountain to crawl under where he can flail himself for the temerity to open his mouth and daring to speak in God's stead, not glad-handing his way through congregational ego stroking.

Never forget this: It is fraudulent doctrine because it cannot be practiced. There is no practical expression that can stand up to the metaphysical assertion. People invent half measures and pay sanctimonious lip service, but the only truly "appropriate response" to these doctrines is utterly passive, grief-stricken, self-imposed, unrelenting sanction. And maybe, God—in His great mysterious wisdom—will occasionally fill the soul with a blessed reprieve. Maybe. . . . But one can never have a self-appointed hope. Any scripture they read on Grace and have the temerity to assume it applies to **them** is a manifestation of fraud. As Dave Harvey so eloquently declared, "As Christians, we must never forget that our remaining sin nature will continually drive us to subordinate the objective truth of scripture to subjective impressions." Since man is self-deceived, this deception includes Eternal Assurance. Since each of us is doomed to our own "cramped, subjective little universe of personal impressions," we should be utterly suspicious of **any** hope that creeps into our decadent and wicked heart. So abandon ye all hope ye who enter here! You can never have a self-appointed hope that you will be saved.

Is the "clear and objective truth" of these doctrines finally plain enough for you? Or are you still trying to evade the logic with the wave of the "I just believe" wand? If you can dodge the conclusions, it is because you are not at all consistent with your own doctrinal loyalty. You pick and choose what you want to believe for your own felt needs payoff, so what follows will be irrelevant.

For those of you who battle endless tides of guilt and despair and no matter how often you try to grasp "Grace" or someone tries to explain your "doctrinal deficiency," or assure you of your "eternal security," know this: **You** are the one exercising integrity—not them. Your spiritual affections have absolutely conformed to the correct rational dead end. And this is why you can find no peace. For you to get free, you must fully grasp the violence you are doing to your own psyche. The human psyche cannot sustain an endless barrage of soul-crushing denigration. Behavioral science journals are filled with case studies of sociopathic and psychopathic tendencies that were environmentally drilled into human subjects. If you want to see what twisted looks like, find a child raised by parents that pick and pick and pick and pick, condemn and condemn and condemn in the name of God everything the child does, everything he says and everything he thinks. That cute tyke will be torturing kittens or whipping himself for penance by sixteen. A moral existence brutalized into deviancy was not born that way; they were created.

Men who seek to fulfill the full logical outcomes of

these doctrines—without filter, caveat or addendum—are warped from within by a self-righteous, self-loathing so corrupting that they have lost connection with existence. This is no snarky euphemistic jab for being a moron. This is the conclusion of the ideas. When man is doctrinally mandated to see the whole of his life damned, the sum of his being a curse, the full measure of his rationality bankrupt, he **must** presume that his senses and his mind betray him. The only appropriate response in light of Pervasive Depravity Eternity is the commitment to pluck out his own eyes, lobotomize his own brain, and immolate his own soul. To be consistent, he is morally required to unhinge himself from the world. The only thing left is a worldview of justified, endless, tormented suffering. He **must** embrace an ecstatic mysticism that descends into fits of weeping, grief, anguish and self-flagellation. Historically, many of the men who taught these doctrines and acted consistent with the metaphysical assertion were exactly that way. Or maybe better said, those who acted on these "Christian" doctrines were socially deviant psychological wrecks.

We would never tolerate such abnormal, socially isolated personalities in positions of Church authority today. If they do in fact occupy positions of governing leadership, the people around them work to hide the pathology from full view. In small doses, it looks super spiritual and makes the glossy brochure seem authentic. But if the self-denouncing, self-destroying, self-loathing ever comes to the forefront the mental imbalance is revealed for all its deviant destructive glory.

We have a collective conniption fit if a preacher has the mildest eccentricity to his presentation and a body full of tattoos. Yet the personality aberration described above has been whitewashed as "Christian piety" and is part of the larger picture of corruption embedded in these doctrines. The reason the whitewash works is because theoretical guilt seduces us into mindless obedience.

You do not have a moral obligation to follow their path.

What Does Healthy Look Like?

Your goal is to get healthy. Depending on how long you have been part of groups that teach the doctrines discussed, it is possible you have never seen what healthy really looks like.

Healthy people:
- Believe that God likes them
- Like the kind of person they are
- Can define what they want
- Can be intentional
- Can take action without direction
- Can accept criticism in context to their wants and desires
- Can express their emotions
- Can accept criticism without feeling the need to change who they are
- Can identify behavior that leads to bondage: spiritual, emotional, physical

I have a friend who is a psychiatrist, Dr. Mark McDonald. We have spent endless hours dissecting the cultural problems and its relationship to individual interpersonal action. In light of Brent Detwiler's comments, I thought it would be appropriate to offer up a professional's take on the nature of well-adjusted mental health. Since psychiatric practice is being denigrated as something evil, unspiritual, and part of a broader failed doctrine, I thought it only fair to see exactly what these masters of deception had to offer. Maybe they really are the devil incarnate. And maybe, a psychiatrist's summation of human mental health is a good one. Let us mentally reflect.

When asked to give insights for this book, Dr. Mark McDonald had the following to say:

A healthy woman displays three qualities:
1. She is kind, confident, and happy. She knows how to express concern so that she does not have to live in fear.
2. She is independent emotionally and financially to better succeed in pursuing a partnership rather than a dependency on her mate.
3. She is sexually uninhibited but monogamous. She has a strong self-identity but presents herself with humility and is always working toward improvement.

About men, he said:

I've been thinking about "healthy men" for a while now. What I've concluded, to my own surprise, is that a healthy man is essentially no different from a healthy woman. I've long subscribed to the view that men and women are fundamentally different, but I don't believe that anymore. I do think that unhealthy men and women think and behave differently (in equally unhealthy ways), but when you look at the healthy examples of both sexes, the differences are less apparent than are the commonalities. Healthy men are sexually vibrant and monogamous, financially and emotionally independent, unafraid to voice disagreement or state important needs, and have developed a personal philosophy of life based on years of experience and reflection.

John Immel

> For both sexes, holistic health requires constant tending to internal and external needs—namely, spiritual development and social integration in the context of a self-aware and emotionally balanced state of being.
>
> Additionally, I think self-awareness and emotional balance are prerequisites to obtaining spiritual development and social integration. People with personality disorders or untreated manic-depression can never be truly healthy, because their state of being is either too turbulent or too eccentric to foster spiritual growth and productive social relationships. Within a salted earth, nothing can grow.
>
> This is something many continue to ignore—that their current and future life will never change course until they address the pervasive deficits that prevent internal growth and mutually rewarding social ties.
>
> How does one succeed in embracing the path of self-reflection, self-criticism, self-awareness while at the same time maintaining an appreciation of the wonder of the experience of life? It's like asking the host to just sit down and enjoy the party. And yet some manage to do it. To be healthy, I think, requires one to embrace the role of observer and participant simultaneously, which is quite a challenge. It requires work, but most people don't want to be bothered.

Mark goes on to add:

> On a more scientific side, I have read over the past year that healthy people (as defined by subjective contentment and objective longevity) tend to be less anxious, more expressive of negative emotions (to better purge them acutely), and more curious intellectually than the average person.

From my own personal experience, I see the healthiest people as those who have defined a sense of purpose and have integrated socially into their community. Humans are spiritual and social creatures, and I believe that for a person to be healthy, both purpose and belonging must be present.

Just look at unhealthy people and see how those qualities are lacking. They usually fail to define a life purpose, because they are unclear about their identity and thus lead a daily ritual of scattered, ineffectual, project-chasing behavior.

They have a limited sense of belonging, because they have failed to find anything they are worthy of giving. Unhealthy people avoid committing to people due to fear of being rejected.

By my definition, even a ditch-digger can be healthy, if he feels his work has purpose, and he feels connected to his family and neighbors. Greatness and health are not correlated, unfortunately. I do think that happiness and health are.

The above sounds positively Satanic, doesn't it? Oh woe is us! The devils of psycho-analytics are going to destroy us all!

Think about where you are now. Can you define your purpose? Can you define what you are worthy of giving? Or more fundamentally, does the idea of you being worthy fill you with shivers. Do you hear endless commentary about indwelling sin and sinful motives in your head? Can you define your identity? Or do you need someone else to tell help you define yourself? Do you feel an overwhelming need to have a pastor look you deep in your eyes, put their hand on your shoulder, and say, "You belong"?

John Immel

If you couldn't give good answers to the above questions, no worries . . . I will show you some steps to take so that you can get there.

"What Do I Want?"

The first step is to be able to define you. Right now you have lost what you looks like. The sum of your identity is built around a corporate image with someone else as arbitrator and director.

To find you, you are going to have to think about what defines you; not what should define you and not what ought to define you. Many of you will be terrified of this exercise. You will feel a powerful, powerful need to proof-text your every thought, word, and action as if the only way you are authorized to act is if you can find a scripture that gives you tacit authority to just exist. There isn't enough space in this book to unravel the failures of the interpretive methodology that has been drilled into your soul. So, I will say this: The Bible was not designed as a battering ram. The very need to micro-measure man's every breath is the deep and abiding core of the leaven of the Pharisees. The endless quest for a doctrinal precision as a means to human validation is as sure a path to bondage as utter debauchery. This very mindset is what Jesus said made men twice the son's of Hell. So, put away the pretense that has been poured into your soul; right this minute there is no agenda, no right or wrong answers.

Sit down with a piece of paper and write that question. Then write the answer.

Many of you will be tempted to write "To do God's will."

>sigh<

OK . . . **specifically**, what is that? Can't tell? Don't know? The only thing that comes to mind is the roiling uncertainty of the whole mess? Can you be very specific about God's will and take clear, subsequent action? If you can, then you probably don't need what follows. If you can't . . . then read on.

Frankly, the bromide "To do God's will" is a wonderfully vague copout on personal choice, desire, and self-appointment. It gives a person the broadest credit for a spiritual sentiment with no responsibility to any specific outcome. The rub of life is always in the doing, it is always in the action. There is no faith without works. I know what most people have been taught about faith and works, and I won't unravel the doctrines now except to say this: You must take ownership of the course of your life. And the only way to really do that is to define who you are and what work you are inclined to do.

Most people have the process of finding the Will of God backwards—which leads to 90 percent of Christian consternation. We look to a guy who calls himself pastor and wait for him to pat us on the head and say, "Yea, verily." The loose logic being, a professional Christian must have a monopoly into God's specific will. Funny thing though, talk to most of these men long enough and you find they are just as blurry on the whole issue as you are. But to be sure, the starting place for their grasp of divine will is **their life**. So, is it really a mystery why they always determine God's will is for **you** to give **them** some part (or all) of you?

As an aside, every pastor I've ever met has said it is my job to submit to them. To illustrate the arbitrary absurdity of that declaration, I finally started saying: "No, it is your job to submit to me. Now give me your tithes."

John Immel

It is too hilarious to watch their faces as they realize I'm as serious as they are.

Anyway . . .

If the pastor thing doesn't work too well in finding God's will, most of us play a variation of divine charades—

two syllables . . .

feel like God is saying . . .

And then we shout out answers desperately hoping someone will tap their nose and point in our direction. For most people, charades quits being fun after the first group date night and men go home with angry wives. "You thought I meant 'churning ice cream' when I'm clearly shooting a **movie**? Have you lost your mind???" And it isn't any more fun when God is gesturing like a Major League Baseball third base coach. At least, the professional baseball player has the advantage of knowing the code. •

Which leads nicely to the issue of the "code" for unraveling God's will. For many people, the logic goes like this: "Well, I feel God wants me to be a missionary. And since I really **don't want** to go to Africa, that must mean that's where God wants me."

So, the definition of divine will is what you **don't want**?

"I just **want** what God wants," and then saying "I **don't want** to do what God is asking . . . therefore, **that** must be his will."

That is really funny and really, really, really absurd.

Spiritual perfection has nothing to do with an absence of self. No matter how it has been portrayed over the last 2,000 years, Christianity is not a Zen, zero religion of human vacuum. The source of this anti-self, anti-personal interest, anti-desire, anti-rational, anti-material doctrine has deep roots in Medieval thought and has made insidious inroads to Christian doctrine and practice. I cannot expose the true non-biblical sources of these doctrines in this work, nor address the modern manifestation of this evil perpetrated by the unwary who have imported Immanuel Kant's philosophy (circa 1750) into Christianity. But your current issues come from Bible ideas hijacked by vain, destructive, death-worshiping philosophies that lead men to believe they are wrong to have any self at all.

There is no such thing as a human vessel perfected with emptiness.

Let me ask you this: For the duration of your time within the Church collective, you strove to be an empty vessel, right? Who filled you up?

If it was God, why do you so desperately crave the affirmations of men?

Do you see the rub? If the empty vessel bit is God's highest ideal, why then are men the determining factor in your spiritual and emotional "substance"? Or maybe the better question: How can there be spiritual "substance"? Anything multiplied by zero is still . . . zero.

Let me ask you this question: In all the accusations of sin**full**ness, uh . . . where is the self? Your identity is borrowed from the group. Your desire to conform is demanded by doctrine. Your mind is filled with ideas approved by other men. The work of your hands, the "service" to the local church, is organized from apostolic central planning. The "character" you have is because leadership enforces your actions. When you seek men to "commend" you to the work of the ministry, you are really looking to garner prestige. And prestige is a product of other people's perceptions. Acceptable pleasures are strictly outlined from someone else's palate.

The self in this equation is a reflection in the mirror of other people's faces.

Every expression of your life, every value you seek to embrace is sourced from outside by the pressures of everyone else's wants, needs, or doctrinal demands. Where is the **you** in that equation? How can you be sinning when **you** are not present? How can you be guilty of a crime when **you** are not there?

Sounds grim when put like that, doesn't it? Makes you sound like an automaton, doesn't it?

You don't want to think that is you, do you?

If you don't think this is you, then I challenge you to answer this question: "What do I want?"

Can you give details in three minutes or less? Can you give details and not once have to modify the declaration with the silent thought, "But what would they think?"

If not, then you don't have a self. You are already empty. And by doctrinal definition, this should be your highest spiritual existence, the source of unspeakable joy, the state of unending satisfaction. At least, that is the marketing and packaging. Well, unless they are telling you to revere death, suffer, suffer, suffer, revere death! In death is life and peace blah, blah, blah, blah.

And yet you are miserable. . . .

Hmmm, interesting. . . .

Tell you what. Let's try something a little more mundane but substantially more effective. Or maybe better said, a little more definable. Start with fessing up to your real heart's desire. Own up to what you **want**: good, bad, or indifferent. Be excruciatingly honest. If you want to tie on a drunk for a year and forget every pain, write it down. Fly to the moon? Write it down. Rule the world? Write it down. Run down the road naked screaming like a little kid? Write it down. Rob a bank with Richard Nixon masks on your head? Write it down. Write a bestseller? Write it down. Create a work of art? Write it down. Invent the hydrogen engine? Write it down. Tour the Amazon jungle? Write it down. This is not for public consumption. The goal is to be as blatantly, brutally honest as you can muster. The goal is to get to the inside of you: the deepest desires, wants, and aspirations buried deep.

Don't skimp on the rewards, or the accolades, or the achievements you desire. This is not an exercise in digging into the cesspool of your soul. This broad tour of your **self** will identify some bad. But most importantly, it needs to reveal the greatness, the virtues, and the hero within. This is the most important element of you that needs identified because this person will love to rise in the morning and go to bed at night in the bliss and security of the wonder of them, without conceit or pretense.

Pretend you are David, standing on the battlefield before he heads out to take on Goliath. Notice that he asked what the reward for killing Goliath was three times. He had ambitions of his own. He wanted the King's daughter and a trip to the Royal Penthouse. Newsflash: David had self-interest and self-ish motives. He was a man after God's own heart.

I suspect that you will be amazed at what hits the page, stealing your breath at honesty you have not expressed in years. The first shock will come as you list all the things you used to **love** to do but haven't done forever. You sacrificed those values only to realize that no one else really valued what you were cutting off. (This single reality has been the greatest source of guilt and frustration.) The longer this sacrifice list gets, the more your anger will grow at how much of you had been lost. Part of you will weep with the joy of meeting yourself again. Your personal honesty will fill you with a vibrancy you may have forgotten, or more significant, discover for the first time.

OK . . . got your list?

Now, identify the illegal and the insane, and tuck those away for a good laugh. This important step is how you know you are rational enough to be a safe member of the human race. If one cannot distinguish this part . . . then . . . well, you have other problems that this book, or maybe any book, cannot help.

>snicker<

The sane amongst us can now move to the next step.

And . . . Action

The reason you feel so powerless is because you have forgotten how to take action. You are so used to having someone filter and dictate and lead that your ability to make decisions has atrophied. You are going to have to build that muscle . . . again. Or maybe you are going to have to build it for the first time.

Many people gravitate to SGM style leadership because they don't like the responsibility of their own faith, their own choices, and their own lives. People will give up enormous freedom to be absolved of responsibility. No man should ask another to make his choices. And no man should be taking up that cause. It isn't their place.

The action you take is directly related to being able to answer the question: What do I want? So, these two sections are inseparable. Every time you find yourself

Blight in the Vineyard

answering the question, immediately go take action to get or do what you want.

But what if what I want is sin?

Well, if you are a Reformed Theology type, I say, how can you want anything else? So, what difference does it make if you take action on it or not? If all sin is the same before a Great and Holy God, what is the difference between wanting and doing?

I know what I just said. . . . It's your doctrine not mine.

If you are not a Reformed Theology type, I ask you, where is your faith? How is it you believe the New Birth so ineffective?

I contend that Christianity has become a twisted aberration of God's intent. We are to be salt and light in the middle of all the human disaster. Yet we are neither because we are not in the middle of anything except the church pews.

It really isn't complicated. We don't trust God. We don't trust him to "lead us not into temptation, but deliver us from evil." We don't really believe that He is gracious and forgiving and forgiving and forgiving. We don't really believe that God actually settled the issue of sin in his own mind. So, we are very sure we must forever revisit our failings before him. We fear that if we don't fear our very motives and desires, we will be led astray. We really don't believe that God meant what he said in Hebrews: ". . . no more **consciousness** of sin. . . ." But most appalling, we really don't believe the Holy Spirit will actually fill us with his fruit. He is the vine and we are the branches, and we will bear much fruit. We should be producing the fruit of the Spirit because it grows in us. That means every resource we will ever need to overcome every temptation grows within us. I suppose running away from temptation works in a pinch, but running isn't overcoming. And Holiness is not that absence of temptation. Holiness is the power to stand in the middle of all temptation and feel no pressure to succumb. That is the power, the treasure that resides in this earthen vessel.

But because of our unbelief, we retreat into the walls of our buildings so very sure that if we venture out, bad things will bite us in the ass and we will sin. If we sin, God will suffer some public shame.

So, it is better not to want. It is better not to risk. It is better to sit like an empty vessel and wait for God to put some motivation in me. The loose logic being, if He moves me like a puppet, there can be no question of the source.

Another thought occurs to me: No member of the biblical Faith Hall of Fame was so vacant. No human being who has ever done anything for God has been so inert.

Let me ask you this: What father really cares if he suffers shame for his children? No good father. What father puts his public image before the health and benefit of his children? No good father. What father gives one good rip what the neighbor thinks when his son or daughter is doing wrong? No good father.

The good father is only concerned with equipping that child in the best method possible to handle life's rigor. The good father is looking for the earliest and quickest path to self-reliance and self-determination.

So, the magic moment has arrived. You have your list of what you want and now you must **work** to get it. Get your car keys, drive to the store, and buy what you **want**. Get that application to the job of your dreams. Go lie on the beach and get a tan—the men lusting after your body

Blight in the Vineyard

can grow up and just deal with their own lust. Yes, men. The homosexuals are just gonna have to learn to deal with their own issues; the issue is not your modesty.

>snicker<

Forget whether it is wise or prudent or someone might object. You are not healthy enough to worry about all of that. Your ability to make decisions, **any** decision, has been stunted.

For many of you, this will be almost impossible. You will be soooo terrified that you might want the wrong thing, so paranoid that you will make a bad choice, so fearful that you will make a mistake, that you won't take any action at all.

Well, welcome to reality.

Let's assume it is all true, that you have wrong wants and make bad choices and mistakes. So what? You are not judged for a failure of omniscience. And only Mystic Despots turn naiveté into a sin and a virtue at the same time. They applaud your simplemindedness as long as you believe what they tell you without question. But they are utterly condemning when you make a self-appointed choice and use that as proof of your failure to conform to the true order of the universe. However, if you take action on what turns out to be a good choice, they want credit for the outcome. It is a scam. Humans are not born omniscient. And you are not condemned as you learn to master yourself in pursuit of life.

Standing inert and motionless, paralyzed by the boogieman of bad choices, is not a superior moral state. It occurs to me that the harshest judgment went to the guy who buried his talent for fear that his risk-taking would bring his master's wrath.

Uhh . . . said another way, he was judged for his paralysis. Conversely, the guy who took the greatest risk was the recipient of the greatest compensation. This is a standard in the Kingdom of God.

The careful, cautious, worrisome Christianity that gets perpetuated from pulpits by fearful men has sucked us dry of our power because we are sooo afraid that we will be wrong.

Trust me, self-appointment is much better. And as for bad choices, no worries; reality will enforce the good and recompense the bad. Since you are the master of your own destiny, the choices you make, the outcomes you create are yours. Own them, relish them, and never, ever demand someone else bail you out.

The Inevitable Pendulum

For some, you have never had freedom. You have never tasted the heady flavor of making a choice and eating the product of what you made. Sometimes the meal is bliss, sometimes it is sorrow, but once you accept the responsibility, the self-appointment is very satisfying.

You will be like the kid leaving the a strict household so impressed by your ability to make your own choices that you lose sight of sense. Unfortunately, I don't think it can be helped. Here is why. You have never been prepared to accept the rigor of your own life. When "leaders" think it is their job to run interference on all the bad decisions that people can make and filter all the bad things they can believe, they do those very people a huge disservice. They stunt their moral and spiritual development.

We are all familiar with the parents who are driven by fear of their children failing, running interference on all things bad. When the kid hits the streets, they can't handle what they encounter. This is horrific parenting.

Blight in the Vineyard

And it is equally horrific leadership. I don't think this is "leadership," but that is another conversation.

The fruit of this kind of "leadership" is in two kinds:
1. Individuals convinced of their utter inability to live effective lives, dependent on others to make decisions. (The spiritual crack addicts)
2. Individuals so hostile to any imposed order or outside counsel that their very own chaos leads them ever closer to impending social, personal, and moral disaster. (The moral anarchists)

Of course, neither course of action is a good result, but I do expect the pendulum to swing for you. I expect you to like defining yourself and acting like a healthy person. And I expect that you will find you've made some choices along the path that might seem to invalidate your self-expression.

It doesn't.

To commit error is human. Not because we are all just sinners, but because we are creatures who grow. We change! Growth in man's existence is expressed in the ongoing process of action and consequence, cause and effect. We are not born omniscient. We are born with a profound ability to change our actions by identifying the failure of bad ideas and adjusting the ideas and the actions accordingly. Actions are a reflection of values. There are only two effective values: things that produce life and things that produce death. Persist in either effort long enough and reality will enforce an outcome: life or death. Freedom is not lawlessness. Self-absorption looks like freedom, but it keeps you in bondage as surely as if you had someone standing over you dictating every move. Changing bad actions to persist in life values IS the power of change given to you at New Birth, and the result is to reap the reward of your own virtue—character, happiness, and identity.

No matter how bad your moment-to-moment choices are, I have this confidence. Between God and you working to adjust your values to reflect life, you will get to the right place, at the right time, healthy and satisfied.

I trust that God is big enough in you to lead and guide you to the right answers to your intentional questions.

The real cool thing about being intentional is you get to look back in life and have no regret. The moment you take responsibility for your actions—good, bad, or indifferent—woulda, coulda, shoulda, disappears.

The Next Generation

And no, this is not a Star Trek reference. This is an ongoing mission to explore the strange world of interpersonal outcomes and find new life. Our enterprise is to boldly talk about kids because this group has the pendulum swing hit them the hardest. The place I notice the wreckage of these ideas manifests with horrifying clarity is in children.

Man is born a ferocious creature fighting and squalling to live; he wants what he wants, when he wants it, and reason, rationality, or any other barrier be damned. This is a good thing, because he was born into an utterly hostile environment that requires that single driving determination to prevail. One of the drawbacks of American culture is we have been so successful at beating back the forces of nature that we have lost touch with what it takes to survive planet Earth. The ability to overcome is essential and important, but the problem is our proportion. So hostile is this world that not even one hundred years ago, American infant mortality rates were over 50 percent. And 30 percent of the children that survived birth died within the first year. People who made it into adulthood were fortunate to live past forty. We are insulted at the injustice of life if **all** of our children do not live to a ripe old age. We live in air-conditioned homes, rarely want for heat, and complain roundly if the sky dares drop water on our heads. So used to mastering our environment are we that presidents are faulted for natural disasters as if the force of his office **should** have stemmed the tides, stilled the ground, and calmed the seas.

So, it is easy for those of us in the current age to look at forceful, self-driven existence of the young and think it a bad thing. We think we inhabit a gentler, kinder world, so why can't Man's nature be the same? Our error is we are mistaking insulation for attitude. Planet Earth is not nicer; its forces are merely controlled . . . sort of. I submit that if Man did not have this ferocious will to live built into his DNA, we would have ceased as a species long, long ago.

Anyway, the little bundle of barbarism is manageable for a brief time mostly because adults are bigger: a factoid that somehow never registers as a disadvantage in a baby's marauding soul. This developmental stage is blessedly short-lived, and mom and dad tend to think it adorable so they are restrained from eating their young. No culture can survive the fresh wave of barbarians that spring from the womb every year unchecked; hence, the rise of the benevolent (hopefully) totalitarian state called family. But all governments are the product of philosophy, and adults indoctrinated into the doctrines at hand bring the full force of ideas to bear on young psyches.

Adults exposed to the Platonist/Augustinian doctrines

use tools that help them bootleg caveats and addendums into the teaching that lets them escape the destructive logical extension. This is why most adults are a basket case of theological inconstancy. For the sake of self-preservation, they seek out mental and emotional hedges to find some peace in their soul. But kids don't have this luxury because they are force-fed the ideas at the same time they are being told Santa Claus gives presents to good little boys and girls. Children accept both ideas with wide-eyed wonder because mommy and daddy are the gods of their barbarian universe. In a few years, the crumb-crunchers will be fully smug knowing that Santa Claus isn't real, but doctrinally sound in believing they "sin" all the time. It must be true because mommy and daddy said so while they are getting spanked.

In the progression of human growth, man does not start philosophical development until later in life. A four-year-old asks why, not because he wants to integrate his metaphysical worldview, but rather because he likes hearing his voice. Mom and dad answer the question, "Just because," and the cute little tyke trots away munching on cookies. A fifteen-year-old asks why and mom and dad haven't figured out that "just because" doesn't work anymore and cookies are not a distraction. Why can't I watch that movie? Why can't I skip school? Why can't I have her as a friend? Why do I have to kiss dating goodbye? Why do we go to church? Why do we believe in God? Why? Why? Why? Why? Why? Why? Why? Why? Why?

And the answer comes back: "Because I said so." And when that doesn't get much traction, parents try for the ultimate authority: "Because the Bible says so." And when that doesn't pass the adolescent so-what test, the parental easy out is: "Because you are a sinner with

Blight in the Vineyard

foolishness bound up in your heart. Spare the rod and spoil the child!" Whack!

The kid is exasperated because they can't get satisfactory answers without reprisal. The parents are panicky because their argument can hardly stand up to the philosophical equivalent of the china shop bull. So, like a matador, they seek to bludgeon the teenager into philosophical submission.

Adolescents make bad choices for a host of reasons that we won't dissect. So, the times when they resist parental edicts that have merit are few and get tossed into the avalanche of misbehavior and written off as teen rebellion. But in their own utterly ham-fisted way, teens are wrestling with the very foundations of their existence. They are asking the questions and testing the limits of them**selves** in a deliberate effort to find an effective identity. The iterative process of action/failure, action/failure, action/success is how they are gaining feedback on what works and what does not. Of course, the inevitable question is "**Why** did it 'work'?"

Platonist/Augustinian doctrines presume that the problem is not a **misapplication** of **self**, but a problem with **having a self** at all. So, dogma-convinced parents decide that their kid's problem is an identity as such and make a relentless effort to destroy that.

When a young mind is pounded with the message of inability and self-doubt, it wrecks this very natural, very essential developmental stage. No matter how precocious the youngster, it takes no real skill to destroy the identity of a teen. I am always amazed at how often adults appoint themselves the destroyers of children who "need to be taken down a peg," and some do it with a stunning relish. It is a marvel that church functions exist with the express intent to batter young minds, wreck the smallest confidence, and demand they weep, wail, and moan in service to filling altar calls. And this despicable event is called "Youth Ministry."

Since the root of their adolescent quest was in service to an effective identity, the teenager's reactions are pretty much the response we discussed in the previous chapter. Just like the adults of our culture, some teens find a voice for their implicit self-loathing. The doctrines affirm their greatest suspicions, and they realize they can be absolved of life choices and responsibility. They like mooching their personality from the collective identity because they cannot be criticized if they have no self to fault. And for a young soul enduring the barrage of adolescence anxiety, this seems like a blessed escape. They don't need much motivation because Daddy "covers" them, so they embrace the pre-adolescent nanny state, expecting that some "authority" will provide the direction and substance of their life.

Parents love having a compliant kid, showing them off in church as models of sound doctrine and receiving the accolades of involved, theologically precise parenting. They count their lucky stars that God granted grace to their tykes, never realizing that the doctrines tended to suit their kids' personalities. And then they wake up one day and realize they have a thirty-something spinster child still living within arm's reach and always underfoot who has no ability to accept life's rigor and no one stepping up to perpetuate the nanny state. That is a sad story. But ultimately, everyone got what they wanted, so it is hard to sustain any real sympathy.

The story that gets all the press is the one that has all the fireworks. The family committed to the local church. They have a pew named after them because they are present every time the door opens. Dad is a deacon or

Blight in the Vineyard

an elder, or some other muckity muck in the congregation. The mother is prim and proper and dresses church approved. Her wee children are in ribbons and lace, homeschooled in pristine, utterly sterile beauty. They are the poster family for the Norman Rockwell of WASP upper middle class Christianity. The fairytale lasts until the dreaded adolescence hits, and then disaster strikes like the colliding of Leviathan against Poseidon.

The kids can smell their parents' fear that information not conforming to the tidy, sterile environment will find its way into their heads. The parents rail against "influences" and "environments," locking the horizon line of experience and exposure down in proportion to parenting terror. But the tide of ideas cannot be held back and wrecks the polite lies used to enforce family control. In a fit of utter doctrinal inconsistency, the parents console themselves that if only "so and so" or "such and such" were not in their child's life, all would be well with the world. They pay respect to Indwelling Sin and preach endlessly of the Man's unruly nature, offering vague portents of doom to terrorize the youth into obedience. But never once do they review the Doctrine of Predestination and say, "Yup, God picked my kid to go to Hell," thus conceding the truth of the doctrine. The only rational conclusion for the prevailing conduct should be that no parental effort will restrain the evil in their child's wicked soul. If God will not restrain them, how will their feeble efforts ever succeed?

No matter how much the parents preach the depravities of man, or demand obedience to God's word, or try to "discipline" a right mind, the kids will have none of it. They cannot wrap their mind around the blanket judgment of depravity when it is apparent that some men are good. And young people refuse to pretend they are not offended at logical inconsistencies. They demand answers to the hard questions and refuse to be patronized even if they are young enough to be their children. The parents might get some reprieve if their public life and private life are mostly the same, but if the public life is an utter hoax, the kids will be inconsolable. Adolescents can smell fake from miles away and have no patience for parents who put on a spiritual face at church and at home they are harsh tyrants fueling the household into emotional chaos. The child is viscerally insulted that the things they like are considered trivial or even evil. Never being allowed to have a passion or interest that isn't church-approved robs them of motivation to pursue anything, and they slump into indolence.

Of course, the kids don't have the ability to explain why they are so frustrated, why they feel so stifled, so compelled to passivity, or that the passivity is killing them. They can't detail why the Augustinian metaphysical worldview grates so hard on their soul. They find it absurd that mom and dad insist they cannot know anything of TRUTH unless it is revealed by a book all the while mom and dad exist in a fictional world of denial about what is obvious. As budding rational beings, they cannot grasp that lies are in service to TRUTH and TRUTH is in service to lies. TRUTH hits them every time they walk out the door and they encounter the substance of creation. How can they be asked to deny what is before them?

They are outmatched in the formal presentation so they are reduced to carping on their parents not "getting" them or rail against not being able to have friends. And when those values fail to get any traction with despot mom and dad, they respond like most adolescents . . .

with silent, sullen defiance: the only defense of individuality available. And this is the central point of the tragedy. Amidst the avalanche of teen anxiety, misbehavior, and parental reprisal was little more than a desperate quest for a **self**-defense . . . for both parties.

The parents were also trying to defend an identity: the corporate accolades of their accepted authority. It really does all boil down to an issue of authority. And the highest expression of Dave Harvey's truth is when parents protect the acquisition of authority at the expense of their children. The parents' identity was utterly tied to the moral narcissism embedded in the doctrines. As a result, they filtered every request, idea, or action through depravity. They measured their child's authentic conduct through the collective church lenses. They demanded the child's attitudes conform to an ideal "biblical" expression, a standard that by doctrinal mandate **no man can sustain** lest he no longer need God's Grace. Some parents even expect that molested children subordinate their self-defense to the pursuit of some lofty doctrinal/spiritual purity. Some churches requiring molested children remain in a hostile environment in the name of forgiveness and repentance.

I cannot imagine anything more demoralizing, anything more overtly **self**-effacing than a body of teaching that persuades grown men to sacrifice the emotional wellbeing of their daughter's or son's. A child has no claim to individuality when their right to feel safe is subordinate to the words: "I'm a sinner like everyone else, so forgive me." Imagine the value judgment that a young mind must internalize when they **must** go to a building at least four times a month knowing that the person who violated their greatest personal boundary will be in the pew just down the way, maybe having suffered no penalty because they "repented." And then insult to injury, that person in time may be given a title of authority because in repenting they had shown "great character."

Even the healthiest, most well-developed of men cannot sustain this kind of interpersonal ongoing violence or integrate the horrific sense of proportion **that** collective dynamic forces upon them. So, it is no wonder that an adolescent acts out against the ideological and interpersonal train wreck being done in the name of God and Church?

Parents, committed first and foremost to their own identity, are mystified by their kid's actions, feeling victimized after having "tried so hard." The House doubles down on the doctrines clinging desperately to the "promise" that "If you raise up a child in the way he should go . . . he will not depart . . . ." But they are secretly, desperately afraid that they will lose their position because ". . . if a man know not how to rule his own house, how shall he take care of the church of God?" And then Leviathan takes the cards and tosses them in Poseidon's face and says, "No, the House doesn't always win," and bolts.

And the disaster continues. The kid hits the streets looking for the very identity that mom and dad summarily wrecked. In the barbarian, philosophical world, this is the easiest integration; girls end up in an endless string of beds to find someone to reflect a self back into their soul, and the boys assume they will get value by an endless campaign of conquering. Since there is no such thing as a righteous pleasure and being conscious is painful, the path of least philosophical resistance is drugging and boozing and sexing their lives into depravity. They reject moral judgment as such

Blight in the Vineyard

because the only morality they've ever heard condemned everything they liked.

Well, at least Poseidon successfully defended his identity. The parents should be applauded the philosophical coup, but victory wasn't that hard to achieve. They pitted the ideological abilities of a teenager against philosophical giants and demanded that their child communicate with the same thoroughness as professional academics. This was hardly fair, considering those same adults couldn't last three minutes and twenty-one seconds in a metaphysical debate with the likes of Plato, or Augustine, or Calvin. And they too would sound like blithering idiots when trying to explain **why** man is morally justified to have friends of his own **self-satisfying free choice** when talking to Immanuel Kant.

But as parents, they wielded the bumper sticker version of that philosophy and theology like a hammer against the naiveté of their fifteen-year-old. This would be like making a ten-year-old enter a WWF cage match against Andre the Giant, Hulk Hogan, The Rock, and the Undertaker for dibs on the right to breathe, and then have the nerve to wonder why the kid ends up hating the world. This would be riotous comedy if it were not such an endless tragedy.

If this is you, your relationship with your kids, you've got work to do. And "I'm really, really, really sorry, I was just doing the best I could," won't be worth much at all without recanting the sum of the doctrines and the full measure of your authority that drove your actions. And then maybe, if there is any hope at fixing the relationship, the only thing that might repair the rift is the restoration of sovereign individuality. That means the members of your family must trust you with interpersonal boundaries. Good luck with that.

And if those were your parents and you bolted into the world of amorality and deliberate abandon of consciousness, here is the reality: You are responsible for the wreckage of your own life. You wanted self-appointment and you got it. The fact that you sucked at the implementation does not change your responsibility to the rigor of your own life.

The reason I put this section after the Inevitable Pendulum is directly related to your reaction. As I said above, to commit error is human, not because we are all just sinners but because we are naïve. We are not born omniscient. So, to survive, to thrive, we must grow. We grow by the iterative process of feedback, action, and consequence. Actions are a reflection of values. There are only two values: things that produce life and things that produce death. Persist in either effort long enough and reality will enforce an outcome: life or death. Freedom is not lawlessness. Self-absorption looks like freedom, but it keeps you in bondage as surely as if you had someone standing over you dictating every move. Changing bad actions to persist in life values is the power of change given at the New Birth, and the result is to reap the reward of your own virtue—character, happiness, and identity.

Now, go be about that.

Your Warped Proportion

Now, I need to hold a mirror up to your face. You need to see some things, namely, your warped sense of proportion.

Church leaders often draw the equation that not being in church—their church—means you are isolated. And if

Blight in the Vineyard

you are isolated, you are somehow prone to error. I find this hysterical because if there was ever a group of people who isolate themselves, it is the local submission and authority church leadership near you. The lives they lead are so sterile, so removed from everyday human interaction that they have no idea how much they stand out at the grocery store or in the work place. Oh, they know they stand out, but they think they are making a profound righteous stand for the benefit of the Gospel. They are not. The preoccupation with sin, sin, sin, and church, church, church, and death and cross, and cross and death isolates as certainly as walking into the wilderness. When the practice of spiritual life makes it impossible to engage people where they are for fear of bad "influence," the Gospel of God has already lost its power. When the power for social impact is synonymous with social condemnation, the "gospel" necessarily becomes a battering ram of force to compel by shame, guilt or (depending on the civil climate) violence. The result is a church at full odds with everyone and everything in every culture. This is a perfect recipe for utter social irrelevance.

So, here is the mirror.

Wash all the cars, and rake all the leaves, and have all the open houses you want. But in spite of the sacrificial service and smiles, "sinners" know they are fully displeasing to Church member sensibilities. They see you biting your tongue when you want to pounce on some idea you don't approve. They see you sniff your derision at whatever they do that is not church approved. They hear your endless accolades for all things church and all things pastor, and all things Jesus, Jesus, Jesus and know they have just walked into the Christian version of used car sales tactics. They will tolerate the treatment as long as the free cookies hold out. But after that, with a wave and an under the breath muttered "right wing nut case," they will be off, glad to be free of the assault. And to console yourself why those good intentions did not bear more fruit, you will commiserate with another pew-sitter and try to say the most profound judgment you can muster: "Well, they just need Jesus."

And here is the tragedy. While you thought you were extending compassion and trying to set a sooooo very righteous standard, what you were really offering was sanctimony. You were chugging down the track of the Interpersonal Train Wreck using perfect strangers like your own personal project, trying to social engineer your status within the Christian collective.

Like I said, this is a mirror. And the "Sinners" knew it.

Here is the reality. You have no sense of proportion. You have been hyper-sensitized. You have been led to believe that taking any pleasure, any satisfaction in anything deemed not church-approved, people are automatically sinning. And anyone who participates in any unapproved pleasure, they are squandering God's grace. Therefore your job is to play social cop and explain the evil ways to all the bad, bad sinners. A truly absurd calling, if one claims rational fealty to Depravity, Predestination, and election. But then again, under these doctrines you have no motive towards rational consistency. Your leading motive is authorized acceptance into the collective. So who cares if you actually listen to anyone? Who cares if they actually want what you are offering. They don't know what they want. How can they? They are depraved and therefore deceived. What they think and what they like is fully irrelevant in light of Eternity.

Blight in the Vineyard

So the choice before you reduces down to an outward condemnation of "the world" or withdraw from the "world."

The result is absolutely no ability to affect the world in which we live. We cannot be around anyone that doesn't emulate our perfect, sterile worldview for fear of it affecting us like cooties.

The result is that you have stunted your moral growth, withered your spiritual strength, and warped your compassion. You need to get a new sense of proportion.

How?

Very simple.

Are you sitting down?

Go to a bar.

That's right . . . you heard me. Go into a bar. (In some states there is no public smoking. So, no matter how terrible I think the law, I can enjoy the freedom to breathe smoke-free air.)

Go into the bar and meet people. Or a pub, or a tavern, or a watering hole. I don't care what you call it. Go to where people socialize and sit and listen and watch. The first twenty or thirty times, you will be so very certain that you are committing a grave error. Sit there as long as you can tolerate it and then run outside and look up. And I guarantee you will see the darndest thing. The sky didn't fall.

And then walk back inside and the second miracle of miracles will occur. Lightning will not strike. You won't even get the smell of ozone. Go back and sit and listen. Smile and nod to people and say hello. Engage them about all things trivial and all things important. You might have to listen through a few dozen nauseating conversations about Jägermeister. But hey, you are not there to do anything but be around people.

But John, what about compromising God's word? What about championing God's cause? What about running from temptation? What about abstaining from the appearance of evil? How about standing apart from the world, be not of this world?

Stop.

Let me address that last objection first, that we must stand apart from the world. Trust me. If you shut up and listen long enough, most non-Christians will mark you as plenty different.

And second . . . this is a stunning Christian presumption that has destroyed our ability to go where just plain people are and hang out with the sinners and the prostitutes and the tax collectors. Let me burst your ego bubble. There is no mandate to defend God anywhere, anytime. Period! God is a big boy and can take care of his own reputation. Thank you very much. God's word suffers no compromise regardless who fails to follow His command. God's word remains forever even if there is no one around.

We are so very sure that our job is to defend Dad, to defend the purity of Christianity that we drive everyone away from us and wonder why? People stay away from Christians and church in droves, and we wonder why. Then we retreat into the four walls of our air castle—we call it church. We escape to a building because we are terrified that bad things will sneak up on us and bite us in the ass and then call ourselves spiritual overcomers. How utterly ridiculous.

"But I might sin."

Yeah . . . you might. And then again you might not sin. Actually, better said, I doubt that you will sin. Tragically, we have manufactured ways to make the rudiments of life sin by turning virtues into vice. This has made us create an endless preoccupation with doing nothing because we have made every desire and pleasure sinful. But so what? What if you do sin? Doesn't God's grace matter? How did location change any of God's grace?

Like I said, if you are the Reformed type, then I think you are stuck with the implications of your own doctrine. Indwelling sin means, by definition, that I am not able not to sin—*non posse non peccare*. So . . . how does location change anything? Your great sin will be just as great in a bar as it is in your house or in a church. There is no difference. Oh, I know people play all sorts of intellectual games to microscopically emphasize or morally equivalize "sin" depending on the argument. But those are intellectual sleights of hand designed to satisfy some theological inconsistency. Under the current theological construct, the fact of sin either means you are just a sinner who will always need God's grace or you are not a Persevering Saint drawn by Irresistible Grace and you are going to Hell anyway because God's election put you there.

>shrug<

If you are not the Reformed type and are therefore free to believe moral growth is possible, it follows that people are then free to choose righteousness. If they can choose righteousness, they then can choose moral strength. And if they can choose moral strength, then they have character. And character is not **location**-specific.

So, again, I ask you. Where is your faith?

How is it you trust God so little to show you how to be temperate, meek, and kind, and all the fruit of the spirit? How is it that you don't believe that God can lead you not

John Immel

into temptation and still be standing beside the temptation? The issue of sin is never location. So, why do you fear the New Birth so inferior?

Well, the answer to your question is this: You have been so sensitized to believe that almost **anything** you do is somehow offensive to God and His great Glory that you are terrified to do anything. This is why you are paralyzed. This is why you fear taking any action. You are in stunning unbelief.

I am going to tell you a secret. God is not offended. God quit being offended when he killed his Son and poured out his warfare for Adam's treason over 2,000 years ago. The issue is your sense of proportion. You have been so hyper-sensitized to "sin" that you have lost the ability to participate in the rudiments of life. You will never get the correct sense of proportion back if you keep barricaded behind the very thin walls of some church, quivering, and cowering from all the bad, bad sinners.

Gag me!

I cannot dedicate the space to discussing the length and breadth of Grace on these pages, so I will leave you with these thoughts. If you cannot sit and eat dinner and drink wine with sinners and tax collectors and prostitutes without making them feel as though they must cater to your prim sensibilities, you have failed to understand Jesus' heart in the matter.

The One Thing I Forbid

I know you can't get over the implicit hypocrisy. A long chapter on self-determination and self-direction, and I have the nerve to forbid you anything.

This is funny. You will find it almost impossible to

comply.

Here it is. Ready? You are forbidden to ask the question, "Where do you go to church?"

Forbidden!

I give you this commandment for one reason. This is the first step on the path of spiritual tyranny. We ask the question so we can figure out the spiritual brand of the person to whom we speak. We ask it so we can judge. (OK . . . so maybe 0.2 percent of the time we are asking for directions, but don't be coy.)

Well, we go to Faith Church.

Well, we go to Power Church.

Well, we go to Worship Church.

Well, we go to Home Church.

Well, we go to Character Church.

Well, I don't go to Church. . . . (Sinner)

I don't care where you go. I don't care if you go. And I submit neither should you. Many of you are so used to trying to assess the content of another's life that you will find it almost impossible to have a conversation without starting down this path. So, stop. Don't even start down that path. If the "Where do you go to church" thing comes up in conversation, avoid it.

I am stone cold serious.

Here is what you will find. The folk who don't go to church will probably be attracted to your peace and calm and genuine interest. Hmmm . . . imagine that.

Those who attend church will be suspicious of your reticence to have the conversation.

I forbid this conversation because it really is a test of your self-appointment, of your self-determination. The whole conversation is a test of Christian authenticity and Christian pedigree in disguise.

Are you born again? If yes, then you have the mark of

circumcision on your heart. You have the Spirit of God on the inside that gives you means to cry Abba, Father. This is your seal of authenticity. Why do you care what **men** say?

Refuse to justify yourself. Refuse! It will not be easy, particularly if you don't have a church, particularly if you are suffering the effects of spiritual crack. You will feel a powerful need to justify why you don't sit in a building four times a month. You will want to pour out your heart and tell them of your very oppressive experience.

I will bet you small amounts of money that you will try to explain anyway. At best, your tale of woe will fall on marginally sympathetic ears and therefore not get the affirmation or absolution you so desperately need. At the tragic worst, you will suddenly find yourself sinking in conversation quicksand.

I figure it will take about ten times for you to waltz down this path, entertaining the "Where do you go to church?" conversation until you finally arrive at my conclusion. You will see all manner of sanctimony breathed in your general direction. You will see people physically recoil like you are infected with disease. They will be sure that **their** church isn't like that. If only you would come see. And you are supposed to be in church, don't you know?

By the way, if their church was truly different, you wouldn't be having the conversation.

But you will persist. You will disregard my words and so desperately try to explain. It is here that the subjective "felt needs" driven church participation will be most glaring. The definition of authentic Christianity will be **their** understanding. Period. They will not be able to appreciate your pain because it cuts so across

Blight in the Vineyard

their experience and the warm fuzzy of their group participation. Whatever doctrine you bring up, they will assume your understanding is wrong. Whatever expectations you held from your church experience, your expectations will be error. Your complaints against human mistreatment will be reduced to a complaint against God, which is forbidden and disqualifying. Whatever interactions you had with church leadership will be irrelevant and the product of men doing bad things, **but at my church** . . . blah, blah, blah. If you dare press them to evaluate the consistency of their own assumptions, you will discover endless contradictions, endless Christian clichés, and a general blank check to believe whatever they choose to believe. This is of course why they cannot be theologically tyrannized because as far as they are concerned, if **they** don't believe it, it isn't true Christianity.

And while this conversation unfolds before you, I want you to step outside your body and say, "This is what John said would happen." And the next thing I want you to think, "This is how I treated people."

And if you actually get to conversation number ten (How hard-headed can you be?), where you are embroiled in all manner of self-justification and mounting frustration and are not fully sickened by all things church and all church people, you might even recover. Sounds grim, doesn't it? Don't doubt me here.

For those of you who will be inclined to heed my words, I'm guessing you're scrambling in your head trying to figure out how to avoid the "Where do you go to church?" conversation. It is strange how often that conversation comes up around churchgoing types. Hmmmm . . . imagine that.

Here is what I say: "I gave it up for Lent." And then

smile and laugh. If they know what Lent is, they will think it a bad joke and there is a critical moment before the laughter dies down that you have to continue. Before they have an opportunity to re-ask the question, say, "My, what a beautiful baby!" And point at **anything**, and then smile again. They will be very sure you are crazy and treat you like a toddler, but it is really fun.

On occasion, you will get a true zealot who thinks he's found someone to evangelize. He will press and push, digging for details of your life like he is entitled.

Here is what I say: "You're not too good at reading nonverbal communication, are you? (Don't pause.) Here, I will help you with the point. Where I go to church, or **if** I go to church, is none of your business." And then look them in the eyes and say **nothing**. You will get a mouthful of babbled sanctimony. You will have hurt their feelings. They were only trying to help. They are just trying to be sensitive to God. Blah, blah, blah.

First of all . . . they were not trying to help. They were seeking a foundation of judgment, and they assumed they had a live one to evangeli—oops, recruit.

And there is no second of all. They are sanctimonious twerps that need to learn to respect someone's personal space. Don't fall for the manipulation that will swell out of their mouths. It is all pretentious self-righteousness. They are not entitled to know the content of your life. Any of it! Treat them with the same disregard you would if someone asked you if you were wearing thong underwear.

None of your beeezzz wax.

For You Ministry Types

Many of you found yourself on the outside of the

Blight in the Vineyard

church "in crowd," with a calling that beats relentlessly in your chest, but somehow you can never seem to "qualify" for participation. At the end of your spiritual tyranny experience, you got booted out the door and now don't know what to do. You naturally incline yourself to helping, teaching, and preaching to people. This is a great thing. But here is the problem. Moving into a position of church leadership now is actually a very bad idea.

To be blunt, you are not healthy enough to help people. And more importantly, your motive won't be to help. Your motive will be to prove that you really are called to minister. If only the leaders had seen you in all your glory. If only they had been willing to embrace the wonder that is you. You will show them. You will create something that even they can envy.

Oh, sigh. . . . You are about to become the very thing that you really hate. Why you would want to become something they would envy is very telling, but . . . whatever. Here is what will happen. You will find yourself speeding down the path of "help," suddenly sounding so very like the leaders that addicted you to spiritual crack.

I saw this repeatedly in Montgomery County, Maryland. Men and women who had callings that were flatly, despicably rejected go participate in another church or start their own gathering. And they were determined to recreate what they left, with their own personal spin. It doesn't work. This is exactly the dynamic of the abusive father that produces abusive sons. Under pressure, the only worldview the son knows is what he has been subject to for his whole life. You are going to have to go detoxify. You are going to have to go get some perspective. And the only way to do that is time

John Immel
and exposure.

What do I mean by exposure?

You need to go be around people. Not Church people. Not Safe people. Not Moral people. Not Faith people. Not Sinful people. You need to go be around people that don't have a descriptor. Go meet them with the intention of doing nothing but being around them. Just listen. Don't preach. Don't counsel. Don't offer advice. Just listen. And this could take a while because Christians are miserable listeners.

Listening With an Agenda

Let me illustrate my point with this story. I was eating lunch with a pastor when he corralled a waitress and wouldn't let her go until he got done preaching to her. During the conversation he asked her what she wanted and then gave her no opportunity to answer the question and filibustered for the next ten minutes. At the first sign of a breath, she, of course, made hasty to withdraw.

He subsequently objected to her unwillingness to listen to his ministry. To which I pointed out that he had asked her questions but hadn't actually listened for her response. The result was inevitable. He was "ministering" about things that were irrelevant to HER.

His reaction, "Well, I was just trying to be led of the Holy Spirit." It never really occurred to him to just pay attention to the woman's words.

This type of interaction with Christians is frighteningly consistent.

With church people, I find that about 97 percent of the time, there is no such thing as a conversation. They are not engaged in an exchange of mutual self-disclosure

Blight in the Vineyard

with the intent to develop a relationship between peers. It takes about fifteen minutes to realize they are logging the conversation with the express purpose of critiquing/evaluating your words on behalf of some church-approved idea. They assume that personal revelation is subordinate to their moral narcissism. There is nothing more tiresome than being invited to share personal thoughts, ideas, and concerns only to realize that the listener's agenda was to find some personal failing and offer correction.

For those of you who wail and moan about the lack of connectedness, a failure of any sense of community, complaining that you can't find people who will engage you on intimate, covenantal levels, here is the reason: You listen with an agenda. And the agenda is to identify some failure that you can correct, some opportunity to preach, some justification to proclaim your actions as divinely intended.

People **hate** this. Not a mild dislike. Not a nagging annoyance. **Hate**: full-blown, vitriolic antagonism. They hate being made vulnerable and then having that vulnerability used against them. The solution is to never offer any real transparency. This is why no one wants to connect with Christians; they don't trust them because we are not trustworthy. Christians treat others like this so often, so habitually we don't notice. Long exposure to spiritual tyranny has created a people that are hypersensitive to bad "unbiblical" ideas. They have lived that overwhelming example of listening with an agenda for so long it is almost impossible to do otherwise. The abysmal inability to just listen to folks, to carry no pretense into a conversation is a symptom of stunning spiritual illness.

In the Arena of Ideas, be as critical as you feel the

need. But when you are engaging another human being for the purpose of intimate human connection, take your pulse. Notice how many times you listened to someone's words and interrupt their commentary to fix a bad idea. Then I want you to pretend that God can raise his own kids. If you have to say it out loud, "God can raise his own kids," and then just listen to whatever the person says. Listen without an agenda.

Until you can listen to real people in the midst of life's sloppiness and maintain your own private counsel, you are not healthy enough to help anybody.

Back to Basics

Most people don't read the Bible and that includes church people. Oh, they re-read some favorite snippets and glance at the page on Sunday morning, but for the most part, they don't actually consume the information within the pages of the Protestant anthology. Lots of reasons for the reluctance exist but the motive usually revolves around a lack of tools to understand. On those occasions when they do read, they go to that scripture that gives them a devotional moment. If asked what the passage "says," their response is: "Well, this means to me . . ." And they are subsequently insulted if anyone challenges their conclusion. They don't like to be told that their interpretive method is really subjectivism. With all of our consternation over the subjectivity beast (in everybody else), we will defend our right to be subjective with impunity.

This kind of subjectivity had lots to do with the driving force of the broader Neo-Reformed movement emerging within contemporary Christianity. When everyone seems to be able to make the Bible "say"

Blight in the Vineyard

anything, men offering biblical "absolutes" sound like "rational" saviors. And since Man is really a rational creature motivated by his philosophical harmony, people gravitate to their teaching by the droves. But however well intended their desire, all they managed to do is hand their loyal subjects a five-hundred-year-old pre-scripted view of scripture that is equally subjective. I doubt that many of you can remember a time where you sat down and just read Bible . . . just the Bible, no John Piper books, no Jerry Bridges books, no books by the author *du jour*, or no Home Group leaders presiding over the Bible-reading.

What this means is, you are being told what the Bible is supposed to say. So, when you read Romans 7, you naturally assume that it is talking about you as a Christian and your never-ending struggle with sin. You hear the word *salvation* and immediately think, "Avoid Hell and go to Heaven." You hear *Christ* and hear a pronoun. You read John the Baptist's "Repent, for the Kingdom of God is at hand," and hear "Renounce moral impurity so you can enter the kingdom." You read of Adam's actions in the Garden and immediately think of "The Fall of Man." You read Peter's exhortation to ". . . not forsake the assembling of yourselves together . . ." and cannot help but hear him say, "Go to church on Sunday." Every single one of these interpretive understanding, and dozens more like it, are the result of a specific Bible-reading method shaped by historic assumptions and presuppositions and filters. The structure of your thinking is so firmly in place that hearing the Bible's words afresh will be close to impossible, without some remedial work.

Everything above could be deconstructed to show the error embedded in the readings, but you would find it

John Immel

almost impossible to hear anything different because the spiritual crack has robbed you of your own spiritual mobilization. And besides, you should have no interest in trading out one intellectual master for another. I could certainly connect the dots for you, but that does no good if you can't honestly say, "Yes, I see those conclusions for myself." To become free, you are going to need to take up the cause of your own spiritual life. You are going to have to start reading the book for yourself.

Step 1A: Get rid of the supplements. Put them in a box and set them aside. Don't throw them away because eventually, you will want to come back to them. Trust me. Set aside the intellectual and spiritual crutches. You need the opportunity to develop your muscles.

Step 1B: There is one supplement that I do recommend. Gordon Fee and Douglas Stuart have a very good introduction to Bible reading: ***How to Read the Bible for All Its Worth***. Get a copy of this book and read it for the methodology. Practice asking the questions: Who is talking? Who is the audience? What is the occasion? And then reread the sections of this book that address Higher Critical Methodology.

Step 2A: Put the NIV and the ESV with all your notes that you have accumulated from exposure to the doctrines discussed. I don't have the time to expand the historical and theological assumptions of the NIV and the ESV, but the translators assumed some theological conclusions as they rendered various passages. Those theological translations lean towards Reformation understanding. Since that is the mindset we are looking to unlearn, reading those translations is counterproductive. Don't get rid of them . . . just put it on the shelf.

Step 2B: Go buy the New King James, the New

American Standard, the Amplified, The Message, and the Jewish New Testament. Get a Strong's Concordance, and if you can swing it, an Interlinear Bible. Try to get red-letter editions with wide margins. This will make your reading and studying easier. This represents about $300 worth of Bible, depending on if you get leather or not. I'd go for leather, because if you are anything like me, once you get to note-taking, you will want the books to be around forever.

Step 3A: Read only the Gospels and Acts. That is right: **only** the Gospels and Acts. Grab any of the translations above and read Matthew through John, or start at Luke and pick and choose. Then get the next translation and the next one. I recommend little note-taking on the first run . . . maybe not even the second. Just read. Just let the narrative fill your mind. If you want to get a little crazy, go find another translation of interest, The Cotton Patch, or Living Bible, or NASB, or whatever, and do the same thing. Depending on how fast a reader you are, this could take up to six months. That is fine, take your time. There is no race here. You are undoing some rather sturdy, intellectual biases.[2] It will take time.

Why only the Gospels? Because it takes very little interpretive skill to see Jesus' primary concerns. The narratives in Matthew, Mark, Luke, John, and Acts tend to read rather simply. Jesus' heart is easy to grasp when coupled with his corresponding action. And ultimately, this should be the foundation of one's interpretive

---

2. If you are still trying to go "fly under the radar" at sound doctrine central, you will only confuse yourself. At some point in this process, you are going to have to decide they are WRONG, and YOU don't belong trying to mediate the middle. You can't do it and it isn't your job. So, get out and go get healthy.

assumptions, presuppositions, and filters. So, familiarizing ourselves with His words seems the most direct route to grasping God's intent and purpose.

Step 3B: If you still believe in such things, I recommend you pray in the Spirit. Yeah, talk in tongues. Do it a lot. A LOT. As much as you possibly can. Some of you have forgotten that you used to do this at will. You've been led to believe that praying in the Spirit is a function of divine determination at best and a spiritual delusion at worst. Whatever. I'm not going to unravel this now. You made the choice to shut off this expression of your spirituality. You can choose to turn it back on. And, if you can **choose** to be spiritual, what does that say about you shutting up the manifestation of the Spirit of God?

If you are not filled with the Spirit and do not have a corresponding manifestation of Tongues . . . and can get past your fears, ask. Say out loud: "I want to speak in tongues. Father God, help me do that." And then keep asking until the Spirit shows up. He will.

Step 4A: Pray these prayers in Ephesians.
Here is what they say:

Ephesians 1:15-20

15 Wherefore I also, after I heard of your faith in the Lord Jesus, and love unto all the saints, 16 Cease not to give thanks for you making mention of you in my prayers; 17 That the God of our Lord Jesus Christ, the Father of glory, may give unto you the spirit of wisdom and revelation in the knowledge of him: 18 The eyes of your understanding being enlightened; that ye may know what is the hope of his calling, and what the riches of the glory of his inheritance in the saints,19 And what is the exceeding greatness of his power to usward who believe, according to the working of his mighty power,20 Which he wrought in Christ, when he raised him from the dead, and set him at his own right

Blight in the Vineyard

hand in the heavenly places,. . . (KJV)

Here is how I pray through them:

Father, you are the Father of Glory. I ask you to give me the spirit of wisdom and revelation—insights into deep, intimate mysteries and secrets—by having the eyes of my heart flooded with light.

Father, I want to understand the hope that you have called me to. I want to know how rich my inheritance is.

Help me to grasp the immeasurable. Help me to obtain the unlimited power that I believe for, that same strength that was demonstrated in the resurrection of Jesus the Anointed.

Ephesians 2:4-8

4 But God, who is rich in mercy, for his great love wherewith he loved us, 5 Even when we were dead in sins, hath quickened us together with Christ, (by grace ye are saved;) 6 And hath raised us up together, and made us sit together in heavenly places in Christ Jesus: 7 That in the ages to come he might show the exceeding riches of his grace in his kindness toward us through Christ Jesus. 8 For by grace are ye saved through faith; and that not of yourselves: it is the gift of God:

Father, in **Ephesians 2:6**, *you said you raised me up together and made me sit together with You in heavenly places in Christ Jesus.*

That's where those blessings are. Thank you, Heavenly Father. Have me receive all You have provided. In Jesus' name. Amen.

Ephesians 3:14-21

John Immel

> 14 For this cause I bow my knees unto the Father of our Lord Jesus Christ, 15 Of whom the whole family in heaven and earth is named, 16 That he would grant you according to the riches of his glory, to be strengthened with might by his Spirit in the inner man; 17 That Christ may dwell in your hearts by faith; that ye, being rooted and grounded in love, 18 May be able to comprehend with all saints what is the breadth, and length, and depth, and height; 19 And to know the love of Christ, which passeth knowledge, that ye might be filled with all the fullness of God. 20 Now unto him that is able to do exceeding abundantly above all that we ask or think, according to the power that worketh in us, 21 Unto him be glory in the church by Christ Jesus throughout all ages, world without end. Amen.

Father, based on this prayer, strengthen my inner man, commensurate with the resources of your Glory. Based on that strength, "anointing" would make its home in my heart. Give me root, foundation, and grounding in LOVE.

This foundation of love will produce a comprehension, an understanding that will cause me to experience that love personally.

I give you glory. Work in me, exceeding abundantly above all that I ask or think.

Step 4B: After you have gotten through the Gospels after about four times, start taking notes. Whatever strikes your fancy, write it down. Practice answering the questions: Who is talking? Who is listening? What is the occasion? It doesn't matter if you get the right answer, just practice. Every time you are tempted to say, "This means to me . . ." stop and ask the questions: Who is talking? Who is listening? What is the occasion? Eventually, you will get the hang of it. Just read the words, and let them represent their own commentary. Don't try to interpret, or translate, or add, or embellish.

Blight in the Vineyard

Read the Red and then say, "Jesus really meant that." If you have done what I recommend, I am positive you will start to have a very different understanding of Christianity. This probably represents about a year of study and thought and detox.

Step 4C: After this period of prayer, Gospel-reading, and the subsequent spiritual crack detox, here is your first Bible study. Find out what Christ means in English, Hebrew, and Greek. Get out your Strong's and notice how many times that word is used in the New Testament. Then read Luke 4:16 through 21 and notice that it is central to the definition. And then every time you read Christ in the Bible, translate the word to your new understanding and then pause and THINK about what that means.

If you get this far, I have every confidence that you will be well on your way to spiritual freedom, with a vibrant life of divine conversation, and revelation brewing in your soul.

Learning to Laugh

This is the last step, I think, the ability to laugh. It took me a long time to get here. For years, the pain, frustration, and anger of PDI/CLC/SGM leadership ground on my soul. I didn't laugh much and consequently, my life was powerless.

I want to point out a progression. Faith works by love. Joy is our strength. So, it occurs to me that if your life lacks power, the issue isn't a lack of faith; it is a lack of joy. This is how I take my own spiritual pulse. If my faith is ineffective, I check my love. If my life is powerless, I re-joy.

How do you do that in the face of abuse? Uh . . . well . . . here is the secret. It is a choice. You should be seeing the theme by now. That doesn't sound like magic, does it? That doesn't sound like one day you will wake up all better like getting over a cold. I don't think that can be helped. I found no remedy for my spiritual illness until I made a choice.

I know . . . some of you are not really sure you can **be** joyful, that you **can** laugh. You've been told for so long that you must be on this ever sober vigil to thwart the sins in life. You are terrified of your sin, of what people might think, of what you really want. You are so terrified of **you** that you have a terrible time enjoying **you**. The result is you don't laugh about what tickles you. Christians are a bunch of sourpusses. We only smile at the most homogenous, pasteurized, bland things.

Most of us had our funny bone removed about a year after we got Born Again. We are not a fun-loving people. We are serious, and offended, and nosy, and prim. People stay away from us in droves. This is a striking reality because by contrast, people could not get enough of Jesus. Whether they loved him or hated him, they didn't seem to go away.

This comes from our own sense of self-importance. We are very sure God needs our help telling people they are sinners. We wouldn't want them to misunderstand after all. We wouldn't want to set the wrong example. Here is the thing. We already are setting an example, and no one wants to follow it. And if Church history is any measure, God doesn't even want to follow it.

Jesus hung out with prostitutes and tax collectors and decidedly non-church folks. But also notice that his disciples hung right there with him. So, every unclean thing Jesus touched, they touched. Jesus was soooo not concerned about them being seduced away from his teaching or righteous action. He felt no need to make sure they didn't misunderstand. Actually, he was very often deliberately cryptic. The people preoccupied with doctrinal precision often did misunderstand because their definitions of spirituality were focused on the purest source of authority. They were scandalized by Jesus' apparent disregard for spiritual propriety.

What does this have to do with laughing? Actually, it is pretty simple. As long as you have yourself wrapped up in believing you must raise God's kids . . . that somehow it falls to you to make sure people get all the right answers, you will never be free to laugh.

Being hyper-sensitized is what has sucked the joy out of your life. You have incarcerated yourself with an endless string of second-guessing motives and outcomes. You have taken on the **care** of your own salvation. Nothing could be more tragic. I've been there and done that. I spent years of my life endlessly analyzing what I'd done wrong, what my failures were, and how I could strategize ways to remedy or repent. I finally gave it up. I finally told God: "It is not my job to fix me. So, if you want someone different, you should have made someone different." Then I went and did what I wanted.

The funny thing is, at that point, my life started to change. Did I err? Did I sin? Sure . . . But who doesn't? We are all just sinners, right?

(I couldn't resist.)

>snicker<

Anyway, suddenly, there was power to be free. I finally was free to fail. And the beauty of that is I immediately became free to succeed. Because there was no longer a premium on being flawless, I could risk. I could try and try and try and try . . . until I got it right. The secret of all success is to fail **faster**. The faster we fail, the more feedback we get, so that we can make corrections. I found that my moral development followed along, and many of the things that tripped me for so many years started to fall into the past like bad habits.

And the true beauty of this kind of life, my stock has gone up dramatically with the sinner. I have people who approach me from the farthest corners who want to talk to the "holy man" or that "spiritual guy" or that "wise man." I have been called all of these things over the years by the un-churched. The labels are irrelevant; they only represent people seeking to define common language so they can talk to someone about spiritual things. I get calls regularly to pray for the sick, the grieving, the hurt, the wise, and the spiritual. I like the company I keep now. We have great conversations about God and about truth and about freedom. I laugh and dance most of the time. I laugh over time when I'm barbecuing sacred cows.

If you've been willing to do some of the things I've said, then try this one. You are in charge of your spiritual development. Since you are the driving force, choose to laugh. Start with anything that strikes your fancy. Be like a little kid and giggle at whatever catches your attention. It's kinda fun. Make something up to laugh about and then let it rip. Go to a comedy club, the rated G version, if you must. Go dance. Not the Charismatic Two Step in the nice safe church where you have to worry someone will get offended and call you "wildfire." Go find live music and kick up your heels, shake it to Booty Call, or do the Electric Slide. Or if that is too racy for you, find the ever sedate USABDA events, or look me up at a West Coast Swing Dance event. Do whatever it takes to learn to laugh. I know from experience that dancing is the fast track to absolute frolicking euphoria!

Some of you struggle with the gravity of your interaction with your church. You struggle to look past the

Blight in the Vineyard

source of your hurt and pain. You struggle to organize the tragedy of the Blight in the Vineyard but cannot find a resolution. Laughing? Dancing? How can this really be a fix? Something must be done. This whole dynamic is an outrage.

You are right. But apart from crafting a very skilled philosophical critique, here is a secret that will save you years of life—outrage cannot be sustained and rage does not work much of anything effective. You won't get the outcome you want by sitting around foaming at the mouth outraged by tyranny. Those who've never been there will nod and run away from the bad energy pouring out of your soul. If they have been where you are, they will join the outrage, and shake their heads and will both be depressed. It doesn't work.

Maybe offending leaders will get a comeuppance. Maybe they won't. It doesn't matter if they ever get an "aha!" moment. It doesn't matter if they ever come crawling on bended knee and beg your forgiveness to your satisfaction. If they do, great. If not, so what? They don't make you or break you. They are NOT the arbiters of your spiritual life. You make you. You are a self-appointed spiritual creature. So, self-appoint.

Your job is you. Your job is getting healthy. Making the choice to laugh will go the greatest distance to putting your life back on the path you so desperately desire. Learning to laugh at the absurdity is far more effective. In the beginning, if you can't muster the courage to laugh at them, just laugh near them.
Peace!

About the Author

In 1987, while watching a black and white TV in a college dorm, John Immel decided that he could write better stories than what dulled his mind into an amusement stupor. He turned the TV off. He turned his powerhouse 5-gigahertz Intel clone PC with amber monochrome monitor on. This event officially began his writing quest. Those early paragraphs of storytelling exertion revealed a singular glaring reality: desire does not make up for craft. For the next twenty years, John relentlessly pursued the elements of writing in all forms and expressions: fiction and non-fiction, artistic and technical, idealistic and scientific. He has since been a freelance writer, ghost writer, and teacher. Today he dedicates his writing skills to evaluating social, political, philosophical, and religious movements. He has achieved his goal from so many years ago; John Immel does indeed write better stories than what dulled his mind. In his spare time, John manages an IT division for one of the top education and training companies in the nation.

www.ingramcontent.com/pod-product-compliance
Lightning Source LLC
Chambersburg PA
CBHW071233160426
43196CB00009B/1046